Aston University

Library & Information Services

Aston Triangle
Birmingham
B4 7ET
England

Email library@aston.ac.uk
Tel +44 (0121) 204 4525

Website http://www.aston.ac.uk/lis

VIOLENCE
AND
TERROR
IN THE
MASS MEDIA

VIOLENCE
AND
TERROR
IN THE
MASS MEDIA

An Annotated Bibliography

Compiled by
Nancy Signorielli
and
George Gerbner

Bibliographies and Indexes in Sociology, Number 13

GREENWOOD PRESS
New York • Westport, Connecticut • London

Library of Congress Cataloging-in-Publication Data

Signorielli, Nancy.
  Violence and terror in the mass media : an annotated bibliography/
compiled by Nancy Signorielli and George Gerbner.
    p. cm.—(Bibliographies and indexes in sociology, ISSN
0742-6895 ; no. 13)
  Includes indexes.
  ISBN 0-313-26120-2 (lib. bdg. : alk. paper)
  1. Violence in mass media—Bibliogaphy. 2. Terrorism in mass
media—Bibliography. 3. Sex in mass media—Bibliography.
I. Gerbner, George. II. Title. III. Series.
Z5633.V56S56 1988
[P96.V5]   87-29556
303.6—dc19

British Library Cataloguing in Publication Data is available.

Library of Congress Catalog Card Number: 87-29556
ISBN: 0-313-26120-2
ISSN: 0742-6895

First published in 1988

Greenwood Press, Inc.
88 Post Road West, Westport, Connecticut 06881

Printed in the United States of America

The paper used in this book complies with the
Permanent Paper Standard issued by the National
Information Standards Organization (Z39.48-1984).

10 9 8 7 6 5 4 3 2 1

Contents

Acknowledgments

We would like to thank all the students and staff at The Annenberg
School of Communications, University of Pennsylvania who have helped
out on this project over the past four years. Special thanks go to
Keya Ganguly, Michael Hindmarsh, Beth Milke, Marilyn Kliman, and Avis
Beck.

Preface

This annotated bibliography began as a project of UNESCO commissioned in the fall of 1984. Over 4,600 requests for research reports, papers, publications, and other information pertaining to the subject of violence and terrorism in the mass media were mailed to scholars listed in the World Directory of Mass Communication Researchers (Library of Knowledge of the Press, Vol. XVII, Cracow, Poland, 1984), the membership list of the International Association for Mass Communications Research, and other international lists. This bibliography is based on material received in response to those requests and a search of major libraries between 1985 and 1987.

Although the majority of studies came from the United States, an effort was made to obtain and include studies from all countries where relevant research has been conducted. Communications research in general and media violence studies in particular have had the widest reach in the United States.

The bibliography focuses upon research and scholarly works relating to violence and terror. It does not attempt to evaulate, methodologically or substantively, the research, publications, or approaches that have been included. Careful reading of the annotations, however, clearly indicate how and where the research converges.

The bibliography examines four major areas: violence and mass media content, violence and mass media effects, terrorism and the mass media, and pornography. Consisting primarily of articles published in scholarly journals and books, this bibliography also includes articles from popular journals, reports published by the U.S. and other governments, as well as some conference papers and relevant dissertations. Each entry consists of the bibliographic citation and a short abstract describing the results.

This bibliography includes most, if not all, relevant articles published through the spring of 1987. For future reference, readers should refer to the following scholarly journals for studies relating violence and terrorism in the mass media: Journal of Communication, Journal of Broadcasting and Electronic Media, Journalism Quarterly, and Public Opinion Quarterly.

Introduction

Violence and terror have long been major themes of mythology, drama, literature, and popular culture. Concern about their role in public life, especially in regard to children, crime, and social control is more recent. Much of the controversy about violence and terror revolves around how to define them and how to test theories about them. Historical perspectives provided by Cater & Strickland (322), Rubinstein (214), Rowland (581) and others demonstrate that definitions, theories, and research on violence and terror have both scientific and political implications.

Reliable observation and systematic analysis usually require limited and objective definitions. Most research studies have defined media violence as the depiction of overt physical action that hurts or kills or threatens to do so. A terroristic act is typically defined as one involving violence by, among, or against states or other authorities in order to spread fear and to make a statement, usually political. Media violence and terror are closely related. They depict social relationships and the use of force to control, dominate, provoke, or annihilate. By demonstrating who can get away with what against whom, factual and fictional representations of violence or terror can intimidate people; provoke resistance, aggression, or repression; and cultivate a sense of relative strength and vulnerability as they portray the social "pecking order."

OVERVIEW OF THE STUDIES

Violence and Mass Media Content

Since the 1930s studies of crime, violence, and group conflict in the media have been conducted by the thousands and summarized by the hundreds in conferences, symposia, and published volumes. Most of that research has been done in the United States where both media penetration and communications research (fueled by both commercial and social concerns) made its most rapid and early advance.

Two comprehensive dissertations, one by Barcus (16) and the other by Goodrich (111) summarized and analyzed early media content studies. These analyses revealed two patterns that endure today: males outnumber females by at least two or three to one in all major media and a predominance of violence.

xi

Introduction

Four out of every ten feature movies made in the 1920s and 1930s contained lethal violence (Dale, 62). Comics (Spiegelman et al., 240; Barcus, 17), police-detective and men's magazines as well as romance magazines (Otto, 189; Greenberg, 118) are usually filled with violence. Two-thirds to three-quarters of all television plays in the 1950s showed violence at the rate of between six and ten incidents per hour in prime-time and about 20 incidents per hour in children's programs (Head, 139).

Crime and Media Violence

Media violence and crime statistics are usually worlds apart. Studies of trends in front page violence in newspapers, about 18 percent of the stories, and news of violence on network television, 26 percent of the stories, revealed no relation to trends in crime statistics (Clark and Blakenberg, 45; Garofalo, 87). Sheley and Askins (224) found that while violent crimes were only one-fifth of all real crimes, media coverage and public estimates reversed the pattern. Likewise, Dominick (67) found that two-thirds of all prime-time television programs contained some violence with assault, armed robbery, and murder accounting for 60 percent. Unlike in real life, violence by strangers was more frequent than violence by family and acquaintances of the victims. Haney and Manzolatti (131) noted that television crime and violence emphasizes greed and other personal characteristics but rarely underlying social conditions.

A review of studies of crime reporting and portrayals (Dominick, 69) concluded that television presents violence from the law-enforcement point of view, emphasizes personal and largely ignores social aspects, does not present an adequate picture of the legal process, and does not provide accurate information about crime, criminals, and real-life violence.

Civil Disorders

The Report of the National Advisory Commission on Civil Disorders (Kerner Commission) (160) was the first to discuss the role of reporting in group violence. It concluded that while initial news reports and television coverage may be exaggerated and inflammatory, and accounts may deviate from events, sensationalism or racial incitation were not the major problems of the coverage. Rather, the major problem was the historic failure to adequately analyze and report racial grievances and tensions. The almost inevitable focus on black-white confrontations and efforts at law enforcement simply continued the historic pattern.

Superficial or stereotypically polarized coverage rather than sheer sensationalism have been enduring features of press coverage of

collective violence. One content analysis of major Los Angeles
newspapers from 1892 to 1968 (Johnson, Sears, & McConahy, 155) revealed
that little attention was given to blacks in the press and that
coverage relative to their increasing proportion of the Los Angeles
population decreased from 1892 until just prior to the 1965 riot.
Nevertheless by early 1966 the increased amount of coverage, due to the
riot, reverted to earlier levels of coverage. Analysis of opinions
held by white residents and leaders revealed a lack of understanding of
the problems of the black community and a racism of indifference or
fear. Warren's (648) study of a 1969 Detroit racial incident resulting
in death and injuries showed that the coverage resulted in a
polarization of perceptions between blacks and whites.

Television Entertainment

Since the 1960s there have been numerous studies, conferences, and
books reporting and summarizing research on television violence. These
include works by Larsen (165), Baker & Ball (13), Comstock (51,52,53),
Murray (535, 536, 539), Cook (56), Rubinstein (214,215), Pearl,
Bouthilet, & Lazar (198), the Canadian Royal Commission on Violence in
the Communications Industry (32,33), the British Broadcasting
Corporation (83, 223), Sveriges Radio (61), and Radiotelevisione
Italiana (203).

Greenberg (119) analyzed dramatic series for three seasons and
found violence (defined as "physical aggression") occurring more than
nine times per hour between 8 and 9 p.m., more than 12 times per hour
between 9 and 11 p.m. and more than 21 times per hour on Saturday
morning children's programs.

One of the longest continuing studies of television content and
its relationship to viewer conceptions of social reality has been
conducted by the Cultural Indicators research team at the University of
Pennsylvania. This project, first commissioned in 1967 by the
U.S. National Commission on the Causes and Prevention of Violence (248)
to study television violence, has continued annual monitoring and
periodic surveys until the present time. It provided the research
evidence on violence for the 1972 Report of the Surgeon General's
Scientific Advisory Committee on Television and Social Behavior (638),
for several Congressional investigations (639), and for the 1982
Surgeon General's "update" (Pearl, Bouthilet, & Lazar, 198)--a report
which also summarized ten years of research on television. This study
consideres physical violence in all contexts, including humorous, as
indicative of social relationships and providing demonstrations of
power.

The results of the trend analysis reported by Gerbner, Gross,
Morgan, & Signorielli (103) revealed that the basic structure of
themes, characterizations, action, and fate in the world of dramatic
television is remarkably stable from year to year. They report an
index of violence that reached its highest level, since the study

began, in the 1984-85 season: eight of every ten prime time programs and practically every weekend-daytime (children's) program contained violence. Moreover, violence occurred at the rate of nearly eight incidents per hour in prime time and 27 per hour in children's programs, the third highest on record. The 19-year averages, by way of comparison, are eight and 21 incidents of violence respectively.

This report also brought up to date the cumulative results of the analysis of violence as a demonstration of power. For every ten male characters on prime time network television who commit violence, there are 12 who fall victim to it. But for every ten female perpetrators of violence, there are 16 victims. As television drama goes down the social pecking order, it raises the price to be paid for getting involved in violence. Minority and foreign women pay the highest price; for every ten perpetrators, they suffer 22 and 21 victims, respectively.

National and Cross-Cultural Studies

A comparative study of American, British, Swedish, and Israeli television conducted for the Surgeon General's 1972 report found that violence was more frequent in American dramatic programming than in programs broadcast in the other three countries, due primarily to the larger number of action-adventure programs broadcast in the United States (Halloran & Croll, 130). In Canada, the Royal Commission on Violence in the Communications Industry commissioned a number of comparative studies finding that the U.S. media tended to place greater emphasis on homicide and other types of physical violence while Canadian media showed more conflict and property damage (Gordon & Ibson, 113; Gordon & Singer, 112). Finally, studies of television content in Australia by McCann & Sheehan (176) found that about 50 percent of the programs contained some form of violence, less than the level in the United States and Japan, and comparable to rates in Canada and the United Kingdom.

Effects of the Mass Media

There have been numerous studies of the consequences of exposure to violence through the media, especially television. The individualized and mostly psychological approach, including numerous studies on aggresion (Bandura, Ross & Ross, 285; Bandura, 279, 280; Zillmann, 670) has had a long life and made numerous contributions to research on media violence. Studies of the social and situational factors in exposure, such as those investigated by Drabman & Thomas (366), are relatively rare. The investigation of possible direct links between media exposure and real life violence, and the study of other potential "lessons" cultivated by exposure to media violence have been more recent developments. In the following sections we shall first

summarize research on media violence exposure (focusing upon
television) and then review the major lines of aggression research and
end with a discussion of the Cultural Indicators perspective.

Exposure and Perception

Television viewing is a time-bound and relatively non-selective
activity. Prime time, when most people watch television has very high
frequencies of violent representations. Violence is, therefore, almost
inescapable for the average viewer. Signorielli (230) found that
program mix is such that the average viewer of network television has
little opportunity to choose among different types of programming at
any one time.

Studies on the audience for and popularity of violent programs
reveal that violence is unrelated to viewers' expressions of liking a
program (Comstock, Chaffee, Katzman, McCombs, & Roberts, 335). Diener
& DeFour (66) found no correlation between violent content and Nielsen
ratings. Other content categories do not predict popularity either,
and the researchers conclude that scheduling of programs is the main
factor in determining preference. Finally, a Canadian Radio-Television
and Telecommunications Commission study (35) of the Toronto television
audience in "family viewing time" reveals that reruns of six-to
eight-year-old situation comedies compete successfully with violent (or
non-violent) action programs. Although highly aggressive males express
preference for or enjoyment of violent programs, most viewers watch
these programs whether they like them or not. Class, neighborhood,
home, age, and sex, more than personality or individual choice,
determine the amount of exposure to violence on television (Randall,
Cole & Fedler, 205; Israel, Simmons, & Robinson, 149; Chaney, 43).

Research on how audiences perceive violence usually assumes that
conscious (or at least reported) reactions to violent content might
reveal something about the uses and effects of that content. Haynes
(447) found that children perceive comic cartoon violence as more
violent and less acceptable than "authentic" cartoon violence. Howitt
& Cumberbatch (458) concluded that adults see fictional and humorous
violence as less violent. Robinson's (576) study suggests that
identification with a character might make the action seem more
violent.

Rubins (582) observed that viewers rate most programs favorably
and violence has little to do with their rating. Greenberg & Gordon
(423) discovered that critics rank programs by degree of violence about
the same as viewers. More importantly, they found that those who are
given a definition of violence will be able to perceive more violence
in the programs.

Introduction

Aggression and Violence

In a series of experiments Bandura (286, 279, 284, 281) examined
the impact of televised violence on preschool children. The results of
these experiments revealed that violence on television or in the movies
affects children by reducing their inhibitions against violence, by
increasing aggressive behavior, and by teaching them how to be
aggressive or attack others. The experiments found that witnessing
real-life aggressive models, a film of the same models, and aggressive
cartoon characters all evoked aggressive behavior in children,
especially in the presence of experimentally-induced frustration.

In another landmark series of experiments, Berkowitz (295, 301,
296, 297, 299, 298) demonstrated that aggressive and violent tendencies
can be stimulated by exposure to filmed and television aggression in
the psychological laboratory. The studies also show that justification
of aggression in media portrayals lowers viewer inhibitions against
aggressive behavior.

A series of long-term cross-cultural studies on television
violence and aggressive behavior in children was conducted by Lefkowitz
et al. (493-495) and by Eron & Heusmann and their associates (374-377).
Two large-scale longitudinal studies conducted in the United States,
Finland, and Austria confirmed the relation between television violence
and aggression. Parents' role and the child's intellectual ability and
social relationships were important variables. Support was found for
the theory that there is a sensitive period--probably up to the age of
ten -- during which the effect of television can be especially
influential on children's behavior.

There also have not been many opportunities to examine what
happens when a media like television is introduced into a culture.
Williams (657) and her collaborators, however, were able to observe
children's behavior during free play and to obtain teacher and peer
ratings of aggression in three Canadian communities: one that had
television continuously, one with limited opportunities to watch
television, and one in which television was just beginning to be
available. These researchers found that the children in the community
that had recently introduced television were both physically and
verbally more aggressive two years after the introduction of television
than they were before, and more so than the children of the other
similar communities who had been exposed to television for some time.
Neither age nor amount of viewing or program preference seemed to make
much difference.

Extensive and varied studies on children and television were
carried out over a period of time by Dorothy and Jerome Singer and
their associates (600-603). They conducted research on the
relationship between television viewing at home and the relationships
between viewing and aggression during free-play situations in preschool
settings. They found that aggressive and also rapid-cut action by
adults on television produces aggressive behavior patterns in children.

Murray (540) in Australia, Greenberg (422) in Great Britain, and Rosengren and his colleagues (579) in Sweden all found significant relationships between television viewing and aggression. The consequences of repeated viewings may not be simply additive. A number of researchers, including Donnerstein (353), Drabman & Thomas (365), Malamuth (512, 514), Linz, Donnerstein, & Penrod (505), Thomas & Drabman (627), Thomas, Horton, Lippincott, & Drabman (628), and Zillmann (670), have demonstrated decreasing sensitivity and responsiveness with repeated exposure to violence in the media. Children took longer to seek adult assistance when confronted with violent behavior of younger children. Violence appeared to be more acceptable and less offensive to adults. Emotional reaction to violent scenes and even to real violence was reduced as a result of media exposure to violence.

A more specific connection between certain acts of television violence and similar acts in real life was found in a series of studies by Phillips and his associates (554, 555, 556, 562). In one study national suicide statistics in the New York Daily News, the Chicago Tribune, and the London Daily Mirror for each month during the period from 1946 to 1968 were used to investigate the impact of front page suicides on suicide trends. The number of suicides increased proportionately with the amount of publicity devoted to a suicide story. In another study, daily motor vehicle fatalities in California, from 1966 to 1973, and front page suicide stories from five major California newspapers were examined to test theories of suggestion and imitation. Three days after a publicized suicide, motor vehicle fatalities increased by thirty-one percent. The more the suicide was publicized, the more the automibile fatalities increased. Further studies documented similar relationships between highly publicized homicides, fictional suicides, prizefights, and court-imposed sentences.

Cultivation Analysis

Research by the Cultural Indicators research team (Gerbner, Gross, Morgan, & Signorielli, 403, 405, 406, 407) has taken yet another approach to the investigation of television and violence, broadening the scope from looking for aggressive or violent effects to inquiring into the wider consequences of living with a media in which complex images of violence are deeply and inescapably embedded.

Cultural Indicators research has developed a conception of television violence as a compelling demonstration of power with many lessons for all regular viewers, though not necessarily the same for all groups. The relative commonality of conceptions among the heavy viewers of otherwise distinct demographic groups, blending in with the main currents of television to which all groups are exposed, is called "mainstreaming." The tendency of viewing to cultivate conceptions relating to stable styles of life and television use is called "cultivation." While the convergence of other research has established that exposure to media violence is related to aggression and can incite and often desensitize, Cultural Indicators findings show that, for most viewers, television's mean and dangerous world tends to cultivate a sense of relative danger, mistrust, dependence, and--despite its supposedly "entertaining" nature--alienation and gloom.

This perspective has also found support from numerous investigators working independently of the Cultural Indicators research team. Doob and Mcdonald (361, 362) reported that media exposure to violence boosts public estimates of crime and violence, although not equally in all groups. Carlson (321) found a significant relationship between exposure to crime shows, approval of police brutality and bias against civil liberties. Bryant, Corveth, & Brown (314) and Zillmann & Wakshlag (667) found that television viewing was related to feelings of anxiety and fear of victimization, although Wober (661) did not find viewers in Great Britain similarly affected. More recently, however, Gunter & Wober (433) found that heavy viewers report higher risks than comparable groups of light viewers from lightning, flooding, and terrorist bomb attacks. A large-scale survey by Research and Forecasts (574) concluded that exposure to violence both in the press and on television relates to expressions of fear. Finally, Haney & Manzolati (439) looked at common themes in crime drama and related them to viewers' conceptions, concluding that television tended to cultivate the presumption of guilt rather than innocence of a suspect, the belief that legal rights protect the guilty rather than the innocent, and the belief the police are not restricted by law in their pursuit of suspects.

Other related studies come from Australia, Switzerland, and Germany. Hawkins & Pingree (444) and Pingree & Hawkins (566) studied cultivation in children in Western Australia. They found that the viewing of U.S., but not other programs, related to beliefs about violence and crime in their own country. Saxer, Bonfadelli, & Hattenschwiler (588) and Bonfadelli (310) reported the results of a cultivation study of adolescents in Zurich. Television viewing showed a significant relationship to conceptions of violence and expressions of fear. Viewer gratifications, reality perceptions, and social characteristics of viewers typically mediated the relationships. Finally, Groebel & Krebs (425) found a number of anxiety measures related to fear-evoking situations in television programs.

Terrorism in the Media

Work by Burnet (725), Alexander (712), Schmid & de Graaf (775), Midgley & Rice (760), and others have reported and summarized studies on the subject of the press coverage of terrorism. Moreland and Berbaum's 1982 bibliography lists about 500 papers (756).

Although international terrorism by and against states receives most attention, terroristic acts in a national context far outnumber the international acts (Bassiouni, 719, 720). Paletz, Fozzard, and

Ayanian (760) analyzed the New York Times' coverage of the I.R.A., the Red Brigades, and the F.A.L.N. during the period from July 1, 1977 to June 30, 1979 and found no basis for the charge that coverage legitimizes the cause of terrorist organizations. Martin (750), however, found that the mass media may quote someone using "terror" or "terrorism" in reference to an act performed by a group toward which the medium is either neutral or opposed. The press, however, will never use these terms in a headline unless it not only disapproves of the act but has no sympathy for its perpetrators.

Elliot, Murdock, & Schlesinger (734) present three points of view on terrorism as mediated by television. The first view, that of officials and authorities, regards terrorism as illegitimate and repression as the only political solution. The second view is that terrorism, while illegitimate in "liberal democracies," may be legitimate in other political systems. The third view, that of opponents of the state, justifies violent action by general condemnation of the existing system or by a claim of self-determination or national liberation.

Hostage crises have also received extensive coverage by researchers. Altheide (714-716) studied U.S. television network news coverage of the 1980 Iranian embassy hostage crisis and found overall similarily among networks in the number of reports devoted to the hostage situation. There was a very limited view of events and issues that did little to provide deeper historical and social understanding. Similar findings were found in work relating to the 1985 Beirut Hostage crisis (Adams, 711).

There is also considerable concern about the relationship between news coverage and terrorist events, examined from a legal or "public's right to know" perspective (713, 721, 765, 772). A conference on Terrorism and the Media (752) revealed that many experts in this field propose guidelines, such as those used at CBS, that leave the media responsible for policing its own actions and using its judgment as to what extent coverage will be given to each terrorist act. Others feel, however, that the media, by virtue of its nature, will not be firm enough and suggest that formal legislation is necessary to keep the media inhand. Participants at the conference voiced strong support for the position that the public's right to know is secondary to the safety of the people involved.

Pornography

As with violence, pornography and obscenity have been almost always been part of our lives and so has the debate about the possible consequences of the portrayals of explicit sex. Although the President's Commission on Obscenity and Pornography (676), created in the late 1960s, found no real scientific basis to support contentions about the possible antisocial effects of pornography, recently there has been a resurge in this topic and research in general has shown that the portrayal of violence and sex in the media has some effects on, at least, some people.

Eysenck & Nias (687) in a comprehensive review of research relating to the effects of sex and violence in the media, found that media violence increases viewer aggression, and perhaps viewer sexual libido; that the effects of pornography, while variable, cannot be disputed; and that the portrayal of violence in the media can incite some viewers to violence.

Donnerstein, Malamuth, and associates (see, 678-685, 691-694) in a series of experiments and and review articles have found that it is difficult to make a straightforward definitive conclusion about the relationship between pornography and aggression toward women. Certain types of pornography can influence aggression and other asocial attitudes and behaviors toward women; others, especially nonaggressive pornography, do not. This work has indicated quite strongly, however, that the aggressive content of pornography is the main contributor to violence against women. They also stress the importance of the cultural climate in determining whether acts of aggression against women are relatively unacceptable or acceptable as well as individual differences in aggressive inclinations and emotional states (693, 694).

Finally, the impact of long-term exposure to pornography on attitudes and arousal has been studied by Zillmann and Bryant (710). In regard to sexual arousal their findings generally provide support for the findings of the Commission on Obsencity and Pornography (676). Their conclusions in regard to attitudes, however, are quite different from those of the commission, suggesting that massive exposure to pornography trivializes rape by portraying women as hyperpromiscuous and socially irresponsible and generally fostering a callousness toward women.

Conclusion

Most research about media violence and terror stems from concern with potential threats to the social order. Recent inquiries and reviews of traditional lines of study, however, suggest that images of media violence and terror function in a variety of media scenarios and contexts. They can incite and desensitize. They can also cultivate lessons about domination and submission, vulnerability and victimization, group relationships, and social and political orientation to conflict, crime, and law enforcement--all highly relevant to issues of violence and social control.

Our review of the numerous content analyses reveals that violence is a staple of the mass media, especially television. These studies also suggest that the major media tend to reflect dominant points of view rather than illuminate sources of conflict and tension. The presentations of differential ratios of violence and victimization also tend to accomodate rather than ameliorate inequalities as they reproduce symbolically the national and global structures of power.

Although few would question that people learn something from mass media, just what is learned is not easy to define and even more difficult to measure. As this bibliography and many other reports indicate, numerous researchers working in diverse settings have found some degree of relationship between violence and the media, especially television. It is obvious that while there are positive correlations between watching media violence and aggressive behavior, people do not become aggressive or violent from watching television or violent movies. Rather, what we find is that the everpresent images of media violence lead to an acceptance of violence as normal behavior. Moreover, violence and victimization demonstrate power: they tell us who is on top, who is on the bottom, who will win, or who will lose. These portrayals convey lessons with important implications for the cultivation of insecurity and dependence, anxiety and alienation, approaches to crime and law enforcement, and the differential allocation of power in society.

This unequal sense of danger, vulnerability, mistrust, and general malaise cultivated by what is called "entertainment" invites not only aggression but also exploitation and repression. Fearful people are more dependent, more easily manipulated and controlled, more susceptible to deceptively simple, strong, tough measures and hard-line postures--both political and religious. They may accept and even welcome repression if it promises to relieve their insecurities and other anxieties. That is the deeper problem of a violence-laden media.

VIOLENCE
AND
TERROR
IN THE
MASS MEDIA

Mass Media Content

1. Abel, John D. and Maureen E. Beninson. "Perceptions of TV Program Violence by Children and Mothers." Journal of Broadcasting, Vol. 20, No. 3, 1976, pp. 355-363.

Schoolchildren aged 10-11 and their mothers completed questionnaires on perceived violence and viewing habits. Results of the analysis contradicted the prediction that the mothers would perceive more violence in the programs than the children. In fact, the children's mean ratings of perceived violence were higher than those of their mothers for 15 of the 21 most violent programs.

2. Adams, William C. and Michael Joblove. "The Unnewsworthy Holocaust: TV News and Terror in Cambodia." In William C. Adams (ed.), Television Coverage of International Affairs, Norwood, NJ: Aben, 1982, pp. 217-226.

Researches amount and analyzes why, network news coverage of Cambodia from the 1975 Khmer Rouge overrun of Phnom Penn until their fall from power in 1979 received such scant treatment.

3. Adoni, Hanna, Akiba A. Cohen and Sherril Mane. "Social Reality and Television News: Perceptual Dimensions of Social Conflicts in Selected Life Areas." Journal of Broadcasting, Vol. 28, No. 1, 1984, pp. 33-49.

Young people in Israel served as respondents in the examination of the perception of social, political, and economic conflicts in society and as portrayed on television news. The results revealed that young people are able to differentiate between social reality and television reality. Contrary to the authors' expectation was the fact that social conflicts in reality were perceived as more intense than in television news.

4. Albert, James A. "Constitutional Regulation of Televised Violence." _Virginia Law Review_, Vol. 64, No. 8, 1978, pp. 1299-1345.

Recapitulates the media violence issue as outlined by research findings and congressional action (the 1977 Report of the U.S. House of Representatives Subcommittee on Communications). This perspective assigns primary responsibility for content regulation to the networks, with secondary responsibility assigned to television production staff, advertisers, station licensees, and the viewing public. The author presents a challenge to legislative inaction. He argues that the Federal Communications Commission has a constitutionally legitimate role to play in regulating program content in the existing regulations concerning licensing, the fairness doctrine, and public service, and lists court decisions supporting this view.

5. Alexander, Yonah. "Terrorism, the Media and the Police." _Journal of International Affairs_, Vol. 32, No. 1, 1978, pp. 101-113.

Asserts that modern media provides terrorist groups with a critical communication instrument which willingly or unwillingly serves their general or specific propaganda and psychological warfare needs. This paper elaborates on the specifics of how and why this occurs. Research results are presented regarding the role the media should take in combating terrorism.

6. Altheide, David L. "Iran vs. U.S. TV News: The Hostage Story Out of Context." In William C. Adams (ed.), _Television Coverage of the Middle East_. Norwood, NJ: Ablex, 1981, pp. 128-158.

The objective of this analysis was to determine the degree to which network news reports reflected "reality" and various production values by examining format, mode of emphasis, themes, topics, and visual images of reports about the holding of American hostages in Iran. Clusters of 375 reports included in network early evening newscasts from November, 1979 to June, 1980 were analyzed. Overall, the content and style of these reports--including emphasis on release of the hostages rather than on socio-political conditions in Iran and emphasis on conflict--served to support official U. S. policy during the crisis, documenting an important role of the media in diplomacy.

7. Altheide, David L. "Three-in-One News: Network Coverage of Iran." _Journalism Quarterly_, Vol. 59, No. 3, 1982, pp. 482-486.

Analysis of a saturation sample of 368 evening newscast reports concerning the holding of United States hostages in Iran. The sample, from the Vanderbilt University Television News Archive, dates from November, 1979 to June 1980. There was overall similarity among networks in the number of reports devoted to the hostage situation and similar patterns of fluctuation in this measure of coverage over the period examined. However, amount of time devoted to coverage varied considerably during sampled clusters of broadcasts for all three networks and, overall, for one network. There was general consistency in emphasis of various topics, with reports about the hostages themselves the most prominent. Activities of Iranian students in the United States received more attention than did internal socio-political events in Iran. The effect of this homogeneity in coverage amounts to a "national news service," which presents a very limited view of events and issues.

8. Altheide, David L. "Impact of Format and Ideology on TV News Coverage of Iran." Journalism Quarterly, Vol. 62, No. 2, 1985, pp. 346-351.

A content analysis of 925 reports about Iran from two waves of selected newscasts broadcast from August 4, 1979 to June 7, 1980 and from July 3, 1980 to January 24, 1981. The Iranian hostage crisis of 444 days received extensive coverage by the major American networks. The reporting of selected events was consistent with production considerations such as accessibility, visual quality, drama and action, and thematic unity. This corresponded with selection of themes resonant with cultural stereotypes and images already familiar to the journalists. In this way, political and ideological value judgments became part of news coverage.

9. Aner, Kerstin. "La Violence et Les Medias." [Violence and the Media]. Revue Internationale de Criminologie et de Police Technique, Vol. 36, No. 4, 1983, pp. 72-83.

This article presents a recommendation adopted by the European parliament concerning methods of reducing violence, and contains part of an associated report on violence and the media. The recommendation addresses such areas as terrorism, the role of the media, violence in sports and the role of education in promoting socially constructive behavior. Results of research on the effects of violence in the media and means of establishing a European strategy to reduce the portrayal of violence in the media are discussed.

10. Atwater, Tony. "Network Evening News Coverage of the TWA Hostage Crisis." Terrorism and the News Media Research Project, Paper No. 6, Louisiana State University (undated).

Study to investigate the nature of the network evening news coverage devoted to the TWA hostage crisis by ABC, CBS and NBC. Questions included amount and percentage of newstime devoted to the crisis, specific topics emphasized, types of stories and locations of report origination. A comprehensive visual analysis of story content indicated 17 days of intensive coverage; 491 stories comprising 12 hours of newstime. Topics characterizing coverage were hostage status and official U.S. reaction.

11. Australian Broadcasting Tribunal. Children's Television Standards: Report and Determination. Sydney, Australia: Australian Broadcasting Tribunal, 1984.

Guidelines set up to ensure better children's programming between 4 p.m. and 5 p.m. each day. One concern was that programs broadcast during this time period did not present images or events in ways that were unduly frightening or disturbing to children.

12. Bailey, George A. and Lawrence W. Lichty. "Rough Justice on a Saigon Street: A Gatekeeper Study of NBC's Tet Execution Film." Journalism Quarterly, Vol. 49, No. 2, 1972, pp. 221-229, 238.

The decisions involved in NBC's production and broadcasting of the famous execution by General Loan (chief of the South Vietnamese National Police) of a captured Viet Cong officer on February 1, 1968 are examined using a cybernetic gatekeeping model. Gatekeeping decisions were influenced by journalistic subcultural norms, by informal and formal communication decision networks, by executive producers' conceptions of audiences, and possible reactions to the newsstory. The study found most gatekeeping decisions in this case were determined by the criterion of taste in editing. The audience response, however, revealed that viewers objected to the film as being in bad taste. None of those surveyed questioned the truthfulness of the NBC film.

13. Baker, Robert K. and Sandra J. Ball. Mass Media and Violence, Vol. 9 (A Report of the Task Force on Mass Media and Violence to the National Commission on the Causes and Prevention of Violence). Washington, DC: U.S. Government Printing Office, 1969.

The research reported in this volume grew out of concern with racial and political disturbances in the United States during the 1960s and media coverage of these disturbances. Discussion of the development of various media and the early role of sensationalism leads into consideration of media access and responsibility for coverage of underlying causes of social conflict. Research is presented concerning the prevalence of violence in television drama in 1967 and 1968 in comparison to real-world statistics, violent content in other media, and effects on behavior and attitudes. The task force called for industry support of research and self-regulation of content.

14. Baker, Robert K. and the Media Task Force Staff. "The Views, Standards and Practices of the Television Industry." In Robert K. Baker and Sandra J. Ball, Mass Media and Violence, Vol. 9. Washington, DC: U.S. Government Printing Office, 1969, pp. 593-614.

Responsibility of the television industry for research on the social consequences of violent content is a major focus of this article. Industry personnel feel they meet this responsibility by evaluating and using relevant research generated outside the industry and by controlling treatment of violent incidents in dramatic programs. The authors discuss the shortcomings of the

National Association of Broadcasters' Code and of network standards and practices departments, citing lack of meaningful sanctions and absence of control of the number of violent programs.

15. Baldwin, Thomas F. and Colby Lewis. "Violence in Television: The Industry Looks at Itself." In George A. Comstock and Eli A. Rubinstein (eds.), Television and Social Behavior, Vol. 1: Content and Control. Washington, DC: Government Printing Office, 1972, pp. 290-373.

Interviews with 48 producers, writers, and directors associated with 18 action series featuring violence. Creative personnel felt that violent conflict was essential in drama, and that the audience both expects and looks for violence. Censors play the role of a buffer between producers, networks, and the public but were unaware of or unconcerned with research dealing with effects of televised violence. Creators of programs did not believe that violent portrayals had a harmful effect upon most children; many subscribed to the catharsis hypothesis.

16. Barcus, F. Earle. "Communications Content: Analysis of the Research, 1900-195." Unpublished Doctoral Dissertation, University of Illinois, 1959.

A "content analysis of content analysis." Includes the history, theories, methodologies, and actual summaries of 1,235 research studies.

17. Barcus, F. Earle. "A Content Analysis of Trends in Sunday Comics 1900-1959." Journalism Quarterly, Vol. 38, 1961, pp. 171-180.

Content analysis of 778 comic strips appearing in Boston newspapers during the sixty-year period revealed a sharp increase in action-adventure strips, from about 5 percent to 25 percent of the total, between 1930 and 1939. The increase peaked during the war years--1940 to 1944. There was a corresponding increase in crime/detection/violence themes and an increase in romance in other comic strips, paralleling a decline in domestic-situation strips.

18. Barcus, F. Earle. Saturday Children's Television: A Report of TV Programming and Advertising on Boston Commercial Television. Boston, MA: Action for Children's Television, 1971.

An analysis of Saturday morning children's programming broadcast by commercial television stations in Boston in mid-1971. About one-quarter of the broadcast time was devoted to announcements (usually commercials). Most of the programs were animated and lacked diversity. About two-thirds of the dramatic programming dealt with crime, the supernatural, or interpersonal rivalry. Almost one-third of dramatic segments were saturated with violence (71 percent included at least one instance of human violence with or without the use of a weapon). Although in 52 percent of the segments violence was directed at humans, only 4 percent of the segments showed death or injury.

19. Baxter, Richard L., Cynthia DeRiemer, Ann Landini, Larry Leslie, and Michael W. Singletary. "A Content Analysis of Music Videos." Journal of Broadcasting and Electronic Media, Vol. 29, No. 3, 1985, pp. 333-340.

A content analysis of a random sample of 62 music videos broadcast during one week in 1984. Violence and crime appeared in more than half of the videos, often depicted in innuendo and stopping short of completion of a violent act.

20. Beattie, Earle. "Magazines and Violence." Report of the Royal Commission on Violence in the Communications Industry, Vol. 4, Violence in Print and Music. Toronto, Canada: The Royal Commission, 1977.

Violence was a significant element in a cross-section of magazines, including family magazines. Police file magazines were a particularly violent medium, featuring beatings and torture. Men's and women's magazines blend violence, sex, and stereotyping in ways that dehumanize and set the stage for violent conflict.

21. Becker, Jorg. "Communication and Peace: The Empirical and Theoretical Relation between Two Categories in Social Sciences." Journal of Peace Research, Vol. 19, No. 3, 1982, pp. 227-240.

In a theoretical discussion of the representation of peace in the mass media, the author observes that the most promising approach begins with perception of the system as an index of structural violence generated by an emerging military-industrial complex. Advertising for the weapons industry in trade journals and crime reporting in the mass media are discussed. Democratization of the media is proposed as a means of changing their function to peace-making.

22. Becker, Jorg. "Methodological Problems of Dealing With Disarmament in the Press." Current Research on Peace and Violence, January, 1983.

Available scientific literature reveals that the press in developing countries reports rather little about the arms race, nuclear threat, disarmament negotiations or the peace movement in the US or in Western Europe. An international and culturally comparable content analysis of the presentation of disarmament and armament in the press makes scientific sense only if it is stringently embedded in an analysis of the historical and social structure of the national system.

23. Boemer, Marilyn Lawrence. "An Analysis of the Violence Content of the Radio Thriller Dramas and Some Comparisons with Television." Journal of Broadcasting, Vol. 28, No. 3, 1984, pp. 341-353.

A content analysis of 25 radio "thriller-dramas" using the methodology and definitions of the Cultural Indicators project. The type and amount of radio violent content was similar to that found on television. Certain aspects of radio violence context reflected a simpler way of life. Values were clearly black or white, rather than subtle shades of gray. In this sample the message of "crime does not pay" was, in many cases, backed by death for the criminal.

24. Bormann, Ernest G. "A Fantasy Theme Analysis of the Television Coverage of the Hostage Release and the Reagan Inaugural." Quarterly Journal of Speech, Vol. 68, No. 2, 1982, pp. 133-145.

A rhetorical critical analysis of the TV coverage of the hostage release and the Reagan inaugural address, using the method of fantasy theme analysis to examine how the dramatization of unfolding events on TV creates a social reality for those caught up in the portrayal. Compares the subliminal impact of the public affairs inaugural coverage and coverage of the hostage release, in working together to reinforce and amplify the core fantasy of Reagan's speech.

25. Bouman, H. and Nancy Signorielli. "A Comparison of American and Dutch Programming." Gazette, Vol. 35, No. 2, 1985, pp. 93-108.

Dramatic prime-time programming from both American and Dutch samples from 1969 to 1980 was subjected to a recording instrument examining different aspects of programming and characterization. Data analysis revealed striking similarities, with violence found in almost every program and used in similar ways - to reveal a power structure with men generally as victors and women generally the victims, and with similar characters populating programs. In both countries, women, the very young and the old were underrepresented in relation to their numbers.

26. Bowers, James R. "Violence on Television and Violent Crime in Japan." Anthrotech: A Journal of Speculative Anthropology, Vol. 5, No. 3, 1981.

Analysis of TV programming in Japan in relation to amount and type of violence, coupled with statistics on actual violent crime, indicates that the positive relationship found elsewhere (for example, in the U.S.) may not typify all countries and cultures.

27. Brody, Stephen R. "Screen Violence and Film Censorship: A Review of Research." London: Home Office Research Unit, 1977.

An extensive review of the directions, findings, and conclusions of research in Britain and the United States concerning violence in film and television programs and its effects. The review is organized in sections pertaining to impact (imitative aggression, anxiety, habituation or desensitization, attitudes), influence of viewer and content variables, violent content, and viewer perceptions of such content. Operation of the British Board of Film Censors is discussed in relation to the issue of media violence.

28. Brown, William J. "Mediated Communication Flows During a Terrorist Event: The TWA Flight 847 Hijacking." Paper presented at the International Communication Association, Montreal, May, 1987.

Potential international effects of a single terrorist event can be augmented by news media mediation and control during such an event. A theoretical approach proposed here describes how the mediation process can alter discourse as it moves through channels of communication that are regulated by the mass media. A case study of the TWA Flight 847 Hijacking of 1985 is used for this analysis. By combining semiotic concepts with an understanding of mass communication flows, this paper analyzes the terrorist discourse disseminated by the news media during this event. The nature of the mass media's role as mediator, and the critical need for communication scholars and government leaders to understand this role is considered.

29. Bryant, Jennings and Dolf Zillmann. "Sports Violence and the Media." In Jeffrey H. Goldstein (ed.), Sports Violence. New York: Springer-Verlag, 1983, pp. 195-209.

Considered are: 1)nature and consequences of sports violence; 2)popular notions, formal proposals and empirical evidence for aggressive play as enhancement of spectator enjoyment and; 3)ways in which the media exploit sports violence. Evidence is given and descriptive statistics reported regarding media exploitation. It is suggested that coverage of violent play is emphasized, that feature articles give unrepresentative attention to violent aspects of sports, and that TV promotions highlight violent content in upcoming programming. It is suggested that depiction of violence in sports continues to escalate in volume.

30. Burnet, Mary. The Mass Media in a Violent World (1970 Symposium Proceedings). Paris: UNESCO, 1971.

Specialists in mass media, sociology, psychology, criminology, social work, and education from 18 countries met to examine the definition of violence, the relationship between real-life and media violence, and the means of expanding the use of reason in the conduct of human relations. Topics included content and impact of civil disturbance and personal violence in news; the dramatic context of violence in media entertainment; and the particular status of media and related problems in developing countries. Participants called for examination of industry

10

processes which determine content and of the political, economic, and social influences of these processes. They also sought media promotion of increased understanding of social and international conflict.

31. Cairns, Ed. "The Television News as a Source of Knowledge About the Violence for Children in Ireland, North and South." Current Psychological Research and Reviews, c.1985.

Two studies explored how much children in different parts of Ireland knew about the civil disturbance in the North of Ireland and examined the role of television news broadcasts in providing such knowledge. In the first study 488 children living in five different areas on a continuum of increasing distance from the actual scenes of violence, were asked to complete an 11-item multiple choice questionnaire concerning detailed knowledge of matters closely related to the troubles and to indicate how often they watched the television news. Results indicated that the closer children lived to the violence the higher their scores, and that the more they watched television news the higher their scores. The results of the second study virtually replicated the first study in that children in the South of Ireland knew less than did children in the North; no difference emerged between the children in the two different areas in the North of Ireland.

32. Canadian Government. Report of the Royal Commission on Violence in the Communications Industry, 7 Vols. Toronto, Canada: The Royal Commission, 1977.

The LaMarsh Commission conducted 61 public hearings and foreign consultations and commissioned 28 independent studies of violent content, its effects, and regulation in several media industries. The Report includes a volume summarizing the conclusions, recommendations, and public comment. Recommendations included decreasing the exploitation of violence by increasing accountability and professionalism; restructuring programming to reflect Canada's own cultural identity; and providing for public input to various media. Reports of research are presented in six other volumes, including an extensive bibliography.

33. Canadian Government. Report of the Royal Commission on Violence in the Communications Industry, Vol. 2, Violence and the Media: A Bibliography. Toronto, Canada: The Royal Commission, 1977.

This volume contains approximately 3,000 citations of research in 26 countries relating to violent content, effects, and regulation of print, music, film, radio, and television.

34. Canadian Radio-Television and Telecommunications Commission (CRTC), Social Communications Division Research Branch. "Violence on English-Language Television in a Canadian City During Periods of High Child Viewing." Ottowa, Canada: CRTC, 1974.

Content analysis of 55 programs broadcast by two urban English language stations revealed 108 violent episodes involving half of major characters with the highest hourly rate of violence in Saturday morning programs. More than 95 percent of the violent episodes occurred in programs not originating in Canada. These imported programs comprised 88 percent of the programs with violence, and the majority were produced in the U.S.

35. Canadian Radio-Television and Telecommunications Commission (CRTC), Social Communications Division Research Branch. "Audience Preferences and Programming Strategies From 4:00 to 8:00 p.m. in the Toronto Area." Ottawa, Canada: CRTC, 1975.

A survey conducted to assess the popularity of violent programming among Toronto's television audience and the proportion of violent programming during "family viewing time." The study included all programming between 4:00 and 8:00 p.m. from September 22 to September 26, 1975. Reruns of six-to eight-year-old situation comedies were very successful in competition with either violent drama or programming in the 4:00 to 6:00 PM time slot. Action drama, either violent or non-violent, competed favorably only in special circumstances during the time periods surveyed.

36. Canadian Radio-Television and Telecommunications Commission (CRTC), Social Communications Division Research Branch. "Three Measures of Public Attitudes Towards Television Violence." CRTC 1975 Symposium on Television Violence, Queen's University. Ottawa, Canada: CRTC (in French and in English), 1976.

The authors report results of studies conducted by the CRTC in assessing the extent of public concern over televised violence. About 40 percent of 532 letters received by the Commission from viewers related to program content. Of these, televised violence was the largest category. A review of Bureau of Measurement diaries indicated that about 4 percent of over 5,000 TV-related comments were negative about televised violence.

37. Canino, Glorisa, Maritza Rubio-Stipic, Milagros Bravo-Corrada, and Juana M. Rodriguez. A Content Analysis of Puerto Rico's Radio and Television Prime Time Programming. San Juan, Puerto Rico: Departamento de Salud, c.1984.

An analysis of samples of Puerto Rican television and radio programming broadcast in 1981 including a week of prime-time (6 p.m. to 9 p.m.) television, and 55 hours of radio news. When compared with mainland U.S. television programming, Puerto Rican dramatic programming was considerably less violent. Fewer characters were involved in violence in Puerto Rican programs, but those involved exhibited patterns of committing violence and victimization similar to those found in studies of mainland U.S. programming. Violence was the third most frequent theme on both Puerto Rican radio and television news programs.

38. Caplan, Richard E. "Violent Program Content in Music Video."
Journalism Quarterly, Vol. 62, No. 1, 1985, pp. 144-147.

Content analysis of 139 music videos (fifteen hours) broadcast on
MTV Music Television in 1983 revealed a mean number of violent
acts per video of .84 or about 10 per hour. This is about twice
as violent as programming on commercial television. Women were
about as likely as men to be portrayed as victims of violence.
These videos appear on several commercial network and cable
television stations.

39. Caron, Andre H. with Marie Couture. "Images of Different
Worlds: An Analysis of English- and French-Language Television."
Report of the Royal Commission on Violence in the Communications
Industry, Vol. 3, Violence in Television, Films and News. Toronto,
Canada: The Royal Commission, 1977, pp. 220-341 (in French) and
pp. 343-463 (in English).

Programming preferences in four Canadian TV markets (Montreal,
Toronto, Ottawa, and Sudbury-Timmins-North Bay) were compared by
demographics with program ratings data for each area. In 1975-76,
locally-produced French language programming was preferred in
Montreal. Areas with large English-speaking audiences such as
Toronto received a greater proportion of American programs,
especially crime drama. In 1975, the proportion of crime drama
varied from 6 percent in Sudbury-Timmins-North Bay to 16 percent
in Toronto and was the third most prominent category after news
and movies. The proportion increased to 10 percent in
Sudbury-Timmins-North Bay in 1976. Content analyses of seven
French-language serials popular in Quebec (teleromans) indicated
that the majority of conflict presented in the serials was
nonviolent--argument, for example. In the 27 percent of conflict
scenes that did involve physical violence, the violence was
usually humorous and off-camera, with the characters involved back
on good terms in the following scene. When serious violence
occurred, it was usually crime-oriented, involving strangers, and
focusing on the repercussions in relationships rather than on the
crime.

40. Catton, William R. "Militants and the Media." Indiana Law
Journal, Vol. 53, 1978, pp. 705-713.

New threats posed by the media's availability to terrorists. The
author addresses the possiblility of preventing terrorists from
taking illicit advantage of the existence and nature of the mass
media. He suggests that denial of access to the media to these
groups challenges the nature of the first amendment of the United
States Constitution. The trends in terrorism and the media's role
in terrorism in light of these issues are examined.

41. Cawelti, John G. "Myths of Violence in American Popular Culture." Critical Inquiry, Vol. 1, No. 3, 1975, pp. 521-541.

Heroic violence has been legitimized in several U.S. popular culture genres--the western, the detective story, the gangster chronicle, and the police melodrama. These genres have perpetuated five violence-related myths: crime does not pay, equality through violence, the code of the duty-driven and unemotional hero, regeneration through violence, and the reluctant, justice-seeking vigilante. Current debate about TV violence should be viewed in the light of earlier controversies about gangster movies and comic books.

42. Chaffee, Steven H. and Albert R. Tims. "Interpersonal Factors in Adolescent Television Use." Journal of Social Issues, Vol. 32, No. 4, 1976, pp. 98-115.

A sample of adolescents and teenagers indicated that they were most likely to view crime, western, and adventure dramas (programs which depict a significant amount of violence) in the presence of a parent. The analysis focuses on the tendency of adolescents to modify their viewing patterns and behavior in a way that reflects the nature of their communication patterns with parents and friends.

43. Chaney, D.C. "Involvement, Realism, and the Perception of Aggression in Television Programmes." Human Relations, Vol. 23, No. 5, 1970, pp. 373-381.

This study examined children's perceptions of the degree of violence and extent of realism in television programs as related to sex, IQ, and record of delinquent behavior. The relationship between these perceptions and degree of involvement in viewing was also analyzed. Based on interviews of twelve-year-olds, there was no relationship between liking and frequency of viewing certain TV programs and demographic variables. However, analysis of involvement in viewing indicated that boys who were highly involved in aggressive aspects of programs were the most likely to believe violent programs were realistic.

44. Clark, Cedric. "Race, Identification and Television Violence." In George A. Comstock, Eli A. Rubinstein, and John P. Murray (eds.), Television and Social Behavior, Vol. 5, Television's Effects: Further Explorations. Washington, DC: U.S. Government Printing Office, 1972, pp. 120-184.

This two-part study consisted of the development of a model based upon racial identification of blacks in the mass media and an experiment to test this model. A sample of 71 teenagers, half white and half black, participated in an experiment where the stimulus was a half-hour tape of a show from a police series featuring a black militant, a black policeman, and a white policeman. Blacks identified with the white policeman more than whites. Evidence also indicated that black subjects rated the two policemen as more friendly than the white subjects.

45. Clark, David G. and William B. Blankenburg. "Trends in Violent Content in Selected Mass Media." In George A. Comstock and Eli A. Rubinstein (eds.), Television and Social Behavior, Vol. 1, Media Content and Control. Washington, DC: U.S. Government Printing Office, 1972, pp. 188-243.

An analysis of summaries of evening television programs listed in TV Guide for one week in October for the years 1953-1969. Violent programs accounted for 17 to 41 percent of the yearly samples. There were no major trends toward overall increase or decrease; but violent content increased in correspondence with profitability for the networks and decreased in correspondence with public apathy or dislike at four-year intervals. Violence in movies, magazines, newspapers, and television news also was examined.

46. Clutterbuck, Richard. The Media and Political Violence. London: The MacMillan Press, 1981.

An examination of the power and role of the media in the context of political violence. The author discusses the influence of television on scenes of violent demonstrations, and asks if one of the aims of such violence is to provoke or discredit the police, and whether the media unwittingly further this aim. He also debates whether the BBC should broadcast interviews with terrorists, and examines the effect of the media on violence in Northern Ireland. Finally, the author discusses the issue of whether the journalistic profession should enforce its own standards, or whether there should be Parliamentary legislation regulating the conduct of the media.

47. Cohen, Akiba A., Hanna Adoni, and Gideon Drori. "Adolescents' Perceptions of Social Conflicts in Television News and Social Reality." Human Communication Research, Vol. 10, No. 2, 1983, pp. 203-225.

This study is based on the assumption that television news coverage distorts social conflicts in terms of complexity, intensity, and solvability. The authors test the hypothesis that age and degree of remoteness from specific social conflicts affect perception of these conflicts. Approximately 1,000 Israeli teenagers differentiated, by age, between television news portrayal and real-world perception of school integration, labor disputes, and political terrorism--older teenagers to a greater degree than younger ones. The greatest differentiation between TV and real-life conflict for both age groups involved conflict surrounding school integration, with which respondents were presumably most familiar in real life. The least amount of differentiation was in relation to political terrorism.

48. Columbia Broadcasting System. "Network Primetime Violence Tabulations for the 1975-76 Season." New York: CBS Office of Social Research, 1976.

   Tabulations of the amount of violence in a full season (13 weeks) of network, prime-time programming. Overall, the amount of violence isolated in this analysis was less than the amount isolated in similar academically-related projects.

49. Comics Magazine Association of America. "The Role of the Code Administrator" and "Applying the Comic Book Code." In Otto N. Larsen (ed.), Violence and the Mass Media. New York: Harper and Row, 1968, pp. 244-252.

   The development of the comic book trade and the origins and objectives of the Comics Code (industry self-regulation) are discussed. The author outlines specific policies concerning depiction of authority figures such as law enforcers and parents, and of violent themes and actions in war, western, and fantasy comics.

50. Comstock, George A. "New Research on Media Content and Control (Overview)." In George A. Comstock and Eli A. Rubinstein (eds.), Television and Social Behavior, Vol. 1, Media Content and Control. Washington DC: U.S. Government Printing Office, 1972, pp. 1-27.

   A summary of TV violence-related research. Data on trends in amount and nature of violence in dramatic programs and the institutional framework which generates and controls this violence in several countries is brought together in a useful, concise report. The author concludes that substantive control of violent content in a competitive, commercial broadcasting structure, such as that in the United States, would require changes in the dynamics of that structure.

51. Comstock, George A. "Violence in Television Content: An Overview." In David Pearl, Lorraine Bouthilet, and Joyce Lazar (eds.), Television and Behavior, Vol. 2, Technical Reviews. Rockville, MD: National Institute of Mental Health, 1982, pp.108-125.

   Traces the development of governmental attention to television's effects on the public from initial congressional hearings in 1952 to the 1982 update of the Surgeon General's Report. Summarizes major research and controversies about methods and results in documenting violent program content and cultivation effects such as fearfulness and pessimism.

52. Comstock, George A., Eli A. Rubinstein, and John P. Murray (eds.). Television and Social Behavior (Technical Reports to the Surgeon General's Advisory Committee), 5 Vols. Washington, DC: U.S. Government Printing Office, 1972.

Five volumes of research supplementing <u>Television and Growing Up</u>, the Report to the Surgeon General of the United States, focusing on media content and control, and effects of televised violence on viewers' attitudes and behavior. Many of these studies are annotated in this bibliography under their respective authors.

53. Comstock, George A., Steven Chaffee, Natan Katzman, Maxwell McCombs, and Donald Roberts. <u>Television and Human Behavior</u>. New York: Columbia University Press, 1978.

An overview of research relating to violence on television. Violence in network television drama emphasizes victimization and the prowess of the white male. Between the late 1960s and 1970s violence remained at consistently high levels, especially in children's programs. Evidence suggests that the amount of interpersonal physical and verbal abuse in programs is unrelated to audience popularity or viewers' expressions of liking a program.

54. Conradie, D. P. and J. C. Malan. <u>Aggression and Violence on TV1, 1976-1981</u>. Pretoria, South Africa: Institute for Communication Research, Human Sciences Research Council, 1983.

A content analysis to investigate the incidence of aggression and violence in samples of television programs broadcast by the SABC on TV1 between 1976 and 1981. The total number of aggressive and violent incidents as well as the number of violent incidents broadcast per hour increased from 1976 to 1981. Most of the increases were found in programs broadcast in the late evening. The most noticeable increase was that of verbal aggression.

55. Cony, Edward R. "Conflict-Cooperation Content of Five American Dailies." <u>Journalism</u> <u>Quarterly</u>, Vol. 30, No. 1, 1953, pp. 15-22.

A test of the hypothesis that newspapers emphasize conflict to a degree that presents a false reality. Six issues of several U.S. daily newspapers were analyzed in 1952. Overall, 53 percent of "relational" stories (involving humans in contact with one another) were conflict-oriented; 43 percent were cooperation-oriented. Crime and politics were the major conflict categories. Natural disasters and accidents accounted for about 5 percent of the stories. There was some difference among newspapers--one or two presented up to 10 percent more conflict than the others.

56. Cook, Thomas D., Deborah A. Kendzierski, and Stephen V. Thomas. "The Implicit Assumptions of TV Research: An Analysis of the 1982 NIMH Report on Television and Behavior." <u>Public</u> <u>Opinion</u> <u>Quarterly</u>, Vol. 47, No. 2, 1983, pp. 161-201.

Compares the 1982 National Institute of Mental Health research program and report, Television and Behavior, to the existing body of research and to a model of television in a context of socio-cultural institutions and processes. The research program placed emphasis on individual psychological effects of televised violence, particularly in regard to children. More attention was given to the pro-social uses of television than in the past. Relatively little attention was given to the structure and functions of the television industry, to institutions that interface with it (advertising, government regulation, advocacy groups), and to leverage for change.

57. Cooper, Anne Messerly. "Third World News on Network Television: An Inclusion/Exclusion Study of Violence ." Presented to the Association for Education in Journalism and Mass Communication, International Division, University of Florida, Gainesville, 1984.

Data from a content analysis of network news in 1978 was compared with newsworthy events in the Conflict and Peace Data Bank (international events classified according to their neutrality or conflict orientation). Violence in Third World regions (Latin America, Africa, Asia, and the Middle East) was only minimally related to inclusion or exclusion of events, failing to support a hypothesis that Third World violence would be used to portray a negative image.

58. Cullingford, C. Children and Television. New York: St. Martin's Press, 1984.

This volume reports survey results from over 5000 children from diverse backgrounds in the US and the UK. Part 1 presents data on children's attention to TV. Part 2 discusses heroes and heroines on TV, the real vs. the fantastic, TV news, violence and style. Part 3 deals with what children learn from TV; recall and recognition, educational TV, information, propoganda and advertising. Part 4 discusses the influence of parents and peers on TV viewing, mass vs. individual responses to television, subliminal content, the development of children's responses, and models of effect. The final chapter presents conclusions, followed by a bibliography on children and television.

59. Czerniejewski, Halina J. "Terrorism and News: In Search of Definable Boundaries." The Quill, April,1977, p. 12.

How news media should handle hostage/terrorist stories, and who should be making news decisions. Problematic guidelines are suggested which do not encroach upon news judgment, that deal with compexities of coverage helping or hindering terrorists or victims, and that clarify the situation for newspersons to deal responsibly with fast-breaking life-and-death situations.

60. Dahl, Asle Gire.   "Norwegian Statement on Violence in the Media."
Typescript, 1985.

   Film censorship and codes for editors and broadcasters have
   limited violence in Norway's media. Of more than 500 articles
   concerning video violence published in daily newspapers in 1982,
   67 percent were negative. Children and young people were the
   focus of 45 percent of the articles. Regulation by authorities
   was recommended in the majority of cases. Legislation enacted in
   1983 requiring censorship of violence in film/video is being
   enforced in the courts.

61. Dahlgren, Peter.   "Television in the Socialization
Process: Structures and Programming of the Swedish Broadcasting
Corporation." In George A. Comstock and Eli A. Rubinstein (eds.),
Television and Social Behavior, Vol. 1, Media Content and Control.
Washington, DC: U.S. Government Printing Office, 1972, pp. 533-546.

   Outlines the structure of Sveriges Radio (broadcasting), a limited
   company, and the policies under which it operates--the Radio Act
   of 1966 and Agreement of 1967. These regulations underlie TV1's
   own policy of avoiding needless brutality in programs and
   attempting to "foster an atmosphere where intolerance and
   prejudice would have no part". TV2 recognizes the existence of
   violence as a real-world fact but insists that the social and
   human context be considered, including explicit motives and
   consequences. Analysis of a week's programming in 1971 indicated
   relatively few violent incidents. These are described and appear
   to meet the guidelines.

62. Dale, Edgar.   The Content of Motion Pictures.   New York:
MacMillan, 1935.

   Content analysis of 1500 feature films from the years 1920, 1925,
   and 1930 indicated that crime and war were significant themes.
   Murder techniques were frequently portrayed, and actual murder was
   depicted in about one-quarter of the films.

63. Davis, David Brion.   "Violence in American Literature." In Otto
N. Larsen (ed.), Violence and the Mass Media. New York: Harper and
Row, 1968, pp. 70-82.

   Explores the presence of violence in American literature from
   Cooper, Poe, Twain, and Steinbeck to Mickey Spillane. The author
   provides thematic interpretations of several types of violent
   characters: brothers or social classes in conflict, the western
   hero, and American Indians and blacks and discusses the
   philosophical view of violence as an "act of creation."

19

64. Davis, F. James. "Crime News in Colorado Newspapers." *American Journal of Sociology*, Vol. 57, No. 4, 1952, pp. 325-330.

Crime stories in four newspapers were sampled over a two-year period. Items concerning theft, rape, murder, assault and so forth were compared to FBI crime reports for the period and to public opinion concerning criminal activity. There was no relationship between changes in actual rates of crimes and amount of coverage of the particular type of crime. Public opinion concerning certain types of crime--theft and violent crimes except rape--was more similar to newspaper coverage than to actual occurrence.

65. Deleon, Dennis L. and Robert L. Naon. "The Regulation of Televised Violence." *Stanford Law Review*, Vol. 26, No. 6, 1974, pp. 1291-1325.

A concise review of laboratory and field studies centering on the issue of the impact of television violence prefaces this outline of the sources of regulation. The author discusses the potential and limitations of the industry and the Federal Communications Commission to control violent content and proposes new legislation, especially in regard to programming for children, which would involve scheduling and censorship. The author argues that such legislation, if carefully drawn by Congress and carefully administered by the Federal Communications Commission, could be consistent with First Amendment freedoms.

66. Diener, Ed and Darlene DeFour. "Does Television Violence Enhance Program Popularity?" *Journal of Personality and Social Psychology*, Vol. 36, No. 3, 1978, pp. 333-341.

No correlation was found between violent content of two evening police/detective action series and Nielsen ratings of the series. Also, no separate objective categories were significant predictors of popularity. More complex factors and/or factors unrelated to content, such as scheduling of programs, are implicated. This research was supplemented by an experiment involving 100 college students. A high-action, low-violence edited version of a police-action program was shown to half the subjects; the others viewed a high-action, high-violence version. Neither episode was preferred significantly to the other. Analysis of subject personality characteristics revealed that highly-aggressive males were most likely to enjoy the violent episode.

67. Dominick, Joseph R. "Crime and Law Enforcement in Prime-Time Television." *Public Opinion Quarterly*, Vol. 37, No. 2, 1973, pp. 241-250.

A content analysis of one week of dramatic and comedy television programs. Two-thirds of prime-time programming portrayed at least one crime and violent crimes were most prevalent. Murder, assault, and armed robbery accounted for 60 percent of TV crimes.

Compared to real life, crimes against property and violent crimes against family members were underrepresented on television.

68. Dominick, Joseph R. "Children's Viewing of Crime Shows and Attitudes of Law Enforcement." Journalism Quarterly, Vol. 51, No. 1, 1974, pp. 5-12.

371 fifth grade children in 4 New York City schools (2 in blue-collar areas and 2 in white-collar areas) completed questionnaires in May, 1972. The amount of time a child spent watching crime and police shows was unrelated to the judged importance of television as an information source. For boys and girls, viewing crime shows was positively correlated with (1) identification with a TV character associated with law enforcement; (2) belief that criminals usually get caught; and (3) knowledge of civil rights when arrested. For both boys and girls the strongest predictors of general evaluation of police were the perceived attitude of friends and family. For boys only, more personal contact with police was associated with negative evaluation. Legal terms and processes frequently seen on TV were better known than those things not commonly portrayed.

69. Dominick, Joseph R. "Crime and Law Enforcement in the Mass Media." In Charles Winick (ed.), Deviance and Mass Media, Beverly Hills, CA: Sage, 1978, pp. 105-128.

A review of content analyses examining the portrayal of crime and law enforcement in newspapers, broadcast news, and broadcast entertainment. Also discusses the special problems of media coverage of terrorism because in many of these episodes the medium itself is manipulated by the individuals or terrorist group involved.

70. Dworkin, Mark. "Theme Usage as an Indicator of Agency Bias." Paper presented to the International Communication Association, Intercultural and Development Communications Division, San Francisco, California, 1984.

An examination of Western wire news services to determine degree of bias in coverage of the Third World. The thirty-three International Association for Mass Communication Research themes were employed in a content analysis of AP and UPI wire stories to Asia during the summer of 1980. Three of five hypotheses that assertions referring to the Third World would be more negative were supported--including the hypothesis that a greater proportion of conflict-oriented assertions would refer to the Third World.

71. Dworkin, Martin S. "'The Desperate Hours' And The Violent Screen." Queens' Quarterly, Vol. 63, No. 3, 1956, pp. 415-423.

The author states that it is not new for films to debate the use of violence, nor to seem to decry the brutality they actually glorify. The nature as well as the number of these films suggests that we may be reaching a climax in the latest cycle of screen violence. At this point it may be possible to clarify what we mean when we judge a film to be gratuitously violent -- and, perhaps, to suggest ways of recognizing the effects violent films have upon us.

72. Dziki, Sylwester, Janina Maczuga, and Walery Pisarek (eds.). World Directory of Mass Communication Researchers. Cracow, 1984.

An international listing of mass communication researchers.

73. Edelstein, Alex S. and Jerome L. Nelson. "Violence in the Comic Cartoon." Journalism Quarterly, Vol. 46, No. 2, 1969, pp. 355-358.

A content analysis of cartoons in the New Yorker and the Saturday Evening Post indicated that cartoons expressed hostile and violent behavior ranging from mild to severe and indirect to direct. There was a tendency for the behavior expressing violence or hostility to be more indirect than direct and more mild than severe in the higher status magazine.

74. Edmunds, Hugh H. and John Strick. "Economic Determinants of Violence in Television and Motion Pictures and the Implications of Newer Technologies." Report of the Royal Commission on Violence in the Communications Industry, Vol. 7, The Media Industries. Toronto, Canada: The Royal Commission 1977, pp. 71-184.

American films account for 91 percent of all film rental fees in Canada. American TV shows attract larger audiences than those produced locally, and they are less costly to acquire for broadcast. Violent material is relatively easy to make. Situation comedy is more difficult but can draw even larger audiences than police drama or action adventure. The dominant position of American productions is the result of a matrix of elements such as audience taste, market size, oligopolistic structures and practices in the communications industry, and economies of scale.

75. Eleey, Michael F., George Gerbner, and Nancy Signorielli Tedesco. "Apples, Oranges, and the Kitchen Sink: An Analysis and Guide to the Comparison of 'Violence Ratings'." Journal of Broadcasting, Vol. 17, No. 1, 1973, pp. 21-31.

An examination of some of the pitfalls one may encounter in trying to use a number of different studies as alternative or complementary approaches to a "violence rating" system.

76. Ellison, Jerome and Franklin T. Gosser. "Non-Fiction Magazine Articles: A Content Analysis Study." Journalism Quarterly, Vol. 36, 1959, pp. 27-34.

Crime stories increased sharply from relative absence in general magazines such as Life, Reader's Digest, The New Yorker, and Ladies' Home Journal between 1947 and 1957.

77. England, Claire. "Violence in Literature for Children and Young Adults." Report of the Royal Commission on Violence in the Communications Industry, Vol. 4, Violence in Print and Music, Toronto, Canada: The Royal Commission, 1977, pp. 115-160.

Death, maiming, and cruelty have been elements of literature since the 16th century. Violence may be exploited by writers under pressure of competition with television and of demands of a child market oriented primarily to TV.

78. Estep, Rhoda and Patrick T. MacDonald. "How Prime-time Crime Evolved on TV, 1976 to 1983." In R. Surette (ed.), Justice and the Media: Issues and Research. Springfield, IL: Charles C. Thomas Publishers, 1984, pp. 110-123.

This study attempts to examine the validity of charges of a recent surge in amount of prime-time tv's portrayal of crime, by analyzing data from 1976-1977, 1978-1979, and 1980-1981 television programming seasons. It was found that television continues to over-emphasize murder, robbery and assault, and minimize property crime, in direct contradiction to crime statistics. The authors conclude that because television continues to portray violent criminals as white, middle-aged, middle-class men who have psychological problems, it ignores the real, social-structural factors which motivate most crimes.

79. Estep, Rhoda and Patrick T. Macdonald. "Crime in the Afternoon: Murder and Robbery on Soap Operas." Journal of Broadcasting and Electronic Media, Vol. 29, No. 3, 1985, pp. 323-331.

Crime in soap operas was assessed through interviews with soap opera viewers (informants) and through a content analysis of issues of Soap Opera Digest published between 1977 and 1984. The depiction of suspects and victims in daytime serials was compared with the image derived from official records. Overall crime in the daytime serials is not presented realistically. Females and whites are represented more often as robbery and murder suspects and victims than would be expected from official records.

80. Feilitzen, Cecilia von, Leni Filpson, and Ingela Schyller. Open Your Eyes to Children's Viewing: On Children, TV and Radio Now and in the Future. Stockholm: Swedish Broadcasting Corporation (in Swedish and in English), 1977.

A review of fifteen years of research concerning children's use of TV and radio, the influence of television programs imported into Sweden, and the lack of resources for children's broadcasting. The summary, directed to the Swedish Commission on Broadcasting, includes proposals to improve the status of programming for children and adults.

81. Fenigstein, Allan. "Does Aggression Cause a Preference for Viewing Media Violence?" Journal of Personality and Social Psychology, Vol. 37, No. 12, 1979, pp. 2307-2317.

College students were classified according to their expression of aggressive or non-aggressive fantasies and then given a choice of film clips for viewing. Aggressive fantasies in males corresponded with preference for viewing violence, and males chose films that were more violent than those chosen by females. Males given an opportunity to be aggressive were more likely to choose violent content than males not given this opportunity. Results are linked to a bi-directional relationship between aggressive behavior and the viewing of media violence.

82. Fishman, M. "Crime Waves as Ideology." In R. Surette (ed.), Justice and the Media: Issues and Research. Springfield, IL: Charles C. Thomas Publishers, 1984, pp. 159-180.

The author suggests that the crime waves which periodically appear in the press are constructs of the mass media, and contribute to an ideological conception of crime in America. Data collected from a television station and two newspapers in New York City (1975-1977) provide basis for arguing that, because journalists depend on one another for their sense of "what's news," a crime theme can spread throughout a news community. Following heavy media coverage, law enforcement authorities can use their power to make news to augment or modify a burgeoning "crime wave."

83. Francis, Richard. "La Politique de la BBC en Matiere de Presentation de La Violence." [BBC Policy Regarding the Presentation of Television Violence]. Revue Internationale de Criminologie et de Police Technique, Vol. 36, No. 4, 1983, pp. 91-99.

Describes guidelines developed by the British Broadcasting Corporation (BBC) concerning the representation of violence on TV. The inclusion of violent scenes in news broadcasts depends on factors such as its importance to the broadcast and public sensibilities. The treatment of stories on terrorism, bomb alerts, and accidents and catastrophies is considered, as well as requests for the suppression of specific information.

84. French, Philip. "Violence in the Cinema." In Otton N. Larsen (ed.), Violence and the Mass Media. New York: Harper and Row, 1968, pp. 59-70.

One of the earliest violent film sequences portrayed the beheading of Mary, Queen of Scots (1893). While violence always has been an element of films and one of interest to the public, disapproval has been expressed since 1897, when criticism arose over early films of prize fighters. The issue is presented as a struggle between reformers/moralists/legislators and artists/exploiters. The author argues that the form and intensity of film violence have changed more significantly than the amount and that different countries have experienced eras in which violence appeared more blatant. An interpretation of a violent theme in two different films reveals that the theme lends itself to exploration as well as exploitation.

85. Fulford, Robert. "Speaking the Unspeakable: Violence in the Literature of Our Time." Report of the Royal Commission on Violence in the Communications Industry, Vol. 4, Violence in Print and Music. Toronto, Canada: The Royal Commission, 1977, pp. 105-114.

Elite literature is not exempt from violent content. The author links it with cataclysmic violent events such as the bombing of Japan in World War II and the decimation of ethnic/economic/political populations.

86. Furnham, Adrian F. and Barrie Gunter. "Sex, Presentation Mode and Memory for Violent and Nonviolent News." Journal of Educational Television, Vol. 11, No. 2, 1985, pp. 99-105.

In this study, 68 undergraduates were presented with violent and nonviolent news stories, either audio-visually, audio only, or in print, and then immediately tested for cued recall of story content. Presentation mode was shown to be significant: recall of news was best from print and worst from audio-visual. Males recalled violent news better than nonviolent, while for females the reverse was true. Males also recalled violent news much better than females in the audio-visual mode, but no such difference occurred in any other mode. Furthermore, the presentation of violent news stories audiovisually can produce especially impaired memory performance among female viewers.

87. Garofalo, James. "Crime and the Mass Media: A Selective Review of Research." Journal of Research in Crime and Delinquency, July, 1981, pp. 319-350.

Documents amount of newspaper and television coverage of crime, including entertainment programs, by reviewing studies from the earliest periods available. Newspaper coverage of crime-related topics has been consistent from the 1930s to 1980 (about 5 to 10 percent of news space), but with variations from area to area and newspaper to newspaper. There is no relationship between amount of crime coverage and number of actual crimes. News media in several countries over-represent violent crimes by individuals, especially murder. Studies dealing with effects of media violence, including effects on behavior and attitudes, indicate that early exposure to TV violence, especially by aggressive males, is related to aggressive behavior later in life.

88. George, W. H. and G. A. Marlatt. "The Effects of Alcohol and Anger on Interest in Violence, Erotica and Deviance." Journal of Abnormal Psychology, Vol. 95, No. 2, 1986, pp. 150-158.

The influence of situational antecedents on viewer interest in video entertainment were investigated in this study. Alcohol expectancy, alcohol content and anger provocation were factorially crossed to investigate their influence on male interest in viewing four types of slides: neutral, erotic, violent and violent-erotic. Alcohol expectancy emerged as most potent of these manipulated variables, facilitating viewing times for the nonneutral slides and overriding the impact of alcohol content. This expectancy effect was more pronounced with the violent erotic slides than with slides that were violent only.

89. Gerbner, George and Larry Gross. "Living With Television: The Violence Profile." Journal of Communication, Vol. 26, No. 2, 1976, pp. 173-199.

Description of Cultural Indicators research project, including findings from Violence Profile No. 7. Findings from the message system analysis of week-long annual samples of prime-time and weekend-daytime network drama revealed that there has been no significant reduction in the overall Violence Index despite some fluctuations in the specific measures and a definite drop in early evening violence in the 1975 season. Findings from the cultivation analyses revealed that those who view four or more hours of television each day were more likely to give "televison answers" to questions about the proportion of people employed in law enforcement, whether or not most people can be trusted, and one's chances of being involved in violence during any given week.

90. Gerbner, George and Larry Gross. "The Scary World of TV's Heavy Viewer." Psychology Today, Vol. 9, No. 11, 1976, pp. 41-45, 89.

Report of ongoing Cultural Indicators research reveals that television dramatically demonstrates the power of authority in society. Violence-filled programs show who gets away with what, and against whom. It teaches the role of victim, and the acceptance of violence as a social reality. Research shows that people who watch a lot of television see the real world as more dangerous and frightening than those who watch very little. Heavy viewers are less trustful of their fellow citizens and more fearful of the real world.

91. Gerbner, George. "Press Perspectives in World Communications: A Pilot Study." Journalism Quarterly, Vol. 38, No. 2, 1961, pp. 313-322.

Comparative study of the coverage of the United Nations 1960 "summit" General Assembly in The New York Times and the Hungarian communist daily Nepszabadsag.

92. Gerbner, George. "Dimensions of Violence in Television Drama." In Robert K. Baker and Sandra J. Ball (eds.), Mass Media and Violence, Vol. 9. Washington, DC: U.S. Government Printing Office, 1969, pp. 311-340.

Report of a content analysis of all network dramatic television programs broadcast during prime-time and Saturday morning during the weeks of October 1-7 in 1967 and 1968. The analysis revealed that some violence occurred in 8 out of every 10 programs. The average rate of violent episodes was 5 per play and 7 per program hour. Violence was often an integral part of the plot and usually serious. There was no decline in violence between 1967 and 1968. The analysis also revealed that at least half of all major characters inflict some violence upon others; there was also widespread victimization.

93. Gerbner, George. "The Film Hero: A Cross-Cultural Study." Journalism Monographs, No. 13, 1969.

Analysis of violent incidents in 341 films from the United States, France, Italy, Yugoslavia, Poland, and Czechoslavakia revealed differences among countries and between the two political-economic blocs represented by these countries.

94. Gerbner, George. "Cultural Indicators: The Case of Violence in Television Drama." The Annals of the American Academy of Political and Social Science, Vol. 388, 1970, pp. 69-81.

Findings of studies of the portrayal of violence in network television drama reveal that violence is not a simple or single dimension of behavior. It is a question of public assumptions about the role of force and the distribution of justice.

95. Gerbner, George. "The Structure and Process of Television Program Content Regulation in the United States." In George A. Comstock and Eli A. Rubinstein (eds.), Television and Social Behavior, Vol. 1, Media Content and Control. Washington, DC: U.S. Government Printing Office, 1972, pp. 386-414.

The Federal Communications Commission and the NAB Code Review Board have authority but little effective power in regard to program content and control. Power lies in the chief client relationships between major national advertisers and the management of the three national networks. With an emphasis on frequency and explicitness rather than on the substance of what violence demonstrates about life, the codes are public relations instruments whose applications protect and enhance the social and commercial functions of programming.

27

96. Gerbner, George. "Violence in Television Drama: Trends and Symbolic Functions." In George A. Comstock and Eli A. Rubinstein (eds.) Television and Social Behavior, Vol. 1, Media Content and Control, Washington D.C.: U.S. Government Printing Office, 1972, pp. 28-187.

Analysis of violent content in TV drama illuminates the power hierarchy of the fictional world. Data for week-long annual samples of prime-time weekend-daytime network dramas were collected in 1967, 1968, and 1969. There were 1355 violent episodes in 281 programs sampled over the three-year period. Although the incidence of killing involving major characters dropped significantly from the earliest sample year, the overall levels of violence as percentage of programs containing violence and rate of violent episodes per hour remained relatively stable. Cartoons increased in violence over the period, remaining the most violent of all program types. Male characters were more than twice as likely as female characters to be involved in violence. However, female characters were more likely than males to be portrayed as victims rather than initiators of violence.

97. Gerbner, George. "Scenario for Violence." Human Behavior, October, pp. 91-96. Also in Robert Atwin, Barry Orton, and William Verterman (eds.) American Mass Media: Industry and Issues, New York: Random House, 1975, pp. 102-107.

A discussion of some of the political issues surrounding the study of violence on television. Notes how the chief social function of symbolic violence is in what it teaches about types of people and power.

98. Gerbner, George. "Death in Prime Time: Notes on the Symbolic Functions of Dying in the Mass Media." The Annals of the American Academy of Political and Social Science, Vol. 447, 1980, pp. 64-70.

The cultural (and media) significance of dying rests in the symbolic context in which representations of dying are embedded. An examination of that context of mostly violent representations suggests that portrayals of death and dying serve symbolic functions of social typing and control and tend, on the whole, to conceal the reality and inevitability of the event.

99. Gerbner, George, Larry Gross, Marilyn Jackson-Beeck, Suzanne Jeffries-Fox, and Nancy Signorielli. "Cultural Indicators: Violence Profile No. 9." Journal of Communication, Vol. 28, No. 3, 1978, pp. 176-207.

A discussion of the diversification of the Cultural Indicators project and findings from Violence Profile No. 9. Detailed content analyses of annual week-long samples of prime-time and weekend-daytime network dramatic programs revealed that the amount of violence decreased in the fall 1977 season. Nevertheless, violence still appeared in more than two-thirds of all prime-time programs and in 9 out of 10 weekend-daytime (children's) programs.

Between 1969 and 1977 63 percent of all major characters were involved in violence with victims outnumbering those who commit violence. Women, minorities, and older women are especially likely to be victimized. Those who commit violence are usually white, middle-class men in the prime of life. Cultivation analyses revealed that more heavy viewers tend to respond in terms of the world of television than do light viewers in the same demographic groups, in regard to questions about violence and mistrust. Analyses of data from a sample of New Jersey school children and the 1975 and 1977 NORC General Social Surveys are presented.

100. Gerbner, George, Larry Gross, Michael F. Eleey, Marilyn Jackson-Beeck, Suzanne Jeffries-Fox and Nancy Signorielli. "TV Violence Profile No. 8: The Highlights." Journal of Communication, Vol. 27, No. 2, 1977, pp. 171-180.

Summary of the annual report of the Cultural Indicators project shows increases in the amount of violence on television, including early evening and weekend-daytime (children's) programs. The profile also reveals the unequal structure of power and risk in the world of television drama, and showed children's particular vulnerability to the effects of television. Heavy viewers revealed a significantly higher sense of personal risk, mistrust, and suspicion than did light viewers in the same demographic groups, exposed to the same real risks of life. The results also showed that television's independent contributions to the cultivation of these conceptions of a "mean world" and other aspects of social reality are not significantly altered by sex, age, education, income, newspaper reading, and church attendance.

101. Gerbner, George, Larry Gross, Michael Morgan and Nancy Signorielli. "Charting the Mainstream: Television's Contributions to Political Orientations." Journal of Communication, Vol. 32, No. 2, 1982, pp. 100-127.

Report of the team's ongoing Cultural Indicators project. The results from the message analysis of annual week-long samples of prime-time and weekend-daytime network dramatic programming revealed that enforcing the law on TV takes nearly three times as many characters as the number of characters in all blue-collar and service worker roles. The average viewer sees over 30 police officers each week. Threats abound and crime, in prime-time, is at least ten times as rampant as in the real world. An average of 5 to 6 acts of overt physical violence involve over half of all major characters. Symbolic violence demonstrates power; it shows victimization, not just aggression, hurt but not therapy; it shows who can get away with what against whom. Results of cultivation analyses focusing upon political orientations reveal that although television brings conservatives, moderates, and liberals closer together on numerous issues, the liberal position is the weakest among heavy viewer. On issues dealing with minorities and personal rights viewing tends to blur traditional differences and blends them into a more homogeneous mainstream.

29

102. Gerbner, George, Larry Gross, Michael Morgan, and Nancy Signorielli. "Gratuitous Violence and Exploitive Sex: What Are the Lessons?" Phila, PA: The Annenberg School of Communications, 1984.

The overall Violence Index for the 1981-82 and 1982-83 seasons remained close to the average rate found in Cultural Indicators monitoring results since 1967. While prime time violence fell slightly below the 17-year average, weekend daytime (children's programs) violence rose far above it. There was a record high for violence in children's programs in 1982-83. The rates of violence per hour and per program remained equally high. Violence continued to reflect the structure of power in society with women, young and old people, and some minorities ranking as the most vulnerable to victimization.

103. Gerbner, George, Larry Gross, Michael Morgan, and Nancy Signorielli. "Television's Mean World: Violence Profile, No. 14-15." The Annenberg School of Communications, University of Pennsylvania, 1986.

This update revealed that the Violence Index for 1984-85 was the higheset and for 1985-1986 the fourth highest on record. The Violence Index for the last two seasons was considerably above the average of Cultural Indicators monitoring since 1967. In addition, in the 1984-85 and 1985-86 seasons, the early evening "family hour" (when most children are in the audience) had the second and third highest Violence Indices ever recorded. Violence continued to reflect the structure of power in society with women, young and old people, and some minorities ranking as the most vulnerable to victimization. Heavy viewers were more likely than comparable groups of light viewers to express the feeling of living in a self-reinforcing cycle of a mean and gloomy world.

104. Gerbner, George, Larry Gross, Nancy Signorielli, and Michael Morgan. "Television Violence, Victimization, and Power." American Behavioral Scientist, Vol. 23, No. 5, 1980, pp. 705-716.

Research conducted as part of the group's ongoing Cultural Indicators project has revealed that violence plays an important role in television's portrayal of the social order. It provides a calculus of life chances in conflict and shows the rules by which the game is played. It demonstrates the relative distributions of power and of the fear of power. In generating among the many a fear of the power of the few, television violence may achieve its greatest effect. The results of adult and child surveys show consistent learning and children's particular vulnerability to television. These results also confirm that violence-laden television not only cultivates aggressive tendencies in a minority, but also generates a pervasive and exaggerated sense of danger and mistrust. Heavy viewers revealed a significantly higher sense of personal risk and suspicion than did light viewers in the same demographic groups.

105. Gerbner, George, Larry Gross, Nancy Signorielli, Michael Morgan, and Marilyn Jackson-Beeck. "The Demonstration of Power: Violence Profile No. 10." Journal of Communication, Vol. 29, No. 3, 1979, pp. 177-196.

Annual progress report sums up findings suggesting that fear and inequity may be television's most pervasive lessons. Message system analyses of week-long samples of prime-time and weekend-daytime network dramatic programs reveal that violence in weekend-daytime children's and late evening programs on all three networks rose to near record levels in the fall of 1978. Violence is the simplist and cheapest dramatic means to demonstrate who wins in the game of life and the rules by which the game is played. It demonstrates who has the power and who must acquiesce to that power. Cultivation analyses revealed that in samples of adolescents in suburban New Jersey and New York City heavy viewers were more likely than light viewers to overestimate the number of people involved in violence, the proportion of people who commit serious crimes, and to express more fear.

106. Gerson, Walter M. "Violence as an American Value Theme." In Otto N. Larsen (ed.), Violence and the Mass Media. New York: Harper and Row, 1968, pp. 151-162.

A discussion of media violence in a socio-cultural context, citing the reciprocal relationship between mass media and public opinion in a democratic society. The dimensions of violence are outlined, along with qualities that distinguish legitimate and non-legitimate forms. Violent real-world events and circumstances contribute to media themes of speed, force, and violence.

107. Ginpil, Stephen. "Violent and Dangerous Acts on New Zealand Television." New Zealand Journal of Educational Studies, Vol. 11, No. 2, 1976, pp. 152-157.

A content analysis of one week of afternoon and evening programs broadcast in New Zealand in 1975. Violent actions were classified to determine the number and type of actions that were most likely to be imitated by children, considering such factors as actual availability of weapons and effectiveness of the dramatic act. The average hourly rate was about 7 violent acts, the majority of which were assaults. About one or two acts during each evening of viewing had an increased probability of being imitated. This study also documented the impact of imported television programs. Of the 99 programs surveyed almost two-thirds were produced in the U.S. (these were above average in violence). Only 5 programs originated in New Zealand.

108. Goban-Klas, Tomasz. "Dyfuzja Informacji O Zamachu Na Jana Pawla II 13 Maja 1981." Zeszyty Prasoznawcze, R. XXIII, nr. 3 (93), 1982.

A survey of 228 respondents conducted by the Polish Center for
Public Studies to establish the rate of news diffusion following
the shooting assault on Pope John Paul in 1981.

109. Goddard, Peter. "Violence and Popular Music." Report of the
Royal Commission on Violence in the Communications Industry, Vol. 4,
Violence in Print and Music. Toronto, Canada: The Royal Commission,
1977, pp. 223-239.

Elements of music performance prone to violent effect are
examined: the sound of certain music, lyrics, stage presentation,
packaging and marketing styles. The evolution of rock music
during successive counter-cultural movements in the 1950s and
1960s is discussed. While the countercultural value of certain
music and performance style can be accepted, such values and
techniques have also been used to manipulate audiences without
concern for social consequences.

110. Goldstein, J. H. (ed.). Reporting Science: The Case of
Aggression. Hillsdale, NJ: Lawrence Erlbaum Associates, 1986.

This collection of essays explores some of the obstacles to mutual
exchange of information when it concerns research and theory on
the socially sensitive issue of violence. Discussed are the role
of the mass media, and the accuracy of information conveyed to the
public.

111. Goodrich, Herbert. "Man and Society in Mass-Media Fiction: The
Pattern of Life in the Mass Media as Revealed by Content Analysis
Studies." Dissertation Abstracts, Vol. 25,1965, p. 4851.

Comprehensive review and analysis with special reference to
demographic and action categories.

112. Gordon, Donald R. and Benjamin D. Singer. "Content Analysis of
the News Media: Newspapers and Television." Report of the Royal
Commission on Violence in the Communications Industry, Vol. 3, Violence
in Television, Films and News. Toronto, Canada: The Royal Commission,
1977, pp. 581-675.

Analysis of 8,000 news items published in 10 large-circulation
newspapers during one week in 1976. Of these, 45 percent were
conflict/violence related. Of 2,400 news items broadcast on 15
Canadian and American TV stations, 48 percent were
conflict/violence related. However, almost 60 percent of lead
items in both media were violence/conflict related. Direct,
physical violence (including natural and man-made disasters) is
about 10 percent more common in TV news than in the newspaper.
Ideological conflict and war are more likely to be depicted in
newspaper accounts than on TV. Television is more likely to
personalize violence in terms of private gain or deviance.
Consequences of conflict/violence are depicted about half the
time, somewhat more often in newspaper accounts. When consequence

is specified, it is death in 40 percent of these items,
particularly on television. Canadian television presented more
conflict/violence items, but U.S. television emphasized physical
violence to a greater degree.

113. Gordon, Donald R. and T. Lynn Ibson. "Content Analysis of the
News Media: Radio." Report of the Royal Commission on Violence in the
Communications Industry, Vol. 3, Violence in Television, Films and
News. Toronto, Canada: The Royal Commission, 1977, pp. 677-703.

A content analysis of 1,400 news items in 140 radio newscasts on
seven Ontario and two American radio stations in 1976. Over 63
percent of the items were violence/conflict related (similar to
the lead item percentage in TV and newspaper news found by Gordon
and Singer). There were other similarities: greater American
emphasis on death, especially murder, and other physical violence
as opposed to Canadian emphasis on nonviolent forms of conflict
and property damage.

114. Gordon, Margaret T. and Linda Heath. "The News Business, Crime,
and Fear." Reactions to Crime, Vol. 16, 1981, pp. 227-251.

A content analysis of 8015 articles about crime in newspapers
published in Philadelphia, Chicago, and San Francisco between Nov.
1977 and May 1978 revealed that crime news is easy news. Crime
stories permit the police to function as gatekeepers. Circulation
figures for these newspapers revealed that crime is competitive
news. Telephone interviews with a random sample of residents in
each city (N=1,389) revealed that the fear of crime among readers
of newspapers that exploit crime as easy, competitive news is
higher than among readers of newspapers that give less prominence
to crime coverage. Data also revealed that more readers of
newspapers that present a lot of crime consider crime to be the
major problem facing their neighborhoods than do readers of
newspapers that present less crime news.

115. Graalfs, Marilyn. "Violence in Comic Books." In Otto N. Larsen
(ed.), Violence and the Mass Media. New York: Harper and Row, 1968,
pp. 91-96.

A 1954 sample of 351 comic books was analyzed for violent content.
Crime comics comprised 28 percent of the total (humor and romance
were other major categories). A violent physical act was
portrayed in 14 percent of the frames (20 percent for crime and
war comics and 6 percent for humor comics). Striking with a
weapon was the most frequently presented type of physical
violence, appearing in 25 percent of violent frames. Another 25
percent of frames depicted death or injury. These findings
pre-dated self-regulation by the comics industry.

116. Graber, Doris A. "Evaluating Crime-Fighting Policies: Media Images and Public Perspective." In Ralph Baker and Fred A. Meyer, Jr. (eds.), Evaluating Alternative Law-Enforcement Policies, Lexington, MA: Heath Lexington Books, 1979, pp. 179-199.

    Comparison of amount of coverage of types of crime in several Midwestern U.S. newspapers and television newscasts with public perceptions concerning the frequency of these crimes during 1976-1977. Reports of political terrorism accounted for 5 percent of press reports and 8 percent of television news reports and ranked 4th out of 8 news topics. Respondents' daily viewing diaries, in which summaries of news items were recorded, revealed a similar pattern.

117.Graber, Doris A. Crime News and The Public. New York: Praeger, 1980.

    Knowledge about the nature of crime news and its impact on the images that people form about crime were the focus of this study. Through field interviews and content analyses of major print and electronic news sources during a one-year period, several hypotheses about learning about politically significant news from the mass media were tested. Results confirmed the hypothesis that exceptionally large amounts of crime information desensitize audiences to the extent that significant amounts are ignored. The opposite was true for the hypothesis that personal images of crime are more strongly influenced by media images than by official crime data.

118. Greenberg, Bradley S. "The Content and Context of Violence in the Mass Media." In Robert K. Baker and Sandra J. Ball, Mass Media and Violence, Vol. 9. Washington, DC: U.S. Government Printing Office, 1969, pp. 423-452.

    A summary of studies on violent content in print media and broadcasting since the early 1950s. Large circulation newspapers and magazines contained about 10 percent violence-related material (crime and accidents), with notable differences among them. About half of paperback books on newsstands featured violence and/or sex in cover illustrations. After 1954, there was a significant increase in the percentage of televised action-adventure programs in late afternoon and evening hours. About half of network programs in major urban areas made violence a predominant means of conflict resolution as of 1968. Characteristics of young people and adults associated with heavy television use generally--and violent content specifically--are listed.

119. Greenberg, Bradley S., Nadyne Edison, Felipe Korzenny, Carlos Fernandez-Collado, and Charles K. Atkin. "Antisocial and Prosocial Behaviors on Television." In Bradley S. Greenberg (ed.), Life on Television: Content Analyses of U.S. TV Drama, Norwood, NJ: Ablex Publishing Corp., 1980, pp. 99-128.

A content analysis of one episode of each prime-time and Saturday
morning fictional television series broadcast during 3 seasons
(1975-76, 1976-77, and 1977-78) to isolate antisocial acts
(physical aggression, verbal aggression, deceit, and theft) and
prosocial acts (altruism, affection, delaying gratification,
controlling other's antisocial behavior, and self-control).
Verbal aggression was the single largest category of antisocial
acts, occurring about 20 times an hour (overall there were about
40 antisocial acts per hour). Antisocial behaviors were committed
by major characters rather than minor ones and were heavily
concentrated among those characters more easily labeled as
villains or lawbreakers. A substantial number of prosocial
behaviors were concentrated among major, regularly-appearing
"good" characters.

120. Greenberg, Bradley S. and Thomas F. Gordon. "Perceptions of
Violence in Television Programs: Critics and the Public." In George
A. Comstock and Eli A. Rubinstein (eds.), Television and Social
Behavior, Vol. 1, Media Content and Control. Washington
DC: U.S. Government Printing Office, 1971, pp. 244-258. See also
Journal of Broadcasting, Vol. 15, 1971, pp. 24-43.

The ranking by degree of violence of 65 network evening series by
sampled TV critics and viewers was fairly stable, regardless of
whether a definition of violence was provided. Ranking was more
stable among critics than among viewers. Respondents given a
definition of violence perceived more violence in the programs.

121. Greenberg, Bradley S. and Thomas F. Gordon. "Social Class and
Racial Differences in Children's Perceptions of Television Violence."
In George A. Comstock, Eli A. Rubinstein, and John P. Murray (eds.),
Television and Social Behavior, Vol. 5, Television's Effects: Further
Explorations. Washington, DC: U.S. Government Printing Office, 1972,
pp. 185-230.

Ten year old children were exposed to different versions of a
45-minute film. There was more acceptance of television violence
and greater perception of such violence as realistic among lower
class boys and among black boys.

122. Gunter, Barrie and Adrian F. Furnham. "Androgyny and the
Perception of Television Violence as Perpetrated by Males and Females."
Human Relations, Vol. 38, No. 6, 1985, pp. 535-549.

Examined 18 female and 22 male British viewers' perceptual
judgments of 12 violent TV scenes from British crime detective
series and American detective and science fiction series in which
either a male assailant attacked a female victim or a female
assailant attacked a male victim. Violence was a shooting or fist
fight/physical struggle. Subjects rated scenes for seriousness of
content. Results show that male violence on a female victim was
rated as more serious than female violence on a male victim, but
only in the British crime dramas. In American and science fiction
contexts the reverse was true. Indications of the importance of

subjects' self-perceived masculinity/femininity and actual sex as
mediators of viewers' judgments about TV violence were also found.

123. Gunter, Barrie. "Personality and Perceptions of Harmful and
Harmless TV Violence." Personality and Individual Differences, Vol. 4,
No. 6, 1983, pp. 665-670.

Examined viewers' perceptions of violent TV portrayals
characterized by different degrees of observable harm to victims
and by different program settings, and related these perceptions
to subjects' scores on the Eysenck Personality Questionnaire
(EPQ). Subjects aged 15-55 years rated brief TV scenes depicting
violence in American crime detective or science fiction settings
that resulted in fatal or nonfatal injury, or in no observable
harm to victims. Harmful violence was rated as significantly more
serious than harmless violence in American crime detective
settings, but was less salient in science fiction settings. Older
subjects and those with lower Psychoticism scores tended to
perceive harmful violence as more violent, frightening and likely
to disturb others than were younger subjects with higher P scores.

124. Gunter, Barrie. Dimensions of Television Violence. New
York: St. Martin's Press, 1984.

This research project examines certain methods of classifying and
weighting the seriousness of violence portrayed in fictional TV
drama. An experimental approach investigates the ways in which
ordinary viewers perceptually differentiate and evaluate a wide
range of violence extracted from current TV drama. Violent
episodes were taken from British made crime-detective shows,
American made crime-detective shows, westerns, sci-fi and
cartoons. Effects on viewers' perceptions of TV violence on the
types of characters involved, types of weapons used, the physical
setting, and the consequences of violent incidences were
systematically explored. They indicate that ordinary viewers can
and do use many different attributes or features of aggressive TV
portrayals when judging how seriously violent they are. This
research demonstrates the complexity and variety of violent forms
on TV, and viewers' appraisals of them.

125. Gunter, Barrie, Adrian Furnham and Gillian Gietson. "Memory for
the News as a Function of the Channel of Communication." Human
Learning: Journal of Practical Research and Applications, Vol. 3,
No. 4, 1984, pp. 265-271.

Sixty female and sixty-eight male 16-18 year olds in the UK were
presented with a sequence of violent and nonviolent news stories
either audiovisually, in audio only or in print, and then tested
for recall of story content immediately. ANOVA showed significant
main effects of presentation medium, content type and sex. Recall
was best from print and worst on audiovisual. Violent content was
recalled better overall than nonviolent, and significantly so in
the audio-only and print modes. Males recalled more than females.
Results indicate that reading the news can produce more effective

retention than does listening to or watching it. Loss of
pictures, however, has a greater effect on recall of certain types
of news stories than on recall of other story types. It is
suggested that verbal material that readily conjures up images may
be more effectively remembered. Sex differences in recall may
reflect differences in interest or background knowledge.

126. Gurevitch, Michael. "The Structure and Content of Television
Broadcasting in Four Countries: An Overview." In George A. Comstock
and Eli A. Rubinstein (Eds.), Television and Social Behavior, Vol. 1,
Media Content and Control. Washington DC: U.S. Government Printing
Office, 1972, pp. 374-385.

A comparison of the studies of broadcasting structure and policies
governing violent content in Sweden, the United States, Great
Britain, and Israel. The author points out the pre-eminence of
"power roles" and corresponding hierarchies of sensitive issues
that transcend broadcasting policy statements in each country.
What is clear from the four content analyses of violence in
programming that accompany the structural analyses is that a
greater proportion of programs produced in the United States
contain violence. Also, programs produced in the United States
tend to dominate program markets in smaller countries.

127. Hagenauer, Fedor and James W. Hamilton. "Straw Dogs: Aggression
and Violence in Modern Films." American Imago, Vol. 30, No. 3, 1973,
pp. 221-249.

A psychoanalytic interpretation of the 1971 movie frequently
considered one of the most violent films ever produced which
relates details of theme and action to complexities of human
aggression and violence. The authors discuss the way in which
violence in this film is used to initiate and structure a change
in a dramatic character and to depict core conflicts in
personality and social relationships.

128. Haines, H. Violence on Television: A Report on the Mental Health
Foundation's Media Watch Survey. Auckland: Mental Health Foundation of
New Zealand, 1983.

Patterns of violent content in Australia generally are similar to
those in the United States and the United Kingdom: 66 percent of
programs sampled contained violence. In the U.S. about 80 percent
of programs contain violence and in the U.K. about 56 percent
contain violence.

129. Hallin, Daniel C. and Paolo Mancini. "Political Structure and
Representational Form in the U.S. and Italian Television News." In
Lars Furhoff and Pertti Hemanus (eds), New Directions in Journalism.
University of Stockholm School of Journalism, 1985, pp. 48-66.

Compares the presentation of television news as related to the political and institutional structure of media in the two countries.

130. Halloran, James D. and Paul Croll. "Television Programs in Great Britain: Content and Control." In George A. Comstock and Eli A. Rubinstein (eds.), Television and Social Behavior, Vol. 1, Media Content and Control. Washington, DC: U.S. Government Printing Office, 1972, pp. 415-492.

A comparison of the non-commercial British Broadcasting Corporation (BBC) and the commercial Independent Television Authority (ITA). Corporate structure (decision-making and accountability, finance, and channels for public influence) and its relation to programming policy is outlined in detail. Content codes are considered guides, but often concentrate on proscribed details rather than a larger context of ideas. Program decision-making is centered on avoiding offense and is a complex of decisions concerning program mix, financing, and competition for audiences. Analysis of one week of late afternoon and evening programming in 1971 revealed that over half the programs contained violence (a larger percentage on BBC than on an independent station). Of programs originating in the U.K., 45 percent contained violence. U.S.-originated programs comprised about 30 percent of total programming in the U.K., and 75 percent of these (generally action-adventure episodes, films, and cartoons) contained violence.

131. Haney, Craig and John Manzolati. "Television Criminology: Network Illusions of Criminal Justice Realities." In Elliot Aronson (ed.), Readings About the Social Animal. San Francisco: W. H. Freeman, 1980.

Common themes in television drama are not representative of criminal justice realities such as frequency of types of crime and underlying causes of crime. Examples of such themes are: criminality as a result of personality traits rather than as a response to social conditions such as unemployment; emphasis on street crime rather than offenses related to intoxication or white-collar crime; and police violations of law as justified in the apprehending of criminals. A cultivation study of several hundred viewers revealed that heavy viewers were more likely to express attitudes reflecting these themes, such as automatic presumption of guilt of a suspect; belief that legal rights protect the guilty rather than the innocent; and the belief that police are not restricted by law in their efforts to apprehend suspected criminals.

132. Hansen, A. and Graham Murdock. "Constructing the Crowd: Populist Discourse and Press Presentation." In V. Mosco and J. Wasko (eds.), The Critical Communications Review, Volume 3: Popular Culture and Media Events, Norwood, NJ: Ablex, 1985, pp. 227-258.

38

In the summer of 1981 serious riots occurred in several major
English cities. This paper attempts to illustrate how definitions
and interpretations were actively constructed out of the raw
materials provided by the available political discourses. The
authors outline the main public discourses in play at the time,
and then look at the way this populist discourse was reconstructed
and reproduced in the national press coverage in the week
following the first weekend of riots. The authors explore how
language and photographic imagery deployed in the news reporting
combined to "close" their presentation of events around the terms
established in populist discourse.

133. Harris, Frank. Presentation of Crime in Newspapers: A Study of
Method in Newspaper Research. Hanover, New Hampshire: Sociological
Press, 1932.

This early analysis of emphasis on crime was conducted using
Minneapolis newspapers in three periods: 1890, 1904-05, and 1921
(years when the largest number of papers were available). The
author found uniformity of coverage of types of crime, with
emphasis on "offenses against the person," particularly murder.
Analysis of emphasis (front-page placement) revealed concentration
on local rather than outside crime, although outside crime was
presented more regularly. Coverage was compared to court records
of percentages of arrests for specific types of crime.

134. Hart, Henry O. "Emergent Collective Opinion and Upheaval in East
Europe and the Role of Radio Communication: A Further Extension of
Basic Models." Munich, 1980.

Theoretical analysis of models of communication in relation to the
role of interpersonal and mass media channels in organizing and
maintaining political dissent, using five Eastern European
communist bloc countries as examples and with particular reference
to events in Poland from 1956 to 1977. The author outlines the
contribution of Radio Free Europe in the containment of civil
violence in conjunction with reinforcement of traditional values
at odds with a new socio-political system.

135. Harvey, Susan E., Joyce N. Sprafkin, and Eli Rubinstein. "Prime
Time Television: A Profile of Aggressive and Prosocial Behaviors."
Journal of Broadcasting, Vol. 23, No. 2, 1979, pp. 179-189.

A sample of 66 regularly-scheduled prime-time programs broadcast
in 1975 was used to study the impact of family viewing time policy
on program content and the appearance of pro-social behaviors.
Violence appeared at an overall rate of about 13 acts per hour.
The level of violence was reduced during family viewing hours but
not during other times. Only two pro-social behaviors appeared
with any meaningful frequency: sympathy and explaining feelings
(about eight acts per hour) and altruism (about four acts per
hour). Both types of pro-social acts were more likely to be seen
between 8 and 9 p. m. (family viewing time).

136. Haskins, Jack B. "The Effects of Violence in the Printed Media." In Robert K. Baker and Sandra J. Ball, Mass Media and Violence, Vol. 9. Washington, DC: U.S. Government Printing Office, 1969, pp. 493-502.

A brief review of violent content analyses and effects studies. The author concludes that laboratory-type experiments of questionable generalizeability indicate a possible triggering effect on a small percentage of the population who are predisposed to violence under certain conditions.

137. Hawkins, Robert P. and Suzanne Pingree. "Uniform Content and Habitual Viewing: Unnecessary Assumptions in Social Reality Effects." Human Communication Research, Vol. 7. No. 4, 1981, pp. 291-301.

Analysis of television's cultivation effect on Australian primary-school children and teenagers in 1977 revealed many differences related to program type, particularly in regard to beliefs about the level of violence in society. Among ten types of program content, viewing of crime programs was most strongly related to belief in a more violent world and lack of trust. Viewing may be more selective than previously thought. These findings, while challenging the hypothesis that messages are consistent across all television programs, supports the cultivation hypothesis and may account for cultivation of different beliefs and attitudes in different segments of a population.

138. Haynes, Richard B. "Children's Perceptions of 'Comic' and 'Authentic' Cartoon Violence." Journal of Broadcasting, Vol. 22, No. 1, 1978, pp. 63-70.

Schoolchildren aged 10-11 were randomly placed in one of two experimental groups. The respondents perceived the actions of comic and authentic cartoons as being significantly different. The comic cartoon was perceived as more violent and less acceptable than the authentic. Violent content in comic cartoons is recognized as violent by children. The findings also point to the possibility that comic violence is seen as more violent, possibly more feared by the child viewer, and less acceptable than violence occurring in authentic cartoon programs.

139. Head, Sydney W. "Content Analysis of Television Drama Programs." Quarterly of Film, Radio and Television, Vol. 9, 1954, pp. 175-194.

A content analysis of 209 episodes of 64 network dramatic series broadcast in 1952. Crime/aggression in children's programs was above the average for crime programs. General drama and situation comedy were low in violence. More than half of acts coded were violent, and more than half of these involved use of weapons. There were 110 homicides. Proportionately, killers were more often major characters than were victims. Compared to real life, homicide was considerably over-represented in television drama. However, real-life events such as birth, health failure, natural death, and rape were not dealt with in TV drama.

140. Higgins, Patricia B. and Marla W. Ray. <u>Television's Action Arsenal: Weapon Use in Prime Time</u>. Washington, DC: United States COnference of Mayors, 1978.

This study was conducted to fill a perceived information gap in TV violence research literature, regarding instruments of violence. 73 hours of prime time "action" shows were observed between March and August of 1977. Weapons studied were limited to those that could be held in the user's hand. Type of weapon, manner of appearance, reason for use, character types of both user and target, and results of weapon use were coded and cross tabulated. Partial findings were that handguns were most common, whites and males were the overwhelming majority of both users and targets, and confrontations were evenly divided between Police officers and "bad guys", although Police more often threatened than actually used their weapons. The report suggests that weapon use on TV is excessive and uncomfortably antiseptic. Little blood letting or suffering accompany weapon use, thus the severity of the results of weapon use is ignored.

141. Himmelweit, Hilde T., A. N. Oppenheim, and Pamela Vince. <u>Television and the Child: An Empirical Study of the Effect of Television on the Young</u>. London: Oxford University Press, 1958.

Content analysis of 20 western and crime programs in Britain revealed stylized presentation of weapons, with infrequent portrayal of moral consquences. These consequences were most remote in westerns, but realistic and personal in crime shows. Crime shows were a preferred program type among children aged 10-14. Children younger than age six often were frightened by violence on television, according to reports by mothers. Beyond that age, media violence was accepted as fantasy. Children were most upset by violence that was similar to their real-life situation. Analysis of ratings of aggressive behavior of children, personality inventories, and viewing habits revealed no relationship between TV viewing and aggressive behavior. While media violence may affect emotionally-disturbed or already aggressive children, a more general effect may be a limitation of children's awareness of consequences of aggression and acceptance of aggression as a means of conflict resolution.

142. Hoge, James W. "The Media and Terrorism." In Abraham H. Miller (ed.), <u>Terrorism: The Media and the Law</u>. New York: Transnational Publishers, 1982, pp. 89-105.

An examination of the media's responsibilities in covering terrorism using specific examples in several countries to back a claim for expanded rather than restricted coverage of such events. While calling for professional restraint and outlining those guidelines that exist among the various news organizations, the author points to the similarity in effect of voluntary guidelines and enforced censorship.

143. Hogg, Peter W. "Constitutional Jurisdiction over Violence in the Mass Media Industries." Report of the Royal Commission on Violence in the Communications Industry, Vol. 7, The Media Industries. Toronto, Canada: The Royal Commission 1977, pp. 229-325.

This article outlines the several jurisdictions involved in regulating content in Canadian film, theatre, print, records and tapes, radio, and television. Included are relevant sections of the 1867 Constitution (the British North American Act) and the parliamentary power of "peace, order, and good government" vis a vis a somewhat limited grant of freedom of speech and press in the Canadian Bill of Rights. The balancing of national and provincial responsibilities regarding media content is explained in a discussion of several specific legal cases involving censorship from 1938 to 1976.

144. Howitt, Dennis and Guy Cumberbatch. "Audience Perceptions of Violent Television Content." Communication Research, Vol. 1, No. 2, 1974, pp. 204-223.

Viewers stratified by social class provided ratings on several descriptive variables for a number of television programs, including violent content, fantasy-reality orientation, and justification of violence. It was hypothesized that these variables might influence the effect of televised violence. Certain types of programs were perceived as less violent than others, despite the actual amount of physical violence depicted. Fictional and humorous violent sequences were rated less violent than violence with a realistic orientation. Viewers also distinguished between justified and unjustified violence.

145. Hughes, Norman and Douglas Jefferson. "Census of Murder." In Martin S. Allwood (ed.), Studies in Mass Communication, 1950-1951, 1951, pp. 26-27.

Analysis of detective magazine character profiles compared to real-life criminals indicated that two-thirds of fictional murderers were college-educated and many were professionals. Three-quarters of real-life murderers, on the other hand, completed only grade school and few finished college.

146. Hutchinson, Bruce D. "Comic Strip Violence 1911-66." Journalism Quarterly, Vol. 46, No. 2, 1969, pp. 358-362.

Examination of yearly samples of over 5,000 comic strips in one U.S. city newspaper revealed that about 30 percent of the strips and 13 percent of the picture panels portrayed actual or threatened violence. There was considerable variation over the 50-year period, ranging from 90 percent in 1918 to 15 percent in 1966 and fairly constant at about 25 percent since 1925. Comparison with samples from several other newspapers revealed some differences of 5 percent or less in amount of violence depicted. These figures were compared to a declining homicide rate between 1930 and 1963.

147. Independent Broadcasting Authority. "Use of Television in Relation to Events in the Environment: More Evidence on Violence." IBA, Audience Research Department, 1980.

There is evidence for a small measure of selectivity of viewing in Northern Ireland. There is less viewing of action/adventure material in Ulster than in other sections of Northern Ireland. Those who view action/adventure programs however, report enjoying them more.

148. Iozzia, Giovanni and Graziella Priulla. Dal Silenzio al Rumore: L'Informazione Quotidiana e Due Delitti di Mafia. [From a Whisper to a Roar: Daily Media Coverage and Two Mafia Incidents]. RAI Radiotelevisione Italiana, Verifica dei Programmi Trasmessi. Rome: RAI, 1984.

A comparative study of the Italian daily press and television coverage at two points in time -- 1980 and 1983 (after the killings of two Sicilian magistrates and of General Dalla Chiesa, Prefect of Palermo, in September 1982). Between 1980 and 1983 television reporting on the Mafia tripled and press coverage was two-and-one-half times as great. There was also greater use of photographs and film clips in 1983. Both Sicilian newspapers and television echoed official versions of events despite the broader coverage allowed by the print media.

149. Israel, Harold, W. R. Simmons and Associates, and John P. Robinson. "Demographic Characteristics of Viewers of Television Violence and News Programs." In George A. Comstock and Eli A. Rubinstein (eds.), Television and Social Behavior, Vol. 4, Television in Day-to-Day Life: Patterns of Use. Washington, DC: U.S. Government Printing Office, 1972, pp. 87-128.

Male heavy viewers of violence are disproportionately from lower income groups and have less education. They also tend to be over 50 and black. Males between 18 and 24 who are high school dropouts are especially heavy viewers of violence. Race seems to be the major determinant of violence viewing among women; education, income, and age play less important roles. Most viewers of news programs are older, regardless of their educational level or overall television viewing.

150. Iwao, Sumiko and Ithiel de Sola Pool. "International Understanding via TV Programmes: The Case of 'Shogun'." KEIO Communication Review, No. 4, 1983, pp. 3-12.

Millions of Americans and Japanese saw "Shogun" on television in 1980-81. Viewers were interviewed in person in Japan and via telephone in the United States the morning after the first episode and again after the final episode. Japanese viewers were most concerned with unfavorable, violent scenes; American viewers were most concerned about how the final episode ended.

151. Iwao, Sumiko, Ithiel de Sola Pool, and Shigeru Hagiwara. "Japanese and U.S. Media: Some Cross-Cultural Insights into TV Violence." Journal of Communication, Vol. 31, No. 2, 1981, pp. 28-36.

A sample of 139 Japanese evening entertainment programs broadcast in 1977 was examined. Half were children's programs, including many cartoons. There were 24 imported programs, mostly from the United States. Violence which arouses viewer compassion, expecially that suffered by good characters, was common in Japanese programs. In most U.S. programs, however, villains are more likely to be subjected to violence. 80 percent of the Japanese programs contained violence (similar to the percentage found in studies of U.S. programming)

152. Jackson, Robert J., Michael J. Kelly, and Thomas H. Mitchell. "Collective Conflict, Violence and the Media." Report of the Royal Commission on Violence in the Communications Industry, Vol. 5, Learning from the Media. Toronto, Canada: The Royal Commission, 1977, pp. 227-314.

A review of U.S. Government-sponsored research on the relationship between media coverage of conflict and violence in society prefaces this analysis data for 19 countries, including Canada. The U.S. finding of no direct relationship is supported by the cross-cultural data. Newspaper coverage in Ontario of 129 incidents of collective violence and 9 incidents involving individuals during 1965-1975 was examined to determine amount of emphasis given these events. Violence- and crime-related items accounted for 20 percent of first-page coverage, including 8 percent relating to political violence. Initial coverage of individual violence was three times as extensive as that of collective violence. The authors recommended policies and practices by which media and law enforcement agencies could limit the potential for aggravating conflict situations.

153. Jaehnig, Walter B. "Terrorism in Britain: The Limits of Free Expression." In Abraham H. Miller (ed.), Terrorism: The Media and the Law. New York: Transnational Publishers, 1982, pp. 106-129.

An examination of media-law enforcement-government relationships in regard to the coverage of terrorism. Violent acts related to the political dispute between England and Northern Ireland is covered specifically. Media self-regulation by the British Broadcasting Corporation is examined against the background of the 1974 Prevention of Terrorism Act and a 1979 agreement with London's Metropolitan Police concerning "sensitive" programming.

154. Jaehnig, Walter B., David H. Weaver, and Fred Fico. "Reporting Crime and Fearing Crime in Three Communities." Journal of Communication, Vol. 31, No. 1, 1981, pp. 88-96.

A panel of 45 adults in each of three communities of different sizes and in different regions was recruited in January, 1976. Data on fear of crime was supplemented by content analyses conducted from January-August, 1976, of each community's major newspaper. The rankings of concern over crime were identical to the rankings of both newspaper emphasis on crime and the number of violent crimes per person in the three communities, suggesting that both fear of crime and newspaper coverage of crime may be more a consequence of the frequencies of all kinds of crime. The percentages also indicate that the level of fear is associated more strongly with newspaper emphasis on violent crime than with the actual frequency of violent crime in the community.

155. Johnson, Paula B., David O. Sears, and John B. McConahy. "Black Invisibility, the Press, and the Los Angeles Riot." American Journal of Sociology, Vol. 76, No. 4, 1971, pp. 698-721.

Content analysis of two major Los Angeles newspapers from 1892 to 1968 indicated that little attention was given to blacks in the press. Coverage relative to their increasing proportion of the Los Angeles population decreased from 1892 until just prior to the 1965 riot. The considerable increase in coverage at the time of the riot was reduced to the earlier level by early 1966, although the focus changed from stereotypical characterizations and activities to role in social activism after World War II to interracial conflict. Analysis of opinions held by white residents and leaders revealed a lack of understanding of the problems of the black community and a racism of indifference or fear.

156. Jones, Dorothy B. "Quantitative Analysis of Motion Picture Content." Public Opinion Quarterly, Vol. 6, 1942, pp. 411-428.

This early content analysis of films focusing on the goals of characters, documented the prominence of mystery/murder and gangster movies as general categories. The quest for safety is presented as a central goal, along with material and psychological benefits. A death rate of 10 percent for heroes and heroines is linked to the dramatic impact of such depictions.

157. Jowett, Garth, Penny Reath, and Monica Schouten. "The Control of Mass Entertainment Media in Canada, the United States, and Great Britain: Historical Surveys." Report of the Royal Commission on Violence in the Communications Industry, Vol. 4, Violence in Print and Music. Toronto, Canada: The Royal Commission 1977, pp. 1-104.

The authors trace violent content of several media from 16th-century pamphlets and newspapers along with legal control of such content from the 19th century Victorian era. Chapters are devoted to discussion of the sensation novel, the American penny press, comic strips, radio, film, and thematic differences in treatment of violence in Canadian and U.S.fiction. An extensive bibliography contains sections pertaining to each medium.

158. Joyce, Edward M. "Reporting Hostage Crises: Who's in Charge of Television?" SAIS Review, Vol. 6, No. 1, 1986, pp. 169-176.

Reviews the debate which deals with the role of television in hostage- taking acts of terrorism. Examples are cited of arguments regarding media coverage as helping or hindering the cause of terrorism, and commenting upon the public's right to information.

159. Katzman, Natan I. "Violence and Color Television: What Children of Different Ages Learn." In George A. Comstock, Eli A. Rubinstein, and John P. Murray (eds.), Television and Social Behavior, Vol. 5, Television's Effects: Further Explorations. Washington, DC: U.S. Government Printing Office, 1972, pp. 253-308.

Boys in the 4th, 5th, and 6th grades served as subjects in this study using 4 versions of a detective program (high-low violence and color-black and white presentation) as the stimulus materials. Overall, the high violence presentation was perceived as significantly more violent than the low violence presentation. Moreover, the color format had no significant effect on perceived violence or on measures of liking the program. After a two-week period the high violence version was rated as significantly more violent than it was rated immediately after presentation. The low violence version was rated at the same level both times. In general, color does not improve the learning of visual material that is central to a presentation.

160. Kerner, Otto (chairman). Report on the National Advisory Commission on Civil Disorders, New York: Bantam Books, 1968.

This commission was first to discuss the role of reporting in group violence. Conclusions that intial news reports and TV coverage may be exaggerated and accounts may deviate from events. Sensationalism or racial incitation were not major problems of coverage, but rather inadequacies in analysis and reports of racial grievances surfaced. Also found that blacks were presented in the news primarily in the context of disorder rather than in ordinary or normal settings.

161. Knight, Graham and Tony Dean. "Myth and the Structure of News." Journal of Communication, Vol. 32, No. 2, 1982, pp. 144-161.

An analysis of Canadian press coverage of the British recapturing of the Iranian embassy in London. The work reveals that myths work through news accounts by developing abstract notions of expertise and legitimacy. The authors compare the accounts of the embassy takeover in two of Toronto's leading dailies -- the Globe and Mail and the Sun.

162. Knopf, Terry Ann. "Media Myths on Violence." Columbia Journalism Review, Spring, 1970, pp. 17-23.

   The media tend to equate bad news with big news and to confuse the obvious with the relevant. The use of the word "riot" and "disturbance" are often used incorrectly by journalists. The system of reporting ensures that errors of fact and interpretation may be repeated, compounded, and reformulated as myths. Different media tend to reproduce rather than examine one another's views.

163. Kohli, Suresh (ed.). Sex and Violence in Literature and Arts. New Dehli, India: Sterling Publishers Private, Ltd. , 1973.

   Sex has been an important part of East Indian literature and arts through the centuries, and violence, the editor asserts, is a mainstay of Indian films. This collection of essays by writers and critics reviews and comments upon the most controversial books and films in Indian society.

164. Krattenmaker, Thomas G., and L. A. Powe, Jr. "Televised Violence: First Amendment Principles and Social Science Theory." Virginia Law Review, Vol. 64, 1978, pp. 1123-1297.

   Review of research on television and violence from a legal perspective. Concludes that available research does not warrant, from a legal or constitutional perspective, the implementation of a regulatory program to inhibit violent programming.

165. Larsen, Otto N. (ed.). Violence and the Mass Media. New York: Harper and Row, 1968.

   An overview of the issue of violent content in media, containing perspectives and reports of research. Most of the articles examine the question of how the nature and incidence of real violence might be affected by exposure to mass media violence.

166. Larsen, Otto N. "Controversies About the Mass Communication of Violence." Annals of the American Academy of Political and Social Science, Vol. 364, 1966, pp. 37-49.

   Few would dispute that American mass communication dispenses large doses of violence to ever growing audiences. Two related controversies stem from this fact. One concerns the question of effects and the other the problem of control. An inventory of relevant research is inconclusive about effects, partly because of varying conceptions of what constitutes evidence. A dynamic opinion process leads to control efforts. Critics play a vital part in defining discontent. A reciprocal relationship emerges between the public, the critic, and the media. American media respond to controversery and threat of censorship with systems of self-regulation. These grow out of public opinion and are sustained by it in a delicate balance dependent somewhat on developing knowledge of the effects of violence.

47

167. Larsen, Otto N., Louis N. Gray, and J. Gerald Fortis. "Achieving Goals Through Violence on Television." In Otto N. Larsen (ed,), Violence and the Mass Media. New York: Harper and Row, pp. 97-111. See also Sociological Inquiry, 1963, Vol. 33 1963, pp. 180-196.

Analysis of 18 TV dramas aimed at audiences of different ages indicated that violence was the most common means used by characters to achieve goals such as property, power, and self-preservation. Violence was used 47 percent of the time in shows with a predominantly child audience, compared to 32 percent of the time in programs directed to adults.

168. Lefkowitz, Monroe M. and L. Rowell Huesmann. "Concomitants of Television Violence Viewing in Children." In Edward L. Palmer and Aimee Dorr (eds.), Children and the Faces of Television: Teaching, Violence, Selling. New York: Academic Press, 1981, pp. 165-182.

Author suggests that findings of the Surgeon General's report and subsequent empirical and observational studies have demonstrated the contribution of television portrayals to the escalation of violence within American society. Four concomitant categories of violence-viewing effect -- aggression, socialization and values, physiological responses, and mood -- are discussed. So far none of this evidence has lead to a significant decrease in television violence. Suggests three possible strategies for regulation: parents' regulation of children's exposure to television, self-regulation of the industry in regard to amount and type of violence presented, and government regulation of violent television programming.

169. Levy, Sheldon G. "A 150-year Study of Political Violence in the United States." In Hugh Davis Graham and Ted Robert Gur (eds.), The History of Violence in America. New York: Praeger, 1969, pp. 84-100.

A quantitative analysis of the historical levels of political violence in the United States. All politically-violent events were coded in a sample of 6,000 issues of the New York Times and the Washington Intelligencer published between 1819 and 1968, all politically-violent events were coded. The number of events and the number of people injured and killed were measured, as well as the motivations for political violence. Adjustments for both newspaper size and population indicate that this period of history did not witness more internal political violence than previous periods, although the absolute number of violent events increased greatly in recent years.

170. Linton, James M. and Garth S. Jowett. "A Content Analysis of Feature Films." Report of the Royal Commission on Violence in the Communications Industry, Vol. 3, Violence in Television, Films and News. Toronto, Canada: The Royal Commission, 1977, pp. 574-580.

An extensive content analysis of 25 feature films released in
Canada in 1975. The great majority of these films were produced
outside of Canada, most notably in the United States. Among the
dimensions analyzed were incidents of conflict, character
profiles, and interpersonal relationships. Of all incidents
involving conflict and anti-social behavior, 50 percent depicted
violence, with an average of 13.5 violent incidents per film.
Non-Canadian films contained about twice as many violent incidents
as those produced in Canada. These incidents occur most
frequently in action films, including crime drama. Thematic
elements of these depictions are examined as well as various
characteristics of the fictional participants. One-third of the
violent incidents occurred between members of different national,
ethnic, or racial groups; one-quarter of the incidents involved
law agents.

171. Lule, Jack. "The Myth of My Widow: A Dramatistic Analysis of News
Portrayals of a Terrorist Victim." Terrorism and the News Media
Research Project, Paper No. 8, Louisiana State University, (undated).

This paper explores news portrayals of terrorist victims and
discusses the implications of such portrayals for public policies.
The Dramatistic analysis suggests a relationship between the news
stories and myth, if myth is defined not as a false or incredible
tale, but as a symbolic narrative that attempts to explain and
give meaning to practices and beliefs. A compelling mythic image
-- the heroic victim -- is given dramatic portrayal by news
accounts of the victim's widow. Mythic images in the news may
help create a powerful climate for prevention and reprisal against
terrorism.

172. Lyness, Paul I. "The Place of the Mass Media in the Lives of Boys
and Girls." Journalism Quarterly, Vol. 29, 1952, pp. 43-55.

An early study of newspaper reader preferences among children and
adolescents employing classroom questionnaires for 1400
respondents in midwestern United States. In this period, prior to
general availability of television, the majority expressed
interest in reading about murders, robberies, and accidents. Boys
were about 10 percent more likely than girls to report these
preferences.

173. Maccoby, Eleanor E. and William C. Wilson. "Identification and
Observational Learning from Films." Journal of Abnormal and Social
Psychology, Vol. 55, 1957, pp. 76-87.

This research analyzed the relationship between children's
identification with particular media characters and recollection
of violent content. Adolescents viewed movies with various types
of characters and later were interviewed. Recollection depended
on subjects' identification choice and the relevance of the
content to their needs. The adolescents tended to identify with
characters of the same sex and of the social class to which they
aspired. Overall, boys remembered aggressive action in the

49

portrayals more than girls did; aggression by female characters appeared to be less salient than other forms of portrayed interaction for adolescent girls.

174. Martin, L. John. "The Media's Role in International Terrorism." Paper presented to the Association for Education in Journalism and Mass Communication, Corvallis, Oregon, 1983.

This study revealed that the mass media may quote someone using "terror" or "terrorism" in reference to an act performed by a group toward which the medium is either neutral or opposed. The press, however, will never use these terms in a headline unless it not only disapproves of the act but has no sympathy for its perpetrators. Five newspapers were studied, four foreign and one American, on five alternate days in late June and early July, 1983.

175. Mattern, Kimberly K. and Bryon W. Lindholm. "Effect of Maternal Commentary in Reducing Aggressive Impact of Televised Violence on Preschool Children." The Journal of Genetic Psychology, Vol. 146, No. 1, 1985, pp. 133-135.

In an experiment, the authors subjected two groups of children and their mothers to viewing a television segment with numerous expressions of violence. In the treatment group, mothers made anti-violence comments during viewing. In the non-treatment condition the mothers made no commments. Data were gathered in two settings following the viewing. Data analysis revealed that treatment condition subjects did not differ significantly in help-hinder behavior, although sex differences were indicated.

176. McCann, T. E. and Peter W. Sheehan. "Violence Content in Australian Television." Australian Journal of Psychology, c.1984.

A content analysis of 80 Australian television programs broadcast in 1981, studied as part of a larger longitudinal study on the relationship between TV violence viewing and aggressiveness in children. About 50 percent of the programs contained some form of violence, which was considerably less than the 80 percent level in the U.S. and Japan, and comparable to rates in Canada and the United Kingdom. About one-third of the violence was unnecessary. Strong sex bias was observed in violence portrayals, and contemporary settings heightened the dramatic context.

177. McCormack, Thelma. "Hollywood's Prizefight Films: Violence or 'Jock' Appeal?" Journal of Sport and Social Issues, Vol. 8, No. 2, 1984, pp. 19-29.

The practice of many psychological experiments on aggression which use prizefight films as their stimuli is questioned. Examining these films from 1939 to 1982, it is suggested that they are primarily about "jock" appeal rather than violence. Jock appeal is defined as male narcissism, in contrast with the professional

athlete who must think and organize as well as do. To the extent
that the films deal with violence, it is the contrast between the
instrumental violence of the ring and the expressive violence of
the fans. The value of jock appeal in discussions of media
experiences and the relevance of this concept in films about
female athletes are discussed.

178. McCormack, Thelma. "Deregulating the Economy and Regulating
Morality: The Political Economy of Censorship." Studies in Political
Economy, Vol. 18, Fall, 1985, pp. 173-185.

The current agitation in Canada for stronger censorship laws
reflects a return to a more conservative political environment,
with emphasis on deregulating the economy and regulating morality.
The preoccupation with "violence" by antipornography activists is
seen here as an attack. It is also suggested that the problem
from a feminist perspective is not the eroticization of violence,
but that of power, which may take many benign forms. The Fraser
report on pornography and prostitution in Canada rejects the claim
that exposure to pornography leads to acts of sexual aggression
such as rape; instead it directs attention to the obstruction of
women's aspirations for equality. The question is raised as to
whether equality and freedom of expression are tradeoffs or are
necessary for each other.

179. Midgley, Sarah and Virginia Rice (eds.). Terrorism and the Media
in the 1980s (Conference Proceedings). Washington, DC: The Media
Institute and Institute for Studies in International Terror, 1984.

A discussion of the relationship between news coverage and
terrorist events. Many experts in this field propose guidelines,
such as those used at CBS, that leave the media responsible for
policing its own actions and using its judgment as to what extent
coverage will be given to each terrorist act. However, others
feel that the media, by virtue of their nature, will not be firm
enough and suggest that formal legislation is necessary to keep
the media in hand. There is strong support for the position that
the public's right to know is secondary to the safety of the
people involved.

180. Miller, Abraham H. "Terrorism, the Media, and the Law: A
Discussion of the Issues." In Abraham H. Miller (ed.), Terrorism: The
Media and the Law. New York: Transnational Publishers, 1982,
pp. 13-50.

A brief discussion of several of the issues relating to media
coverage of terrorism. Media access to sources, relationships
with government and law enforcement are examined, including ways
in which these relationships are moderated by the law. Specific
terrorist incidents are used to elucidate areas of conflict
between institutions. The author also provides an overview of
questions concerning the depiction of terrorists in the media.

181. Miller, Judith Beinstein. "Television Viewing and Cultivation of Interpersonal Mistrust." Manuscript. Oberlin College, Department of Communication Studies, 1984.

Data from the National Opinion Research Center General Social Surveys of 1975, 1978, and 1980 were used to examine the relationship between peoples' mistrust of others and their satisfaction with interpersonal relationships, and to discover whether satisfaction would condition the relationship between their mistrust and exposure to television. Results indicated that in each year, satisfaction with friends, family, and marriage accounted for significant portions of variance in their mean world scores, as did their exposure to television. The greater their satisfaction with interpersonal sources of support, the lower their mean world scores.

182. Miller, N. L. "Media Liability for Injuries That Result from Television Broadcasts to Immature Audiences." San Diego Law Review, Vol. 22, No. 1, 1985, pp. 377-400.

The author argues that, when a child or a third party is injured as a result of the child's imitative act of television violence, the broadcaster should be held subject to liability. As with parents, teachers and neighbors who might contribute to a child's ability to commit an act of violence, the issue of whether the broadcaster exercised reasonable care in the particular case should be presented to a jury for determination.

183. Mirams, Gordon. "Drop That Gun!" Quarterly of Film, Radio and Television, Vol. 6, No. 1, 1951, pp. 1-19.

Analysis of crime and violence in 100 feature films in New Zealand in 1950, the majority of which were U.S. productions. About 85 percent contained one or both of these elements, with an average of 6.6 acts per film. The rate of crime and violence in U.S. films was about twice that in British films. Of 659 instances of crime and violence, 168 were murders or attempted murders--a considerable proportion of which occurred in 17 Westerns. Heroes contributed over one-third of the deaths, in bringing criminals to justice or in self-defense.

184. Morcellini, Mario and Franco Avallone. Il ruolo dell' informazione in una situazione di emergenza - 16 marzo 1978: il rapimento di Aldo Moro. [The role of information in an emergency situation - March 16, 1978: The Kidnapping of Aldo Moro]. Rome: RAI Radiotelevisione Italiana, Verifica Programmi Trasmessi, 1978.

A content analysis of news reporting in public and private broadcasting and in both the Italian and foreign press on March 16-17, 1978. On this day, Aldo Moro, president of the Christian Democratic Party, was kidnapped and his escorts killed by the Red Brigades.

185. Morcellini, Mario. "L'Informazione Periodica in Televisione" and "L'Attualita' Televisiva: Struttura Dell'Offerta Informativa Sul Territorio." In RAI Radiotelevisione Italiana, Terrorismo e TV, Vol. 1, Italia. Immagini del Terrorismo nel Rotocalco Televisivo. Rome: RAI, Verifica dei Programmi Trasmessi, 1982.

   Results of content analysis on terrorism in evening information and cultural programs on Italian television networks during November 1980 - August 1981. Terrorism accounted for slightly more than 2 percent of the thematic content. Terrorism in other countries (particularly Ireland and Germany) was given wide coverage.

186. Moreland, Richard L., and Michael L. Berbaum. "Terrorism and the Mass Media: A Researcher's Bibliography." In Abraham H. Miller (ed.), Terrorism: The Media and the Law. New York: Transnational Publishers, 1982, pp. 191-215.

   The fields of communications, journalism, law, psychology, and sociology are represented in this bibliography of approximately 500 works relating to media violence and the coverage of terrorism.

187. Murray, John P. "Children and Television--What Do We Know?" In A. Burns, J. Goodnow, R. Chisolm, and J. P. Murray (eds.), Children and Families in Australia: Contemporary Issues and Problems. Sydney, Australia: Allen & Unwin, 1985.

   An overview of various aspects of television and its effects on child viewers, with particular reference to televised violence. Summarizes results of research in several countries, including Australia and the U.S., concerning levels of TV violence and the relationship between viewing and aggressive attitudes and behaviors. The author points to the important influence of individual personality and environmental factors on response to media content.

188. National Coalition on Television Violence. NCTV News. Champaign, IL: NCTV, 1980 to date.

   This newsletter reports on many aspects of violence in society: research on media content and effects, ratings and reviews of programs, scholarly and popular commentary, citizen and governmental action relating to media, industry viewpoints, and crime statistics vis-a-vis TV portrayal. Monitoring results of violent content--classified by network, program, and sponsor--are a regular feature, along with reviews of current theatre films. NCTV also expresses concern about other aspects of violence and aggression in society, including violence-related toys and games, sports, pornography, and interpersonal aggression.

189. Otto, Herbert A. "Sex and Violence on the American Newsstand."
Journalism Quarterly, Vol. 40, 1963, pp. 19-26. Also in Otto N. Larsen
(ed.), Violence and the Mass Media. New York: Harper and Row, 1968,
pp. 82-90.

> Analysis of print material available at a city newsstand in 1961
> to determine the extent of coverage of sex and violence. A
> significant increase was found for the preceding ten years in the
> number of magazines specializing in sexual and violent themes.
> Police-detective and men's magazines contained the largest amount
> of violent incidents--including torture and rape--followed by
> romance magazines, which frequently linked sex and violence.
> Examination of paperback book covers revealed that these books,
> including those in the police-detective category, were more likely
> than similar type magazines to portray sexual themes; while
> violence was a less significant element. On the sample day, the
> ten major daily newspapers allotted about 5 percent of column
> inches to violent topics--including war (the most common
> category). One newspaper contained a significantly greater amount
> of violence-related material (33 percent).

190. Ozyegin, Nejat. "Construction of the 'Facts' of Political
Violence: A Content Analysis of Press Coverage." Unpublished Master's
Thesis, The Annenberg School of Communications, University of
Pennsylvania, 1986.

> A study of the role played by the Turkish press in the creation of
> public images of political violence during five years of rising
> political turbulence prior to the 1980 military coup.

191. Paczkowski, Andrzej. "Few Remarks on the Subject of Violence in
Polish Mass-Media." Manuscript, 1985.

> The problem of the presentation of violence in the Polish media
> appears to be more complicated than in those instances where the
> media are guided by more-or-less commercial principles observing
> laws of demand and supply. Criminal violence is considered
> separately from political violence. Polish media, particularly
> those with a national range, avoid providing any information about
> criminal violence if it takes place in Poland or another socialist
> country.

192. Paddock, Alfred H. "Psychological Operations, Special Operations,
and U.S. Strategy." In Frank R. Barnett, B. Hugh Tovar, and Richard
H. Schultz (ed.), Special Operations in U.S. Strategy. New
York: National Strategy Information Center, 1984, pp. 231-251.

> A comparison of the Soviet media and American media. The former
> adheres strictly to the Bolshevik concept of socialist realism --
> reporting not what is, but what should be. The latter is passive,
> leaving itself vulnerable to terrorist exploitation.

54

193. Paletz, David L., John Z. Ayanian and Peter A. Fozzard. "Terrorism on TV News: The IRA, the FALN, and the Red Brigades." In W. C. Adams (ed.), Television Coverage of International Affairs, Norwood, NJ: Aben, 1982, pp. 143-165.

> Histories, ideologies, goals and tactics of these three terrorist groups are presented, and a content analysis done on every story ABC, CBS and NBC evening news carried in their regard, from July 1, 1977, to June 30, 1979. Dimensions of news content were coded, explanations for depictions offered and explanations of media effects suggested.

194. Paletz, David L., Peter A. Fozzard, and John Z. Ayanian. "The I.R.A., the Red Brigades and the F.A.L.N. in The New York Times." Journal of Communication, Vol. 32, No. 2, 1982, pp. 162-171.

> This study analyzes the New York Times' coverage of the I.R.A., the Red Brigades, and the F.A.L.N., during the period from July 1, 1977 to June 30, 1979. The authors found that despite charges from several quarters, there is no evidence to suggest that media coverage (as exemplified by that of the Times) legitimizes the cause of terrorist organizations. Although violent organizations can influence frequency of news coverage by the nature of their actions, authorities hold greater influence over how violence is portrayed because of the frequency with which they are sources and the interpretations they offer.

195. Paletz, David L. and Robert Dunn. "Press Coverage of Civil Disorders: A Case Study of Winston-Salem." Public Opinion Quarterly, Vol. 33, No. 3, 1969, pp. 328-345.

> The civil unrest on which this study centers occurred two years after major racial disturbance in Los Angeles. The authors present the view that guidelines designed to restrict sensational coverage of urban riots may have unexpected and possibly negative consequences and outline details of the 1967 Winston-Salem riot as a case study. Coverage of the four-day riot by one local, racially-progressive newspaper was analyzed and compared to coverage by two other newspapers, including the New York Times, and to interview data provided by press personnel and participants in the riots. The role of local media in maintaining a sociocultural consensus, in delaying rather than inciting violent conflict, is revealed in this analysis. However, the authors interpret such a role as a subtle, possibly inadvertant form of hostility in that it fails to contribute to better understanding of the black community.

196. Palmer, Edward L. and Aimee Dorr (eds.). Children and the Faces of Television: Teaching, Violence, Selling. New York: Academic Press, 1981.

Violence, one of three "faces" of television, is examined in one section of this book. Included is a historical perspective, examination of research on violence and television, and issues relating to social policy.

197. Palmerton, Patricia R. "Terrorism and Institutional Targets as Portrayed by News Providers." Paper submitted to the Speech Communication Association, Mass Communication Division, 1985.

Terrorism, to be an effective strategy depends upon coverage by the news media for part of its impact. This study examined the news media's portrayal of terrorist action upon governmental representatives and institutions. Includes an analysis of CBS evening news coverage of the taking of American hostages in Iran from 1979-1981. Results indicated that CBS news' image of the situation showed that while actions taken by the United States were responsible for whatever happened to the hostages, control over the outcomes of actions remained external to the United States.

198. Pearl, David, Lorraine Bouthilet, and Joyce Lazar (eds.). Television and Behavior: Ten Years of Scientific Progress and Implications for the Eighties, Vol. 2, Technical Reviews. Rockville, MD: National Institute of Mental Health, 1982.

These technical reviews form the documentation for the update of the Surgeon General's Report. A perspective by Eli A.Rubinstein prefaces major studies relating to televised violence--its forms and its contributions to the socialization process. The projects address past problems and differences in research design and indicate the direction of the most current research.

199. Potts, Richard, Aletha C. Huston and John C. Wright. "The Effects of Television Form and Violent Content on Boys' Attention and Social Behavior." Journal of Experimental Child Psychology, Vol. 4, No. 1, 1986, pp. 1-17.

Investigated the independent effects of TV violence and action level on children's attention to programs and their postviewing social behavior. 32 pairs of 39-75 month old boys participated in 2 experimental sessions in which they saw animated and live TV programs varying in violence and action levels. They then played with toys containing cues for either aggressive or prosocial interaction. Results show that rapid character action facilitated visual attention to programs; violent TV content did not facilitate attention. Strong effects of toy cues were found independently of TV treatment effects; aggressive and prosocial toys produced aggressive and prosocial behavior, respectively. Violent TV content led to changes in subjects' style of interaction and was also associated with increases in some prosocial behavior. Results are discussed within the theoretical frameworks of observational learning and general arousal. Implications for children's TV programming are also discussed.

200. Pritchard, David. "Race, Homicide, and the News: A Longitudinal Study." Paper presented to the Association for Education in Journalism and Mass Communication, 1984.

Report of a longitudinal study examining the hypothesis that the race of homicide suspects and victims influences the way in which newspapers cover these events. The study includes an examination of the coverage of 90 non-vehicular prosecutions in Milwaukee between January 1981 and June 1982. All available police and court records on each case were reviewed. The main finding indicated that homicides allegedly committed by blacks or Hispanics were likely to be covered less extensively than homicides allegedly committed by whites. Results also showed that the race of the suspect was a far better predictor of coverage than the race of a victim.

201. Quarantelli, E. L. "Realities and Mythologies in Disaster Films." Communications: The European Journal of Communication, Vol. 11, No. 1, 1985, pp. 31-44.

This paper examines 36 films with substantial footage on disaster phenomenon, excluding war/terrorism films, science fiction films and comedies. Considerably more time was devoted to preimpact period than to trans or postimpact periods. Disaster agents portrayed were usually highly unlikely, with frequently occuring natural disasters seldom depicted. Disaster agents rarely appeared unexpectedly.

202. Rabe, Robert L. "The Journalist and the Hostage: How Their Rights Can Be Balanced." In Abraham H. Miller (ed.), Terrorism: The Media and the Law. New York: Transnational Publishers, 1982, pp. 69-75.

An argument for the primacy of law enforcement agencies in responding to terrorist actions, citing court decisions which limit the constitutionally-granted freedom of the press. These decisions involve restricting access to information. This perspective, in which the safety of hostages is central, calls for limiting the media's role to factual reporting of information made available by police public information offices.

203. RAI Radiotelevisione Italiana. Metodi di Ricerca e Risultati Sul Rapporto Tra Violenza in Televisione e Criminalita'. [Research Methods and Results Concerning the Relationship Between Violence in Television and Criminality]. Torino, Italy: ERI, 1975.

The record of proceedings of a meeting in Florence in September, 1974, organized by the Prix Italia Secretariat. Various studies conducted in several countries were discussed at this meeting.

204. Randall, Donna M. "The Portrayal of Corporate Crime in Network Television Newscasts." Journalism Quarterly, Vol. 64, No. 1, 1987, pp. 150-153.

Network coverage of corporate crime over a decade (1974-1984), was analyzed using iterative content analysis. Analysis dealt with number of stories, type of crime reported, stage of criminal justice, time devoted to story, placement in the news block, change over time, and network differences. Findings show a relatively large amount and frequency of corporate crime coverage, with 40 percent of sampled broadcasts containing at least one such story. A full spectrum of criminal processing and type of crime were found.

205. Randall, Murray L., Richard R. Cole, and Fred Fedler. "Teenagers and TV Violence: How They Rate and View It." Journalism Quarterly, Vol. 47, No. 2, 1970, pp. 247-255.

Teenagers categorized violence into three types (physical, mental, and verbal) and defined it as senseless and occurring without good reason. High and low users of violent content were identified to determine which variables best predict the use of violent television content and differentiate between them. Sex was the best predictor of violence viewing. Alienation and viewing of violent content, however, bore little relationship to each other. Telephone interviews revealed that few of the teens in this sample spent a lot of time watching television.

206. Rarick, David L., James E. Townsend, and Douglas A. Boyd. "Adolescent Perceptions of Police: Actual and as Depicted in Television Dramas." Journalism Quarterly, Vol. 50, No. 3, 1973, pp. 438-446.

A Q analysis revealed that adolescents' image of television police is not correlated with their image of actual police. Perceptions of actual police are diverse, ranging from highly favorable to openly hostile. Perceptions of television police are relatively homogeneous and positive. Adolescents adjudicated delinquent perceive television police in much the same way as non-delinquents. They also do not have more negative impressions of actual police.

207. Rarick, Galen and Barrie Hartman. "The Effects of Competition on One Daily Newspaper's Content." Journalism Quarterly, Vol. 43, No. 3, 1966, pp. 459-463.

The authors examined a sample of issues from one daily newspaper during three different periods: 1948-49, when there was no competition; 1953-54, when there was intense competition with another daily; and 1962-63, when competition was minimal. During the period of high competition, sensational news items (including human interest as well as crime and disaster stories) received a significantly greater amount of non-advertising space.

208. Rath, Claus and Dagmar Jacobsen. "Produzione di immagini sul terrorismo alla televisione tedesca occidentale." [Production of Images on Terrorism in the TV of West Germany]. In RAI Radiotelevisione Italiana, Terrorismo e TV, Vol. 2. Rome: RAI, Verifica dei Programmi Trasmessi, 1982.

Research on television portrayal of terrorism in West Germany examined programs broadcast from May to October in 1981. Examination of the creation of these mass media events proceeds from reflection on the concept and history of Germany's political system and the concept of political violence to dominant forms of violence on German television and the nature of terrorism as it functions in a specific society. These perspectives are incorporated into a matrix which provides a cohesive framework for the image of terrorism presented on television.

209. Rehman, S. N. and Reilly, S. S. "Music Videos: A New Dimension of Television Violence." The Pennsylvania Speech Communication Annual, Vol. 41, 1985, pp. 61-65.

Music videos were rated for violent content and arranged in two different orders -either ascending or descending order of violence- and then shown to groups of college students to see if their perception of the violent content of the videos rose and declined as the actual level of violent content rose and declined. Two-tailed t-tests revealed that the violence was rated higher by women than by men. In descending exposed group, as violence decreased so did the subjects' violence ratings. In the ascending exposed group, however, ratings did not increase along with violent content. The authors accepted an alternative hypothesis that desensitization to violence does occur.

210. Robinson, Deanna Campbell. "Young Adults' Assessment of Dramatic Television Violence." Manuscript based on 1980 presentation to the International Communication Association, Acapulco, Mexico, 1981.

A study designed to assess what viewers, rather than researchers or activist groups, consider to be television violence. 258 young adults rated the violence of edited television program segments. Questionnaires provided data on subjects' demographic characteristics, media habits, and attitudes. Segment ratings indicated that response to TV action as violent is greater when viewers identify with the plight of the characters involved. In addition, viewers regard some shows generally considered violent as silly and unreal.

211. Robinson, Deanna Campbell, Jerry F. Medler, and B. K. L. Genova. "A Consumer Model for TV Audiences: The Case of TV Violence." Communication Research, Vol. 6, No. 2, 1979, pp. 181-202.

A telephone survey of viewers in Eugene, Oregon and Syracuse, New York employed a consumer behavior measure developed by A. O. Hirshman to explore attitudes about TV violence and behavior related to those attitudes. Excessive violence was one of four distinct viewer complaints. Notable concern was also expressed about sexual content, which was perceived as displacing some degree of violence. However, concern about TV violence did not correspond to altered viewing habits or to complaints to the television industry.

212. Roshier, Robert J. "Selection of Crime News by the Press." In Stanley Cohen and Jock Young (eds.), The Manufacture of News, Beverly Hills, CA: Sage Publications, 1973, pp. 28-39.

A content analysis of crime news in the press and a survey of adults in a town in Great Britain. Selection of crime news by the press involves two processes: (1) the extent to which crime news is selected for publication in competition with other categories of news and (2) the way particular types of crimes (and criminals) are selected for publication out of the total pool of potentially reportable crime. The findings suggest that although the press do present a consistently biased impression of crime and criminals through their process of selection, there is little evidence to suggest that this is found in public perceptions of, and opinions about, these phenomenon.

213. Rubins, William. "Sex and Violence on TV." Journal of Advertising Research, Vol. 21, No. 6, 1981, pp. 13-20.

Bias and superficiality of many polls of attitudes concerning television violence are cited by the author, who reports results of a Roper Organization survey supplemented by two follow-up studies of 2400 adult viewers. Attitudes about violence in 17 TV entertainment programs were solicited. Only two programs were associated with positive or negative attitudes of more than 5 percent of the sampled viewers, and considerably larger percentages of viewers rated the programs very favorably. Three percent or fewer of the respondents felt that certain programs should be taken off the air for either violent or sexual content. The follow-up surveys revealed some differences in results caused by variation in the format of the questions posed to viewers.

214. Rubinstein, Eli A. "Television Violence: A Historical Perspective." In Edward C. Palmer and Aimee Dorr (eds.), Children and the Faces of Television: Teaching, Violence, Selling. New York: Academic Press, 1980, pp. 113-128.

An historical overview of research on television violence conducted since the early 1950's. Discusses numerous Senate hearings, the Eisenhower Commission, the Surgeon General's Program of Research, as well as some of the public campaigns against television violence. Notes that most of the research has indicated that television violence is harmful to viewers and that television is both an important positive and negative influence upon children.

215. Rubinstein, Eli A. "Television and Behavior: Research Conclusions of the 1982 NIMH Report and Their Policy Implications." American Psychologist, Vol. 38, No. 7, 1983, pp. 820-825.

Research on television and behavior in the 1970s has recently been reviewed and evaluated in a report from the National Institute of Mental Health (NIMH). The general conclusion is that TV is an important influence on child development in ways well beyond earlier findings which focused on violence and aggression. Media focus and public emphasis on violence as the major issue has masked an even larger issue. Rather than concern with violent content, there is a need to see the totality of TV viewing as a continuing form of informal education. Government regulation is undesirable and more industry creativity unlikely, so the need is for a continuing process to facilitate the translation of research knowledge into policy-making actions.

216. Savarese, Rossella and Antonio Perna. "Strategic Arms and Guerrilla Weapons: A Content Analysis of Articles from Italian Newspapers of the 70s." Paper presented to the International Peace Research Institute Association, Orillia, Canada, 1981.

A critical discussion of the Italian press' coverage of armament issues and the uses of conventional or nuclear weapons for acts of terrorism. The authors hold the view that the Italian daily press lacks an appropriate communication strategy concerning these issues, and that its main objective is to "make news" and attract readers. An analysis of about 2,700 headlines of the Corriere della Sera, the independent mass circulation newspaper and one of the most important newspapers of Italy, is included.

217. Scarry, Elaine. The Body In Pain: Unmaking and Making the World. New York: Oxford University Press, 1985.

A study of the inexpressibility of physical pain, including the political and perceptual complications. The author discusses torture, using publications and files from Amnesty International (with their depictions of torture methods, practices, and rationales), statements by Henry Kissinger and others, as well as the Old Testament (e.g., the sacrifice of Abraham and Isaac), the works of Marx, and U.S. Court Cases.

218. Schlesinger, Philip. "'Terrorism', the Media, and the Liberal-Democratic State: A Critique of the Orthodoxy." Social Research, Vol. 48, No. 1, 1981, pp. 74-99.

The role of the state (the United Kingdom) in advancing anti-terror images is explored in this complex interpretation of the relationship between terrorists and the media. The author also examines the similarities in effects of industry self-regulation and legislative control.

219. Schramm, Wilbur. "The Nature of News." Journalism Quarterly, Vol. 26, 1949, pp. 259-269.

   Early research on use/gratifications of newspaper readers indicated two basic interests: stories yielding immediate reward (crime, corruption, accidents, disasters, sports, recreation, social events, and human interest) and those yielding delayed reward (public affairs, economic matters, social problems, science, education, and health). Another factor was the ability to identify one's self or family with subjects of the news story. Interest in delayed reward stories increased with education while interest in immediate reward stories declined.

220. Schuetz, Stephen and Joyce N. Sprafkin. "Portrayal of Prosocial and Aggressive Behaviors in Children's TV Commercials." Journal of Broadcasting, Vol. 23, No. 1, 1979, pp. 33-41.

   An examination of the portrayal of prosocial and aggressive behaviors in a sample of 414 children's commercials. The commercials contained about 3 times the number of aggressive acts and double the number of altruistic acts found in TV programs. More than a third of the altruistic acts, however, appeared in public service announcements usually aired before 8 a.m. The commercials also rarely presented characters controlling aggressive impulses or trying to rectify damage caused by their violent behavior. All human aggression was performed by males. White characters were portrayed as more aggressive than black and nonblack minority characters. There were no race differences in the presentation of altruistic behaviors. Finally children were more likely than adults to perform both aggressive and altruistic acts.

221. Shaheen, Jack G. The TV Arab. Bowling Green Ohio: Bowling Green State University Popular Press, 1984.

   A review and examination of the portrayal of Arabs during eight seasons of TV shows reveals that TV perpetrates four myths about Arabs: they are all very wealthy, barbaric and uncultured, sex maniacs, and revel in acts of terrorism.

222. Shapiro, M. E. and L. B. Schofield. "How Proximity, Circulation and Geographical Distribution Influenced Coverage of Miami's Overtown Disturbance." Newspaper Research Journal, Vol. 7, No. 4, 1986, pp. 55-61.

   On news coverage of the violence that occurred in the mainly black Overtown section of Miami in December 1982, the authors analyzed the news content in all sections of the Miami "Herald" and the Miami "News" published from December 29, 1982 to January 3, 1983. Results of the analysis supported earlier findings: proximity of an event played an influential role in the newspaper editorial process.

223. Shaw, Irene S. and David S. Newell. "Violence on Television: Programme Content and Viewer Perception." London: British Broadcasting Corporation, 1972.

An analysis of the amount and nature of violence in British television programs broadcast between November 1970 and May 1971 revealed that violent behavior was found in films and series. Programs imported from the United States were among the most violent. Cartoons, of which there were relatively few, were also quite violent. The second half of this study was a series of surveys that explored the significance of viewing violence. These surveys examined the extent to which viewers were aware of violence, their emotional responses to the programs, and especially the "uses" to which they put the programs.

224. Sheley, Joseph F. and Cindy D. Askins. "Crime, Crime News, and Crime Views." Public Opinion Quarterly, Vol. 45, No. 4, 1981, pp. 492-506.

Analysis of images of crime portrayed on television and in print, 1974 crime data from police records, and attitudes concerning crime in New Orleans. Violent crime accounts for 20 percent of police index crimes, while property offenses account for 80 percent. This pattern is reversed somewhat in press accounts and to a very significant degree in television accounts. Public estimation of the frequency of certain types of crime approximated media rankings more closely than police rankings, particularly the newspaper profile.

225. Sherizen, Sanford. "Social Creation of Crime News: All the News Fitted to Print." In Charles Winnick (ed.) Deviance and Mass Media, Beverly Hills, CA: Sage Publications, 1978, pp. 203-224.

A study of crime reporting in Chicago finds that the news gathering process, relying on police as sources, constructs an artificial picture of crime and violence in society.

226. Sherman, Barry L. and Joseph R. Dominick. "Guns, Sex & Rock and Roll: A Content Analysis of Music Television." Report delivered to the Speech Communication Association, Chicago, 1984.

A systematic and objective look at rock videos using content analytic techniques. MTV, WTB's "Fast Tracks", and NBC's "Friday Night Videos", were analyzed for seven weeks from April 6 to May 18, 1984. The most striking finding was the male-oriented and male dominated nature of music videos. Seventy-five percent of the solo acts and eighty-two percent of the groups were males. The male-orientation was also seen in the way females were portrayed in videos; half of all women who appeared were dressed provocatively. It is suggested that in many cases, women were presented as upper class sex objects for lower class males with visions of upward mobility.

63

227. Sherman, Barry L. and Joseph R. Dominick. "Violence and Sex in Music Videos: TV and Rock 'n' Roll." Journal of Communication, Vol. 36, No. 1, 1986, pp. 79-93.

Comprehensive examination finds that, like television, concept videos contain violence but women and nonwhites are more equitably treated.

228. Shinar, Dov with Pnina Parnes and Dan Caspi. "Structure and Content of Television Broadcasting in Israel." In George A. Comstock and Eli A. Rubinstein (eds.), Television and Social Behavior, Vol. 1, Media Content and Control. Washington, DC: U.S. Government Printing Office, 1972, pp. 493-532.

Description of the institutional structures and control processes of Israeli television and a content analysis of one week of programming. American and British action programs were the most violent.

229. Signorielli, Nancy. "The Measurement of Violence in Television Programming: Violence Indices." In Joseph R. Dominick and James E. Fletcher (eds.), Broadcasting Research Methods. Boston: Allyn & Bacon, 1985, pp. 235-251.

Overview of most of the research conducted to assess the amount of violence on television, including a description of the Cultural Indicators Project.

230. Signorielli, Nancy. "Selective Television Viewing: A Limited Possibility." Journal of Communication, Vol. 36, No. 3, 1986, pp. 64-76.

Analyses of sample years from a 15 year period show that prime time TV presents a consistent portrayal of the world across program genres, and offers few scheduling alternatives to avoiding the violence-laden adventure programs. This analysis examines selective viewing in regard to relative frequency of various program genres, and similarities or differences between them. With violence removed, programs are found to be overwhelmingly similar on dimensions of program content and characterization. Heavy viewers are heavily exposed to violence and selective viewing must be recognized as a limited entity.

231. Signorielli, Nancy, Larry Gross and Michael Morgan. "Violence in Television Programs: Ten Years Later." In David Pearl, Lorraine Bouthilet, and Joyce Lazar (eds.), Television and Social Behavior, Vol. 2, Technical Reviews. Rockville, MD: National Institute of Mental Health, 1982, pp. 158-173.

A focus on the methodological aspects of assessing television violence. Content analysis and ratings systems are defined, and examples of research employing these methods are provided. Particular reference is made to the Cultural Indicators Project, which has analyzed trends in television content since 1967. Definition, unitization, and sampling are discussed, with examples given of different approaches. The standardized, reliable statistics on television violence provided by the Cultural Indicators Violence Index from 1967 to 1979 are included. Over the twelve-year period, an average of 71 percent of prime-time programs contained violence; 94 percent of weekend daytime programs contained violence. The hourly rate of violence was 4.8 for prime time and 5.8 for weekend daytime dramatic programs. Finally, cultivation of beliefs and values in subgroups of viewers is discussed, with descriptions of the processes of resonance (attitude reinforcement) and mainstreaming (channeling of attitudes toward the norm emphasized on television).

232. Silj, Alessandro. Brigate Rosse-Stato: Lo scontro spettacolo nella regia della stampa quotidiana. [Red Brigades-State: Confrontation Spectacle Directed by the Daily Press]. Firenze: Vallecchi, 1978.

Analysis of coverage of the kidnapping of Aldo Moro, president of the Christian Democratic Party, in five Italian newspapers indicated that the press was used by various political forces for ideological ends. Results indicated that political ideology was the basis for immediate beatification of Moro in the press and denial of the authenticity of letters from the "People's prison."

233. Silj, Alessandro. Stampa, Radio e TV di Fronte Al Processo Moro, Ai Casi La Torre, Delcogliano, Cirillo e Ad Altre Storie Di Terrorismo. [Press, Radio and Television Before the Moro Trial, the Cases of LaTorre, Delcogliano, Cirillo, and Other Stories of Terrorism]. Rome: RAI Radiotelevisione Italiana, Verifica dei Programmi Trasmessi, 1982.

A study comparing the RAI information on the problems of Italian terrorism with information published in nationally-distributed newspapers. The study shows that the information on terrorism broadcast or published by eight media groups during a four-week period in 1982 seems to be neither a response to a concern for an exhaustive review of terrorism and related events nor, in the majority of the cases, a response to orientations and choices that are continual and coherent. It is suggested that this type of information has not yet found its own code of behaviors and that the performance of broadcast groups and newspapers is often the result of conflict.

234. Singer, Benjamin D. "Violence, Protest, and War in Television News: The U.S. and Canada Compared." Public Opinion Quarterly, Vol. 34, No. 4, 1970-1971, pp. 611-616.

A comparative content analysis of the United States' CBS news and Canada's CBC "national news". Newscasts from both nations were taped, transcribed, coded, and tabulated for "aggression items". The amount of time occupied by each item was also gauged. The major finding was that the American television news show exceeded the Canadian program in aggression items for every one of the 21 consecutive days monitored.

235. Slaby, Ronald G., Gary R. Quarfoth and Gene A. McConnachie. "Television Violence and Its Sponsors." Journal of Communication, Vol. 26, No. 1, 1976, pp. 88-96.

This study assessed the rate of violence in a 1974 sample week of network television programming and determined how much violence could be attributed to major commercial sponsors. The rates of violence sponsored by the 65 major advertisers on network stations ranged from a high of 22.5 violence episodes for MacDonalds Corporation to a low of no violent eposides per hour for Sperry-Hutchinson Company.

236. Slade, Joseph W. "Violence in the Hard-Core Pornographic Film: A Historical Survey." Journal of Communication, Vol. 34, No. 3, 1984, pp. 148-163.

Analysis of erotic films in the Kinsey Institute archive (dating from 1920 to 1970) and of loops sampled in Times Square arcades during the early 1980s indicate that about 10 percent of these films combine violence and sex. The degree of violence in these films increased somewhat after the mid-1970s, generally avoiding brutal force. The author posits that eroticism has unique dramatic requirements and that while graphic aggression is a standard element of "legitimate" feature films, it has been accepted only on the fringes of the pornography market. However, a new genre -- pornographic feature films -- may blend sex and violence in increasing amount and degree.

237. Smith, James R. "Television Violence and Driving Behavior." Educational Broadcasting Review, Vol. 3, No. 4, 1969, pp. 23-28.

Data collected from matched groups of 68 "good" and 68 "bad" drivers supports the hypothesis that "bad" drivers have a greater preference for violent TV programming than "good" drivers.

238. Smith, Susan J. "Crime in the News." British Journal of Criminology, Vol. 24, No. 3, 1984, pp. 289-295.

Interview data from a household survey in Birmingham, England and from seven months' content analysis of a Birmingham daily newspaper are used to examine conclusions about crime news presented by Jason Ditton & James Duffy, namely that: 1)the newspaper is a main agent in revealing crime news; 2)some newspapers distort official data on crime; and 3)distortion may cause unrealistic dimensions of fears about crime. Distortion is found in the percentage of types of crimes which actually occur, versus what is reported, and in the unjustified linking of crimes with ethnic minorities.

239. Soley, Lawrence C. and Leonard N. Reid. "Baiting Viewers: Violence and Sex in Television Program Advertisements." Journalism Quarterly, Vol. 62, No. 1, 1985, pp. 105-110, 131.

An analysis of 806 program advertisements from eight regional issues of TV Guide published during the introductory periods of the 1982 and 1983 seasons. The ads for network programs were larger, appeared more frequently, and were more likely to emphasize sex and violence than the ads for programs broadcast on affililate or independent stations.

240. Spiegelman, Marvin, Carl Turwilliger, and Franklin Fearing. "The Content of Comics: Goals and Means to Goals of Comic Strip Characters." Journal of Social Psychology, Vol. 37, 1953, pp. 189-203.

A three-week sample of 1950 Sunday comic strips was analyzed to determine the amount and nature of depicted violence. Among characters in these strips, 18 percent of the males and 9 percent of the females employed violence as a means of achieving a goal. This violence was generally portrayed unsympathetically, particularly for female characters.

241. Sprafkin, Joyce N., Eli A. Rubinstein, and Arthur Stone. "A Content Analysis of Four Television Diets." Stony Brook, NY: Brookdale International Institute for Applied Studies, State University of New York, 1977.

A review of content differences in four distinct viewing diets (prosocial, aggressive, neutral, and unclassified), using a sample of 100 television programs. The social behaviors coded in the analysis generally discriminated among the four categories, with crime drama predominant in the aggressive diet. The researchers also found no relationship between frequencies of prosocial or aggressive behaviors and Nielsen ratings of the programs.

242. Stephens, Lowndes F. "Press and Public Reaction to 'Special Bulletin'." Paper presented to the Association for Education in Journalism, International Communication Division, 1983.

An evaluation of "Special Bulletin", a made-for-television movie about a group of anti-terrorists who take hostages. Episodes in the movie were analyzed as a television news scenario. The script was also analyzed to determine if the fictitious news scenario had a structure similar to "real world" accounts of similar activities.

243. Straubhaar, Joseph D. "Television and Violence in Brazil: The Impact of Imported American Programs, Brazilian Industry and the Brazilian Gov." Paper presented at the Northeast Conference on Latin American Studies, Dartmouth, NH, 1980.

Analysis of sample weeks of TV programming broadcast in Sao Paulo at two-year intervals from 1963 to 1977 revealed that imported programming peaked in the late 1960s and early 1970s, and that Brazilian programs are attracting larger adult and child audiences. While imported violent action series are still popular with Brazilian viewers, they have been displaced into fringes of the evening broadcast schedule.

244. Suchy, John T. "British Television and Its Viewers." _Journalism Quarterly_, Vol. 31, 1954, pp. 466-472.

BBC television programming broadcast between August 12 and August 25, 1953 had about half as much violence as a sample of television programs broadcast in New York City in January 1953. Dramatic programs, especially children's, were most violent in both samples. There was more violence per hour in the children's hours than during evening adult or afternoon housewives' time segments on both television systems. Guns, as weapons of violence, were less popular on BBC programs than on U.S. programs; clubs and sticks were used more often than guns on BBC programs.

245. Swanson, Charles E. "What They Read in 130 Daily Newspapers." _Journalism Quarterly_, Vol. 32, 1955, pp. 411-421.

This project covered the period 1939-1950 and employed about 50,000 personal interviews of adult readers of large- and small-circulation newspapers in many regions of the United States. Of over 40,000 news/editorial/feature items, comics had the largest readership (attracting 56 percent of readers). War and defense items, disaster stories, human interest stories, and weather reports were the next largest categories (each attracting approximately 30 percent of readers). Crime stories and accidents attracted about 20 percent of readers. Males were about 10 percent more likely to be interested in war and political or international relations items than females.

246. Taylor, James. "Television Crime Drama: A Mythological Interpretation." In _Report of the Royal Commission on Violence in the Communications Industry_, Vol. 3, _Violence in Television, Films and News_. Toronto, Canada: The Royal Commission, 1977, pp. 157-219.

The author uses the Canadian folklorist Maranda's definition of myth to preface his structuralist interpretation of several TV crime dramas: "myths display the structured, predominantly culture-specific, and shared semantic systems which enable the members of a culture area to understand each other and to cope with the unknown." The most important effects lie beyond considerations of immediate behavior, in ideology rather than realism. Symbolic violence represents contradictions about important moral structures. Use of violence is justified by the importance of its messages about institutions and motives, such as "security lies in bureaucracy." TV exploits only the surface potential of the crime drama form and should, instead, expand artistic respect of the genre and assure availability of other forms of artistic expression.

247. Tumber, Howard. Television and the Riots. London: British Film Institute Publishing, 1982.

An investigation of British television's coverage of the 1981 riots in a number of inner-city areas within Mainland Britain. News bulletins between July 3 and July 16 were content analyzed to assess systematically the amount and type of news devoted to riot coverage, the location of the report, how rioters were described, and causes given for the disturbances. There is no convincing evidence to support claims that television coverage of acts of violence such as riots incites further acts of violence.

248. United States Government. "Commission Statement on Violence in Television Entertainment Programs." National Commission on the Causes and Prevention of Violence (Eisenhower Commission). See also Robert K. Baker and Sandra J. Ball, Mass Media and Violence Vol. 9 (a Staff Report to the Commission). Washington, DC: U.S. Government Printing Office, 1969, 1969.

The Commission's interpretation of the research they sponsored led to their conclusion that television violence can be imitated by children to the extent that they identify with characters and that the portrayed behaviors are perceived as justified and effective in a situation. Young children, new to the television experience, are particularly vulnerable to this effect. The Commission suggested that the industry eliminate violent cartoons and reduce the time given to violent programs; that the context of portrayed violence be altered; and that research be conducted on effects. The Commission also recommended parental supervision of child viewers and public contacts with television stations.

249. United States Government. Television and Behavior: Ten Years of Scientific Progress and Implications for the Eighties. Vol. 1, Summary Report. See also David Pearl, Lorraine Bouthilet, and Joyce Lazar (eds.), Vol. 2, Technical Reviews. Rockville, MD: National Institute of Mental Health, 1982.

A brief account of the U.S. Government's interest in televised violence and its effects on the public. Summarizes trends in violent content, results of research dealing with effects on behavior and attitudes, and the cultivation of conceptions of violence and mistrust. Methodological issues such as definition and unitization of violence are outlined. A description of the Cultural Indicators Project and a useful bibliography are included.

69

250. Valbuena, Xiomira de, and Marta Colomina de Rivera. "Los Medios de Comunicacion de Masas en una Sociedad Capitalista: El Caso Venezolano." [Mass Communication Media in a Capitalist Society: The Case of Venezuela]. In The Faces of Violence (23rd International Seminar in Criminology). Maracaibo, Venezuela: Centro de Investigaciones Criminologicas, Universidad del Zulia, 1974, pp. 239-292.

This study explores the ways in which mass media transmit supposedly stereotyped characteristics of the delinquent and how these depictions compare to the perceptions of media users. Local and national press, comic books, and television drama were examined, revealing a close association between stereotypes and the ideology of the dominant social class.

251. Wakshlag, Jacob, Virginia Vial, and Ronald Tamborini. "Selecting Crime Drama and Apprehension About Crime." Human Communication Research, Vol. 10, No. 2, 1983, pp. 227-242.

Subjects' initial apprehension about crime was manipulated via exposure to a specially-edited crime documentary or control film. They were then given an opportunity to select films to be viewed from a list of film descriptions that varied in the degree of featured victimization and restoration of justice. Analysis of the victimization scores revealed that the apprehensive subjects chose films with less victimization than the control group subjects. Analysis of the justice restoration scores indicated that apprehensive subjects chose films that featured more justice than did the control group.

252. Wardlaw, Grant. Political Terrorism. London: Cambridge University Press, 1982.

The author examines the relationship between terrorists and the media, which is described as a symbiotic one. In this perspective, terrorists gain attention to their cause, and media reap the commercial benefits of sensational coverage.

253. Williams, Tannis MacBeth, Merle L. Zabrack, and Leslie A. Joy. "Content Analysis of Entertainment Television Programming." In Report of the Royal Commission on Violence in the Communications Industry, Vol. 3, Violence in Television, Films and News. Toronto, Canada: The Royal Commission, 1977, pp. 1-155. See also Journal of Applied Psychology, 1982, Vol. 12, pp. 360-380.

Analysis of 109 of the television programs most popular with three age groups of Canadian viewers revealed that 76 percent of them were produced in the U.S. and 22 percent were produced in Canada. The rate of physical, verbal, or psychological aggression in these programs was approximately 9 per hour. Aggression was mostly incidental to the plot, and consequences were seldom portrayed. Aggression was effective--frequently appearing as direct attack, often with ordinary objects as weapons. Few resolutions were negotiated, even in arguments. Rather, conflicts were suspended

voluntarily or in response to authority. Aggression was usually
unpunished. When punishment occurred, it was frequently death.
The amount and severity of violence was affected by the type of
program in which it appeared: 27 percent of animated and crime
show segments contained aggression, usually physical in nature.
Although 40 percent of situation comedy segments contained
violence, it was usually verbal--half comic, half serious
argument.

254. Wilson, Bryan. "Mass Media and the Public Attitude to Crime."
Criminal Law Review, June, 1961, pp. 376-384.

An examination of the persuasive function of mass media in terms
of attention to specific topics, diffusion of ideas, instilling of
fantasies, and tolerance of deviance. The author provides
examples of hostile acts inspired by the dramatic publicity given
to previous, similar incidents, which can act as an incentive.
Such publicity can affect public opinion about crime more than the
specific crimes.

255. Winick, Charles. "Censor and Sensibility: A Content Analysis of
the Television Censor's Comments." Journal of Broadcasting, Vol. 5,
pp. 117-135. Also in Otto N. Larsen (ed.), Violence and the Mass
Media. New York: Harper and Row, 1968 1961, pp. 252-269.

Describes the origins of censorship in classical literature and
social theories as a preface to consideration of communications
industry self-regulation, which began with a code for radio in
1934. Particular application to television is presented in an
analysis of comments about deletions and changes contained in
monthly reports of a network program-screening department during
1956. Comments pertaining to violent content represented about 10
percent of the total, with details of murder or assault and
sadistic descriptions the most frequent category (about third in
rank after sexual material and flippant references to mental
illness).

256. Withey, Stephen B. and Ronald P. Abeles. Television and Social
Behavior: Beyond Violence and Children. Hillsdale, NJ: Erlbaum, 1980.

This collection of essays examines a number of issues relating to
television that go beyond the obvious focus on violence and
children. It presents reports of study groups organized by the
Committee on Television and Social Behavior, including one on the
need for developing and using indicators of televised violence (a
violence profile).

257. Wober, J. Mallory. "Who Views Violence in Britain?" Journal of
Communication, Vol. 28, No. 3 1978, pp. 172-175.

Younger viewers watched more programs containing violence and the strength of the association increased with higher amounts of viewing.

258. Wober, J. Mallory. "War and Conflict: Do People Think That News Coverage Is Fair, Or That It Takes Sides?" IBA Research Paper, October, 1983.

For a week in September, 1982, London television viewers were sent questions on partiality in TV news. Views differed on whether different political events were covered fairly on British television. The clearest distinction was made concerning the conflict in Afghanistan, with the largest number of people reporting bias in coverage.

259. Wober, J. Mallory. "Broadcasting and The Conflict In Ireland: Viewers' Opinions Of Two Series, And Their Context." Manuscript, 1981.

A study of viewers' evaluations of two Irish television series, The Troubles, and Ireland: A Television History, both historical and political accounts of Ireland and Northern Ireland. The survey assessed the significance of these two series for the audience, and explored the programs' roles in the formation of impressions of life in Ireland. The two series were both positively evaluated overall. Protestant viewers in Northern Ireland were less likely than Catholics to have considered the series accurate and were more likely to believe that it might encourage violence. Overall, however, the idea that either series might encourage violence was rejected.

260. Wober, J. Mallory,. "See As You Would Be Seen By: 'Video Nasty' Antagonists In A Personality Mirror." Psychology News & In Mind, 1984, pp. 7-8.

A discussion of the controversy surrounding TV "video nasties," video cassettes featuring sadistic sexual violence. There is a division between those who are alarmed by "video nasties" and who wish to challenge them, and those who realize their unsavory nature but who believe that it is much more important to avoid legislation against freedom of cinematic expression.

261. Wober, J. Mallory,. "Viewers or Vigilantes: Options on Violent Pornography." InterMedia, Vol. 12, No. 2, 1984, pp. 20-23.

A comparison of American and European approaches to the regulation of "video nasties," pre-recorded sexually-violent video cassettes. In the United Kingdom, the government is currently supporting a radical extension of statutory licensing powers that would be more rigid than the ones now in force. The British tradition of voluntary, self-regulatory film censorship and the tenets of the First Amendment of the American Constitution are discussed as ideological hindrances to statutory regulation. These issues are

debated in light of recent findings on the aggression-arousing
elements of violent pornography.

262. Wober, Mallory and Barrie Gunter. "Television and Personal
Threat: Fact or Artifact? A British Survey." British Journal of Social
Psychology, Vol. 21, 1982, pp.239-247.

Analysis of diaries and opinion questionnaires from 322 viewers in
the United Kingdom supported the hypothesis that a more general,
deep-seated personality factor underlies both TV viewing and
attitudes measured by the fear/mistrust variable. This
personality factor ("locus of control") relates to subjects'
belief in mastery by the self as opposed to belief in fate.

263. Wurth-Hough, Sandra. "Network News Coverage of Terrorism: The
Early Years." Terrorism, Vol. 6, No. 3, 1983, pp. 403-521.

Using the Vanderbilt News Archive, this study examines the image
of terrorist activities in reports by ABC, CBS, and NBC. Includes
a comparison of story emphasis and depiction, frequency, length of
coverage, and location of newscasts. Results indicate that the
electronic media influence public opinion by defining which
national and international issues become significant.

264. Wurtzel, Alan and Guy Lometti. "Determining the Acceptability of
Violent Program Content at ABC." Journal of Broadcasting, Vol. 28,
No. 1, 1984, pp. 89-97.

The authors outline the operation of the Broadcast Standards and
Practices Department at the American Broadcasting Company.
Elements of dramatic programs--violent content, for example--are
evaluated on a continuing basis. Established guidelines and
critical professional judgments are used to classify and score
threats, assaults, accidents, and violence occurring in nature.
Excessive and gratuitous violence are identified, using baseline
scores for each series as a standard of measurement. Changes are
negotiated between department editors, producers and writers.

265. Wurtzel, Alan and Guy Lometti. "Researching Television Violence:
Television at the Crossroads." Society, Vol. 21, No. 6, 1984,
pp. 22-30.

In this paper, two members of the ABC Network's Social Research
Unit provide detailed analysis of the 1982 National Institutes of
Mental Health (NIMH) report, Television and Behavior: Ten Years of
Scientific Progress and Implications for the Future, concerning
the relationship between television violence and aggressive
behavior and social attitudes. The authors argue that the NIMH
findings do not support the conclusion of a causal relationship
between tv violence and aggressive behavior, that there is not a
clear consensus among most researchers in this regard, that there
has been a decrease in the overall amount of television violence
in recent years, and that the research does not support the

conclusion that TV significantly cultivates viewer attitudes and perceptions of social reality. Also included is a summary of ABC Broadcast standards and practices, policies and procedures, which are the network guidelines to ensure responsible handling when depicting violence in entertainment programming.

266. Yadava, J. S. "Communicators' Perception of Social Tensions: A Study." Indian Institute of Mass Communication,D-13, South Extension Part II, New Delhi, India, 1980.

Indian Institute of Mass Communication (New Delhi) 1979 survey of journalists presents views on reporting "social tension" (mostly communal strife). Sources of tension, types of coverage, policies of reporting, presumed impact noted.

267. Zusne, Leonard. "Measuring Violence in Children's Cartoons." Perceptual and Motor Skills, Vol. 27, No. 3, 1968, pp. 901-902.

The frequency and duration of violent episodes in children's animated cartoons broadcast between August 30 and September 7, 1968 on the ABC and CBS affiliates in Tulsa, Oklahoma were measured. There was a significant difference in the amount of violence between the two networks and, on both networks, dramatic cartoons were, on the average, more violent than comic (slapstick) cartoons.

Mass Media Effects

268. Adoni, Hanna, Akiba A. Cohen and Sherril Mane. "Social Reality and Television News: Perceptual Dimensions of Social Conflicts in Selected Life Areas." Journal of Broadcasting, Vol. 28, No. 1, 1984, pp. 33-49.

Young people in Israel served as respondents in the examination of the perception of social, political, and economic conflicts in society and as portrayed on television news. The results revealed that young people are able to differentiate between social reality and television reality. Contrary to the authors' expectation was the fact that social conflicts in reality were perceived as more intense than in television news.

269. Albert, Robert S. "The Role of Mass Media and the Effect of Aggressive Film Content upon Children's Aggressive Responses and Identification Choices." Genetic Psychology Monographs, Vol. 55, 1957, pp. 221-285.

An experiment testing the effects of children's identification with film characters and of the fictional outcome of characters' aggressive actions. Children aged 8-10, categorized as high- or low-aggressive, were shown versions of a Western featuring different outcomes or sanctions for aggressive behavior (either the hero won, the villain won but was not punished, or the victory was ambiguous). All versions resulted in a decrease of aggression among high-aggressive children, but not among low-aggressive children. Younger children and those with lower IQs were affected more than were older children.

270. Andison, F. Scott. "TV Violence and Viewer Aggression: A Cumulation of Study Results 1956-1976." Public Opinion Quarterly, Vol. 41, No. 3, 1977, pp. 314-331.

This review of 67 studies involving more than 30,000 subjects conducted between 1956 and 1976 documents a slight-to-moderate relationship between viewing of televised violence and violent behavior. The relationship is strongest in laboratory settings, with adult subjects, and in studies conducted in the United States--where viewers are exposed to more television violence than are viewers in other countries.

271. Aner, Kerstin. "La Violence et Les Medias." [Violence and the Media]. Revue Internationale de Criminologie et de Police Technique, Vol. 36, No. 4, 1983, pp. 72-83.

This article presents a recommendation adopted by the European parliament concerning methods of reducing violence, and contains part of an associated report on violence and the media. The recommendation addresses such areas as terrorism, the role of the media, violence in sports and the role of education in promoting socially constructive behavior. Results of research on the effects of violence in the media and means of establishing a European strategy to reduce the portrayal of violence in the media are discussed.

272. Arnetz, Bengt B., Bengt Edgren, Lennart Levi and Ulf Otto. "Behavioral & Endocrine Reaction in Boys Scoring High on Sennton Neurotic Scale Viewing an Exciting & Partly Violent Movie & Importance of Social Support." Social Science & Medicine, Vol. 20, No. 7, 1985, pp. 731-736.

This study examined psychoendocrine and behavioral effects elicited by viewing an exciting and partly violent movie in forty-two 12-year-old boys in Stockholm. The boys were divided into groups varying on anxiety test scores and previous psychiatric treatment. Reactions to the movie were assessed by self-ratings, direct observations, and urinary analysis. Results suggest that psychosocial factors and access to social support are important variables in predicting psychological effects of watching potentially arousing movies.

273. Atkin, Charles K. "Effects of Realistic TV Violence versus Fictional Violence on Aggression." Journalism Quarterly, Vol. 60, No. 4, 1983, pp. 615-621.

A comparison of the impact of real news violence and fictional violence on aggressive responses of pre-adolescents. Three versions of a specially prepared television stimulus tape were presented to randomly assigned groups of 98 10-13 year old children in a Michigan school. Athough both types of TV violence increased aggression above the baseline of the nonexposed group, violent incidents presented as realistic news had greater impact on aggressiveness than the same scene portrayed as fantasy entertainment.

274. Atkin, Charles K., John P. Murray, and Oguz B. Nayman. "The Surgeon General's Research Program on Television and Social Behavior: A Review of Empirical Findings." Journal of Broadcasting, Vol. 16, No. 1, 1972, pp. 21-35.

An annotated guide to the surgeon general's research program.

275. Atkin, Charles, Bradley Greenberg, Felix Korzenny, and Steven McDermott. "Selective Exposure to Televised Violence." Journal of Broadcasting, Vol. 23, No. 1, 1979, pp. 5-13.

This project tests the selective exposure hypothesis, which states that TV violence is selected by viewers predisposed to aggressive behavior. Subjects were 227 children aged 9-13. Data on their exposure to programs containing physical and verbal aggression and on their aggressive behavior were collected from self-reports and interviews with mothers in 1976 and again in 1977. Children's level of aggression at the first testing was a strong predictor of level of exposure to violent programming. This relationship was strongest for younger children and boys, and for children with relatively unrestricted access to television.

276. Bailyn, Lotte. "Mass Media and Children: A Study of Exposure Habits and Cognitive Effects." Psychological Monographs, Vol. 73, No. 1, 1959, pp. 1-48.

The viewing habits of children aged 10-11 were related to psychological characteristics and environmental factors in this study. As compared to lighter viewers, heavier viewers, particularly among boys, showed more rebellious attitudes, were less subject to restricted television viewing, and preferred aggressive heroes. The psychological determinants were somewhat more important than amount of viewing.

277. Baker, Robert K. and Sandra J. Ball. Mass Media and Violence, Vol. 9 (A Report of the Task Force on Mass Media and Violence to the National Commission on the Causes and Prevention of Violence). Washington, DC: U.S. Government Printing Office, 1969.

The research reported in this volume grew out of concern with racial and political disturbances in the United States during the 1960s and media coverage of these disturbances. Discussion of the development of various media and the early role of sensationalism leads into consideration of media access and responsibility for coverage of underlying causes of social conflict. Research is presented concerning the prevalence of violence in television drama in 1967 and 1968 in comparison to real-world statistics, violent content in other media, and effects on behavior and attitudes. The task force called for industry support of research and self-regulation of content.

77

278. Baldwin, Thomas F. and Colby Lewis. "Violence in Television: The Industry Looks at Itself." In George A. Comstock and Eli A. Rubinstein (eds.), Television and Social Behavior, Vol. 1: Content and Control. Washington, DC: Government Printing Office, 1972, pp. 290-373.

Interviews with 48 producers, writers, and directors associated with 18 action series featuring violence. Creative personnel felt that violent conflict was essential in drama, and that the audience both expects and looks for violence. Censors play the role of a buffer between producers, networks, and the public but were unaware of or unconcerned with research dealing with effects of televised violence. Creators of programs did not believe that violent portrayals had a harmful effect upon most children; many subscribed to the catharsis hypothesis.

279. Bandura, Albert. "What TV Violence Can Do to Your Child." In Otto N. Larsen, Violence and the Mass Media. New York: Harper and Row, 1968, pp. 123-139.

Discussion of a series of experiments carried out at the Stanford psychological laboratories to provide a basis to evaluate the impact of televised aggression on preschool children. Results indicate that violence on television or in the movies affects viewers by reducing their inhibitions against violence, by increasing aggressive behavior, and by teaching them how to be aggressive or attack others.

280. Bandura, Albert. "A Social Learning Theory of Aggression." Journal of Communication, Vol. 28, No. 3, 1978, pp. 12-29.

This theory of aggression stresses that people are not born with preformed repertoires of aggressive behavior; rather they must learn them. A complete theory of aggression must explain how aggressive patterns are developed, what provokes people to behave aggressively, and what sustains such actions after they have been initiated. The theory stresses the importance of observational learning in this process. In both laboratory and controlled field studies exposure to filmed violence shapes the form of aggression and increases interpersonal aggressiveness in children and adolescents.

281. Bandura, Albert. "Psychological Mechanisms of Aggression." In M. von Cranach, K. Foppa, W. Lepenies, and D. Ploog (eds), Human Ethology: Claims and Limits of a New Discipline. Cambridge, MA: Cambridge University Press, 1979.

A review of social-psychological research on aggression. The neurobiological and psychological mechanisms of aggression are explored. Aggression is discussed as a multifaceted phenomenon that has many determinants and serves diverse purposes. The author outlines a schema of three components of aggression in social learning theory; the origins of aggression, the instigators, and the regulators of aggressive behavior.

282. Bandura, Albert. "Self-Efficacy Mechanism in Human Agency."
American Psychologist, Vol. 37, No. 2, 1982, pp. 122-147.

Reviews research showing that the self-efficacy mechanism may have
wide explanatory power. Perceived self-efficacy helps to account
for such diverse phenomenon as changes in coping behavior produced
by different modes of influence, level of physiological stress
reactions, self-regulation of refractory behavior, resignation and
despondency to failure experiences. The influential role of
perceived collective efficacy in social change is analyzed, as are
the social conditions conducive to development of collective
inefficacy.

283. Bandura, Albert. "Social Diffusion and Innovation." In Social
Foundations of Thought and Action, Englewood Cliffs, NJ: Prentice-Hall,
1985.

A discussion of the impact of the electronic media on social
diffusion. Understanding how new ideas and social practices
spread within a society, or from one society to another, has
important bearing on personal and social change. Extraordinary
advances in technology of communications, which expands the range
of social influence, have transformed the social diffusion
process. Social practices are not only being widely diffused
within societies, but ideas, values, and styles of conduct are
being modeled worldwide.

284. Bandura, Albert, Bill Underwood, and Michael E. Fromson.
"Disinhibition of Aggression through Diffusion of Responsibility and
Dehumanization of Victims." Journal of Research in Personality,
Vol. 9, 1975, pp. 253-269.

This study tested derivations from social learning theory on the
disinhibition of aggression. Subjects were provided with
opportunities to aggress when confronted with groups of people who
treated them in either a respectful, neutral, or dehumanizing way.
Subjects were further divided into two groups of lesser or greater
responsibility. Both dehumanization and lessened responsibility
enhanced aggressiveness, with dehumanization the more potent
disinhibitor. The uniformly low level of aggression directed at
humanizing groups, regardless of variations in responsibility,
attested to the power of humanization to counteract punitiveness.

285. Bandura, Albert, Dorothea Ross, and Sheila A. Ross. "Imitation of
Film-Mediated Aggressive Models." Journal of Abnormal and Social
Psychology, Vol. 66, No. 1, 1963, pp. 3-11.

Subjects in this experiment observed either real-life aggressive
models, a film of the same aggressive models, or aggressive
cartoon characters in conjunction with experimentally-induced
frustration. Imitative and non-imitative aggression in a
different experimental setting was then measured. Evidence of
both facilitation and modeling influence in relation to media

content was found. Effects of media exposure also are a function of the sex of the child and the reality cues of the model.

286. Bandura, Albert, Dorothea Ross, and Sheila A. Ross. "Vicarious Reinforcement and Imitative Learning." Journal of Abnormal and Social Psychology, Vol. 67, No. 6, 1963, pp. 601-607.

Nursery school children who saw an aggressive model rewarded preferred to emulate the successful aggressor and demonstrated imitative aggression, while children who saw the punished aggressive model did not. Boys' behavior was influenced by seeing aversive stimuli given to the model; girls were influenced by the demonstration of prosocial behavior.

287. Barlow, G. and A. Hill. Video Violence and Children. New York: St. Martin's, 1986.

This book contains findings of a Parliamentary Group Video Enquiry set up in July, 1983, in Britain, to produce factual evidence regarding effects on children of viewing violence on television. Discussed are the sociopsychological phenomenon of violence, primary findings of British and American research in this area and its historical background. Results of several surveys are presented, along with psychiatric case studies of the nature of effects on children and adolescents. A review of the findings of the academic Working Party which undertook this research are presented.

288. Barnes, Gordon E., Neil M. Malamuth and James Check. "Psychoticism and Sexual Arousal to Rape Depictions." Personality & Individual Differences, Vol. 5, No. 3, 1984, pp. 273-279.

Hypothesized that high scorers on the Psychoticism(P) subscale of the Eysenck Personality Questionnaire(EPQ) would be more sexually aroused by erotic material of a violent nature than low scorers. The EPQ was administered to 145 male undergraduates in the UK who were assigned to 1 of 4 versions of audiotaped stories that were manipulated along dimensions of violence and pain to women. Self-reported arousal was measured, penile tumescence was monitored, and a postexperimental questionnaire was administered. Results show a significant interaction between P and level of violence - high-P scorers showed greater sexual arousal to rape as compared to nonrape depictions. The opposite pattern occurred for low-P scorers.

289. Baron, James N. and Peter C. Reiss. "Same Time, Next Year: Aggregate Analysis of Mass Media and Violent Behavior." American Sociological Review, Vol. 50, No. 3, 1985, pp. 347-363.

Recent research on the mass media as determinants of homicide, suicide and other violent behavior has asserted that imitation of such behavior as reported in the mass media is an important cause of violence. This article points to criticism of both research methods and conceptualizations employed in reaching this conclusion. Several studies are critiqued, and a model is proposed in which apparent imitation effects are statistical artifacts of mortality data, timing of media events and methods used in past research.

290. Baron, Larry and Murray A. Straus. "Sexual Stratification, Pornography, and Rape in the United States." In Neil M. Malamuth and Edward Donnerstein (eds.), Pornography and Sexual Aggression. Orlando, FL: Academic Press, 1984, pp. 185-209.

Despite the theoretical importance attributed to macrostructural factors (political, economic, and ideological institutions) in the feminist explanation of rape, research using social system level data is sparse. Three hypotheses are tested. It is suggested that rape is precipitated by the combination of social characteristics denoted by the struggle to secure equal rights for women, the large readership of sex magazines which potentially legitimize violence, and a societal context with a high level of nonsexual violence. Social policies designed to mitigate the role of these factors are proposed.

291. Baron, Larry, Murray A. Straus, and David Jaffe. "Legitimate Violence, Violent Attitudes, and Rape: A Test of the Cultural Spillover Theory." Annals of the New York Academy of Sciences, in press, c. 1987.

An examination of the relationship between cultural support for "legitimate violence," and the incidence of rape in the 50 American states and the District of Columbia. Legitimate violence was measured by an index combining 12 indicators of noncriminal violence, and by a Violence Approval Index. A theoretical model hypothesizing the relationship of these two measures of cultural support for violence (and seven control variables) to rape was developed and tested using path analysis. The results show that legitimate violence is directly related to the rape rate. The degree of social disorganization, urbanization, economic inequality, and percent of single males are also directly related to rape. The youthfulness of the population and the percent black affect rape indirectly through their association with legitimate violence. These findings are interpreted as providing support for structural explanations of the origins of cultural support for violence, and for a "cultural spillover" theory of rape.

292. Bassiouni, M. Cherif. "Terrorism, Law Enforcement, and the Mass Media: Perspectives, Problems, Proposals." Journal of Criminal Law and Criminology, Vol. 72, No. 1, 1981.

Comparison of the scope of impact of acts of terrorism with that of a widespread condition, such as common crime, suggests that the psychological effect of terrorism is more significant than the specific violent action. This effect may be more a creation of the media than an intrinsic element of such violence.

293. Bear, A. "The Myth of Television Violence." Media Information Australia, Vol. 33, 1984, pp. 5-10.

Examination and questioning of the interpretation of research indicating a positive relationship between television viewing and aggressive behavior.

294. Belson, William A. Television Violence and the Adolescent Boy. Westmead, England: Saxon House, 1978.

This CBS-funded survey of long-term viewing and behavior profiles of 1,565 teenaged boys in London documents a positive relationship between heavy exposure to televised violence and aggressive or violent behavior. Of the 50 percent who reported involvement in violence during the preceding six months, 12 percent were involved in ten or more serious acts. High-violence viewers were more often involved in serious violent behavior than were low-violence viewers. Violence depicted in the context of close personal relationships corresponded most strongly with serious violent behavior. Differences in historical setting, amount of justification, and centrality to the plot did not appear to moderate the relationship between violent content and aggressive behavior.

295. Berkowitz, Leonard. "Violence in the Mass Media." In Leonard Berkowitz, Aggression: A Social Psychological Analysis. New York: McGraw Hill, 1962, pp. 229-255.

A cohesive review and evaluation of many early experimental studies and surveys concerning short- and long-term effects of media violence. The author covers effects on behavior and attitudes; viewer identification with characters, predisposition to aggressive behavior, and ability to distinguish between fantasy and reality; the influence of justification of aggressive acts and other "cues" in media portrayals. The overall conclusion documented by this body of research is that there is no positive relationship between viewing media violence and commission of serious violence, except for a small number of particular individuals under certain conditions.

296. Berkowitz, Leonard. "The Effects of Observing Violence." Scientific American, Vol. 210, No. 2, 1964, pp. 35-41.

Results from a number of experiments suggest that aggression depicted in television and motion picture dramas, or observed in actuality, can arouse certain members of the audience to violent action.

297. Berkowitz, Leonard. "Some Aspects of Observed Aggression." Journal of Personality and Social Psychology, Vol. 2, No. 3, 1965, pp. 359-369.

In 3 experiments male college students were either angered or treated in a neutral fashion by a person who had been labeled either as a college boxer or a speech major, and they were then shown a short film. Expts. I and II were designed to test the thesis that the anger instigator would evoke the strongest overt hostility from the frustrated subjects when he had been introduced as a boxer and they had seen a prize-fight film; by associating this person with the aggressive scene, the "boxer" label had presumably heightened his cue value for aggressive responses. Expt. I, employing questionnaire ratings as the hostility measure, confirmed this theoretical expectation. In Expt. II, using electric shocks as the aggressive response, however, there was also an indication that the label "boxer" could have strengthened the person's cue value for aggression regardless of the nature of the film witnessed by subjects. The findings in Expt. III confirmed the results obtained in earlier investigations by showing that the angered subjects' inhibitions against aggression varied with the apparent justification for the observed aggression.

298. Berkowitz, Leonard. "Some Determinants of Impulsive Aggression: The Role of Mediated Associations with Reinforcements for Aggression." Psychological Review, Vol. 81, No. 2, 1974, pp. 165-176.

A review of research documenting the influence of certain characteristics of media events in eliciting aggressive behavior. Among these characteristics are prior association of the stimulus with reinforced (rewarded) aggression and cues linking the target of aggressive behavior with the portrayed aggressive action.

299. Berkowitz, Leonard, and Joseph T. Alioto. "The Meaning of an Observed Event as a Determinant of its Aggressive Consequences." Journal of Personality and Social Psychology, Vol. 28, No. 2, 1973, pp. 206-217.

Angered college males demonstrated more aggression if the observed filmed aggression (sports contests) was described as involving justified intent to injure rather than as a match between professionals. Subjects also were more aggressive after viewing a war scene described as realistic rather than fictional, while perception of media events as unreal allows dissociation between the viewer and these events.

300. Berkowitz, Leonard, and Russell G. Geen. "Film Violence and the Cue Properties of Available Targets." Journal of Personality and Social Psychology, Vol. 3, No. 5, 1966, pp. 525-530.

88 male university students were either angered or treated in a neutral fashion by the experimenter's accomplice who had been introduced either as "Kirk" or "Bob." Subjects then saw either a 7-minute prize-fight scene, in which the actor, Kirk Douglas, received a beating, or an equally long exciting movie about a track race. Finally, all subjects were given a socially sanctioned opportunity to administer electric shocks to the accomplice. The greatest number of shocks were sent by the angered men who had witnessed the prize-fight and who had been informed that the accomplice's name was Kirk. The latter's name-mediated association with the witnessed aggression had apparently heightened his cue value for aggressive responses causing him to evoke the strongest volume of aggression from the men who were ready to act aggressively.

301. Berkowitz, Leonard, and Edna Rawlings. "Effects of Film Violence on Inhibitions Against Subsequent Aggression." Journal of Abnormal and Social Psychology, Vol. 66, No. 3, 1963, pp. 405-412.

This study examines the effects of existing emotional state and justification of aggression in portrayal on viewer aggressive behavior. Half of the college students serving as subjects were angered by means of insult prior to viewing justified or unjustified violence in a short film of a prize fight. The subjects who had been insulted and viewed justified violence demonstrated more aggression (measured by rating their antagonist) than other subjects. Viewing unjustified aggression did not have this effect. Media justification of aggression in portrayals lowers viewer inhibitions against aggressive behavior in real life, or lack of justification increases restraints against such behavior.

302. Berkowitz, Leonard, Ronald Corwin, and Mark Heironimos. "Film Violence and Subsequent Aggressive Tendencies." Public Opinion Quarterly, Vol. 27, No. 2, 1963, pp. 217-229.

An experimental test of the influence of existing anger and of seeing violence that is justified or unjustified on behavior, employing attitude measures of 90 college males. Subjects who were angered and who then viewed a film in which aggressive action was justified displayed more aggression than subjects who viewed relatively unjustified aggression.

303. Berkowitz, Leonard, Ross D. Parke, Jacques-Philippe Leyens, and Stephen G. West. "Reactions of Juvenile Delinquents to 'Justified' and 'Less Justified' Movie Violence." Journal of Research in Crime and Delinquency, Vol. 11, No. 1, 1974, pp. 16-24.

This experiment was designed to determine whether juvenile delinquents' response to justified or unjustified filmed violence approximates that of non-delinquent subjects. Delinquents who were angered (insulted by the experimenter) and who then viewed justified violence administered stronger electric shocks to a confederate than delinquents who saw no film. There was less difference in aggression between those who saw justified violence and those who viewed a version of the film in which violence is unjustified. There were no significant differences among non-angered subjects. These findings are similar to those for non-delinquents.

304. Bjorkqvist, Kaj. "Vakivaltaelokuvat, ahdistuneisuus ja aggressiivisuus." [Violent Films, Anxiety and Aggression]. Psykologia, Vol. 20, No. 1, 1985, pp. 9-12.

This article summarizes a collection of experiments conducted by the author and colleagues (1983, 1984), in which the effect of violent film viewing on levels of anxiety and subsequent aggression and on the relationship between anxiety and aggression were studied.

305. Blanchard, D. Caroline, Barry Graczyk and Robert J. Blanchard. "Differential Reactions of Men and Women to Realism, Physical Damage, and Emotionality in Violent Films." Aggressive Behavior, Vol. 12, No. 1, 1986, pp. 45-55.

This study investigated the relation between reactions to media violence and self-reports of experience of violence in community college students. Subjects rated brief segments of violence from films selected to represent a variety of approaches to the depiction of violence. Men saw these sequences as more enjoyable, amusing, realistic and emotional then did women. Men also showed less inclination to restrict showing of such sequences to children on TV or by X-rating. While no sex differences appeared in ratings of suffering or overall appraisals of violence, women's enjoyment ratings declined precipitously for films rated as depicting more suffering, while those of men did not. For men, enjoyment of violent media excerpts and self-reports of recent physical violence were unrelated, while women showed highly significant positive relations for the two variables. The sex difference in these evaluations appeared to be largely emotional rather than cognitive.

306. Bogart, Leo. "Violence in the Mass Media." Television Quarterly, Vol. 8, No. 3, 1969, pp. 36-47.

The author expands consideration of the effects of media violence to include the diffusion of anxiety within a society.

307. Bogart, Leo. "Warning: The Surgeon General Has Determined That TV Violence is Moderately Dangerous to Your Child's Mental Health." Public Opinion Quarterly, Vol. 36, No. 4, 1972, pp. 491-521.

A review of the history of this project and the 5 volumes of studies that contributed to the final report.

308. Bollen, Kenneth A., and David P. Phillips. "Suicidal Motor Vehicle Fatalities in Detroit: A Replication." American Journal of Sociology, Vol. 87, No. 2, 1981, pp. 405-412.

Daily Detroit mortality statistics from 1973 to 1976 and front page suicide stories appearing in the two large Detroit daily newspapers were studied; earlier findings, in which Phillips found that publicized suicide stories trigger a rise in suicides (1979), were replicated.

309. Bollen, Kenneth A., and David P. Phillips. "Imitative Suicides: A National Study of the Effects of Television News Stories." American Sociological Review, Vol. 87, 1982, pp. 404-412.

Using a quasi-experimental technique and regression analysis to examine the relationship between U.S. daily suicides between 1972 and 1976, and concurrent television news coverage of the events, the authors found that the effect of a publicized suicide might extend as far as the 75th day following the report. Results also suggested that the rise in suicides occurs after and not before the appearance of a televised suicide story.

310. Bonfadelli, Heinz. "Der Einfluss des Fernsehens auf die Konstruktion der Sozialen Realitat: Befunde aus der Schweiz zur Kultivierungshypothese." Rundfunk und Fernsehen, Vol. 31, 1983, pp. 415-430.

A 1980 cultivation analysis in Zurich of 348 fifteen-year olds revealed a relationship between heavy TV viewing and exposure to televised violence and fear. However, viewer gratifications from the medium were more significant in explaining cultivation than amount of viewing. The influence of user gratification, social framework, and perception of the reality or unreality of the television world mediate the cultivation effect.

311. Bowers, James R. "Violence on Television and Violent Crime in Japan." Anthrotech: A Journal of Speculative Anthropology, Vol. 5, No. 3, 1981.

Analysis of TV programming in Japan in relation to amount and type of violence, coupled with statistics on actual violent crime, indicates that the positive relationship found elsewhere (for example, in the U.S.) may not typify all countries and cultures.

312. Brody, Stephen R. "Screen Violence and Film Censorship: A Review of Research." London: Home Office Research Unit, 1977.

An extensive review of the directions, findings, and conclusions of research in Britain and the United States concerning violence in film and television programs and its effects. The review is organized in sections pertaining to impact (imitative aggression, anxiety, habituation or desensitization, attitudes), influence of viewer and content variables, violent content, and viewer perceptions of such content. Operation of the British Board of Film Censors is discussed in relation to the issue of media violence.

313. Bryant, Jennings and Dolf Zillmann (eds.). Perspectives on Media Effects. Hillsdale, NJ: Lawrence Erlbaum Associates Publishers, 1986.

Empirical mass communication research has been focused on media effects; the social, cultural and psychological impacts. Few general scholarly monographs or anthologies exist. This volume serves as a comprehensive collection of 'state of the art' reports on mass media effects.

314. Bryant, Jennings, Rodney Corveth, and Dan Brown. "Television Viewing and Anxiety: An Experimental Examination." Journal of Communication, Vol. 31, No. 1, 1981, pp. 106-119.

Two groups differing in measured anxiety were exposed to "light" versus "heavy" doses of televised fare for six weeks. At the conclusion of the six week period, measures of anxiety were obtained; three independent assessments of viewers' voluntary selective exposure to further action-adventure fare were also made. Overall, heavy viewing of action-adventure programs increased anxiety and fearfulness even among initially less anxious viewers. A steady diet of programs in which justice is not served especially affected anxiety.

315. Burnet, Mary. The Mass Media in a Violent World (1970 Symposium Proceedings). Paris: UNESCO, 1971.

Specialists in mass media, sociology, psychology, criminology, social work, and education from 18 countries met to examine the definition of violence, the relationship between real-life and media violence, and the means of expanding the use of reason in the conduct of human relations. Topics included content and impact of civil disturbance and personal violence in news; the dramatic context of violence in media entertainment; and the particular status of media and related problems in developing countries. Participants called for examination of industry processes which determine content and of the political, economic, and social influences of these processes. They also sought media promotion of increased understanding of social and international conflict.

316. Cairns, Ed. "The Television News as a Source of Knowledge About the Violence for Children in Ireland, North and South." Current Psychological Research and Reviews, c.1985.

Two studies explored how much children in different parts of Ireland knew about the civil disturbance in the North of Ireland and examined the role of television news broadcasts in providing such knowledge. In the first study 488 children living in five different areas on a continuum of increasing distance from the actual scenes of violence, were asked to complete an 11-item multiple choice questionnaire concerning detailed knowledge of matters closely related to the troubles and to indicate how often they watched the television news. Results indicated that the closer children lived to the violence the higher their scores, and that the more they watched television news the higher their scores. The results of the second study virtually replicated the first study in that children in the South of Ireland knew less than did children in the North; no difference emerged between the children in the two different areas in the North of Ireland.

317. Cairns, Ed, Dale Hunter, and Linda Herring. "Young Children's Awareness of Violence in Northern Ireland: The Influence of Northern Irish Television in Scotland." British Journal of Social and Clinical Psychology, Vol. 19, 1980, pp. 3-6.

This study gauged Northern Irish childrens' awareness of violent events outside of Northern Ireland. They were tested via an indirect, picture story method, in which they were asked to interpret violent scenes based on their own experiences. It was hypothesized that children from a virtually troublefree area of Northern Ireland would respond similarly to children from a South London suburb. The results indicated, however, that the young children in the quiet Northern Irish town did appear to be influenced by violent events outside of Northern Ireland. The two groups differed in the way they used violent terms; most of the references by the Northern Irish children to bombs had obvious terrorist connotations while several London children mentioned "bombs dropped from airplanes a long time ago."

318. Canadian Government. Report of the Royal Commission on Violence in the Communications Industry, 7 Vols. Toronto, Canada: The Royal Commission, 1977.

The LaMarsh Commission conducted 61 public hearings and foreign consultations and commissioned 28 independent studies of violent content, its effects, and regulation in several media industries. The Report includes a volume summarizing the conclusions, recommendations, and public comment. Recommendations included decreasing the exploitation of violence by increasing accountability and professionalism; restructuring programming to reflect Canada's own cultural identity; and providing for public input to various media. Reports of research are presented in six other volumes, including an extensive bibliography.

319. Canadian Government. Report of the Royal Commission on Violence in the Communications Industry, Vol. 2, Violence and the Media: A Bibliography. Toronto, Canada: The Royal Commission, 1977.

This volume contains approximately 3,000 citations of research in 26 countries relating to violent content, effects, and regulation of print, music, film, radio, and television.

320. Canadian Radio-Television and Telecommunications Commission (CRTC), Social Communications Division Research Branch. "Violent Motion Pictures; Crime Radio Programs, and Crime Comic Books -- 3 Controversies in the Scholarly and Popular Press 1909-1953." CRTC 1975 Symposium on Television Violence, Queen's University. Ottawa, Canada: CRTC, 1976.

Current controversy over behavioral effects of television has similarities to and differences from previous controversies about motion pictures, radio, and comic books. Each medium generated concern about short-term and long-term social consequences of anti-social behavior elicited by particular content as well as anxiety over parental/adult supervision of children in competition with what was perceived as an intruding, impersonal agent of socialization.

321. Carlson, James M. "Crime Show Viewing by Pre-Adults: The Impact on Attitudes toward Civil Liberties." Communication Research, Vol. 10, No. 4, 1983, pp. 529-552.

A positive relationship between heavy viewing of crime shows and bias against civil liberties was found in a study of 619 teenagers. Heavy viewers of crime shows had more conservative attitudes relating to punishment and bail, and use of brutal and unconstitutional tactics by police. This relationship also was influenced by age, social class, and total amount of television viewing. The strongest effect was on older and middle- or upper middle-class families.

322. Cater, Douglass and Stephen Strickland. TV Violence and the Child: The Evolution and Fate of the Surgeon General's Report. New York: Russell Sage Foundation, 1975.

A concise history of the Surgeon General's Advisory Committee on Television and Social Behavior and its 1972 Report--from concerns about media influence voiced during Senate hearings on television and juvenile delinquency in the 1950s and 1960s to a second round of hearings concerning the Report in 1974. Included is a candid discussion of the politics and compromises between and within various interest groups involved in the preparation of the Report (representatives of government, the broadcasting industry, and the various sciences and researchers). Major studies commissioned by the Committee are summarized.

323. Catton, William R., Jr. "Value Modification by Mass Media." In Robert K. Baker and Sandra J. Ball, Mass Media and Violence, Vol. 9. Washington, DC: U.S. Government Printing Office, 1969, pp. 285-299.

A sociological perspective on the role of various media in the establishment of a literate elite and in the socialization process, including a review of research on attitudes concerning crime and violence and their relationship to media content.

324. Chaffee, Steven H. "Television and Adolescent Aggressiveness (Overview)." In George A. Comstock and Eli A. Rubinstein (eds.), Television and Social Behavior, Vol. 3, Television and Adolescent Aggressiveness. Washington DC: U.S. Government Printing Office, 1972, pp. 1-31.

Comparative overview of 8 field studies of adolescents examining the relationship between televised violence and aggression among teenagers. Concludes that viewing is one of several variables that show a mild positive association with such behavior.

325. Chaffee, Steven H., et al. "Defending the Indefensible: Television at the Crossroads." Society, Vol. 21, No. 6, 1984, pp. 30-35.

This is a reply to the SOCIETY article by Wurtzel and Lometti, in which the authors refute the findings of the NIMH report on effects of televised violence. In this article, the authors conclude that the Wurtzel and Lometti statement is neither rigorous nor objective, focusing on only one portion of the NIMH review, rather than examining the larger pattern of effects, resulting in conclusions that obscure the issue and deceive the reader.

326. Charters, W. W. Motion Pictures and Youth: A Summary. New York: The Macmillan Company, 1933.

Summarizes the main findings of the Payne Fund Studies regarding attitudinal and behavioral effects of motin pictures on children. These studies were conducted in the 1920s, and concluded that "the commercial movies are an unsavory mess," and that "the producers ought to have a heart" over their bad influences on children. They placed an emphasis on quantitative, experimental and survey methodologies, but still made use of more qualitative approaches. These pioneer studies helped establish the field of media research within the perspective of science.

327. Cline, Victor B., Roger G. Croft, and Steven Courrier. "Desensitization of Children to Television Violence." Journal of Personality and Social Psychology, Vol. 27, No. 3, 1973, pp. 360-365.

Boys aged 5-14 viewed a 14-minute sequence of film segments including violent and nonviolent action. Continuous recording of physiological responses indicated that those subjects with significant previous exposure to violent television drama were less affected emotionally by violent sequences.

328. Cohen, Akiba A., Hanna Adoni, and Gideon Drori. "Adolescents' Perceptions of Social Conflicts in Television News and Social Reality." Human Communication Research, Vol. 10, No. 2, 1983, pp. 203-225.

This study is based on the assumption that television news coverage distorts social conflicts in terms of complexity, intensity, and solvability. The authors test the hypothesis that age and degree of remoteness from specific social conflicts affect perception of these conflicts. Approximately 1,000 Israeli teenagers differentiated, by age, between television news portrayal and real-world perception of school integration, labor disputes, and political terrorism--older teenagers to a greater degree than younger ones. The greatest differentiation between TV and real-life conflict for both age groups involved conflict surrounding school integration, with which respondents were presumably most familiar in real life. The least amount of differentiation was in relation to political terrorism.

329. Cohen, Akiba A. and Hanna Adoni. "Children's Fear Responses to Real-Life Violence on Television: The Case of the 1973 Middle East War." Communications: International Journal of Communication Research, Vol. 6, 1980, pp. 81-94.

This study examined the fear response of children to televised war films. 96 Israeli children were shown war-related film clips or neutral scenes, after which each subject was asked to respond verbally to four questions designed to measure tension. The results supported the hypothesis that authentic background war sounds increased fear. The pattern of sex differences found in the study fully supported the hypothesis that girls would verbally express more fear than boys, but would not show it facially. Hypotheses regarding age and social class were not supported.

330. Collins, W. Andrew, Thomas J. Berndt, and Valerie L. Hess. "Observational Learning of Motives and Consequences for Television Aggression: A Developmental Study." Child Development, Vol. 45, No. 3, 1974, pp. Q799-802.

The authors examined the relationship between age and level of cognitive development of viewers and nature of evaluation of characters and characters' behaviors in action-adventure programs. Subjects were primary school children and 10- and 13-year olds who viewed an aggressive TV program. The youngest children recalled aggressive behaviors concretely or along with consequences; their evaluation of characters was based on these factors only. Older children recalled character motives as well as aggressive behaviors and the consequences and made corresponding evaluations.

These cognitive factors may affect behavioral response to media violence.

331. Comstock, George A. "Types of Portrayal and Aggressive Behavior." Journal of Communication, Vol. 27, No. 3, 1977, pp. 189-198.

Variations in results of research on the relationship between televised violence and imitative behavior is explained in terms of attention to details of portrayal that increase the likelihood of imitative or other aggression in certain viewers. Summarizes findings relating to these factors: reward or lack of criticism of the violent model; and portrayal of violence as intentional, justified, with similarities in setting or character to the viewer, in a highly exciting manner. Cartoon violence, though somewhat less effective than realistic portrayal, still increases the probability of aggressive behavior.

332. Comstock, George A. "New Emphases in Research on the Effects of Television and Film Violence." In Edward L. Palmer and Aimee Dorr (eds.) Children and the Faces of Television: Teaching, Violence, Selling. New York: Academic Press, 1981, pp. 129-148.

The empirical study of the influence of film and television violence has supported the hypothesis that such portrayals increase viewer aggressiveness. While there is no compelling demonstration that such portrayals contribute to harmful crime and violence, we cannot interpret this as null evidence because such linkages are likely to be quite complex. Even if effects seldom transgress the boundary from tolerable interpersonal aggression into proscribed action, one may question whether additional abrasiveness is a social good.

333. Comstock, George A. "Violence in Television Content: An Overview." In David Pearl, Lorraine Bouthilet, and Joyce Lazar (eds.), Television and Behavior, Vol. 2, Technical Reviews. Rockville, MD: National Institute of Mental Health, 1982, pp.108-125.

Traces the development of governmental attention to television's effects on the public from initial congressional hearings in 1952 to the 1982 update of the Surgeon General's Report. Summarizes major research and controversies about methods and results in documenting violent program content and cultivation effects such as fearfulness and pessimism.

334. Comstock, George A., Eli A. Rubinstein, and John P. Murray (eds.). Television and Social Behavior (Technical Reports to the Surgeon General's Advisory Committee), 5 Vols. Washington, DC: U.S. Government Printing Office, 1972.

Five volumes of research supplementing Television and Growing Up, the Report to the Surgeon General of the United States, focusing on media content and control, and effects of televised violence on viewers' attitudes and behavior. Many of these studies are annotated in this bibliography under their respective authors.

335. Comstock, George A., Steven Chaffee, Natan Katzman, Maxwell McCombs, and Donald Roberts. Television and Human Behavior. New York: Columbia University Press, 1978.

An overview of research relating to violence on television. Violence in network television drama emphasizes victimization and the prowess of the white male. Between the late 1960s and 1970s violence remained at consistently high levels, especially in children's programs. Evidence suggests that the amount of interpersonal physical and verbal abuse in programs is unrelated to audience popularity or viewers' expressions of liking a program.

336. Cook, Thomas D., Deborah A. Kendzierski, and Stephen V. Thomas. "The Implicit Assumptions of TV Research: An Analysis of the 1982 NIMH Report on Television and Behavior." Public Opinion Quarterly, Vol. 47, No. 2, 1983, pp. 161-201.

Compares the 1982 National Institute of Mental Health research program and report, Television and Behavior, to the existing body of research and to a model of television in a context of socio-cultural institutions and processes. The research program placed emphasis on individual psychological effects of televised violence, particularly in regard to children. More attention was given to the pro-social uses of television than in the past. Relatively little attention was given to the structure and functions of the television industry, to institutions that interface with it (advertising, government regulation, advocacy groups), and to leverage for change.

337. Copeland, G. A. and Dan Slater. "Television, Fantasy and Vicarious Catharsis." Critical Studies in Mass Communication, Vol. 2, No. 4, 1985, pp. 352-362.

The authors argue that the catharsis hypothesis - that the desire or need to exhibit aggressive or hostile behaviors is reduced by a release of those desires through vicarious participation such as television viewing - has been researched on an unsound formulation of how catharsis functions, one which ignores the degree to which viewers are able to fantasize. A discussion of the construct of television viewing suggests that fantasy is not in the media content but in the person, and assumptions in previous catharsis research are challenged.

93

338. Court, John H. "Correlational and Cross-Cultural Studies on Pornography and Aggression." In Neil M. Malamuth and Edward Donnerstein (eds.), Pornography and Sexual Aggression. Orlando, FL: Academic Press, 1984, pp. 143-172.

The possibility of a negative correlation between the availability of pornography and the incidence of sexual offenses was widely accepted in the 1970s; this position now lacks experimental support. Porno-violence is identified as a subcategory of pornography which is especially powerful in its potential to generate antisocial sexual behavior and attitudes. Experimental work suggests that porno-violence directly affects specific types of response and attitude change. In other respects, a ripple effect (propagation of a hostile, exploitive view of women) is believed to occur. The containment of porno-violence, especially in view of the increasing exposure of young people to pornography, is advocated.

339. Cullingford, C. Children and Television. New York: St. Martin's Press, 1984.

This volume reports survey results from over 5000 children from diverse backgrounds in the US and the UK. Part 1 presents data on children's attention to TV. Part 2 discusses heroes and heroines on TV, the real vs. the fantastic, TV news, violence and style. Part 3 deals with what children learn from TV; recall and recognition, educational TV, information, propoganda and advertising. Part 4 discusses the influence of parents and peers on TV viewing, mass vs. individual responses to television, subliminal content, the development of children's responses, and models of effect. The final chapter presents conclusions, followed by a bibliography on children and television.

340. Dahlgren, Peter. "Television in the Socialization Process: Structures and Programming of the Swedish Broadcasting Corporation." In George A. Comstock and Eli A. Rubinstein (eds.), Television and Social Behavior, Vol. 1, Media Content and Control. Washington, DC: U.S. Government Printing Office, 1972, pp. 533-546.

Outlines the structure of Sveriges Radio (broadcasting), a limited company, and the policies under which it operates--the Radio Act of 1966 and Agreement of 1967. These regulations underlie TV1's own policy of avoiding needless brutality in programs and attempting to "foster an atmosphere where intolerance and prejudice would have no part". TV2 recognizes the existence of violence as a real-world fact but insists that the social and human context be considered, including explicit motives and consequences. Analysis of a week's programming in 1971 indicated relatively few violent incidents. These are described and appear to meet the guidelines.

341. Davis, F. James. "Crime News in Colorado Newspapers." American Journal of Sociology, Vol. 57, No. 4, 1952, pp. 325-330.

Crime stories in four newspapers were sampled over a two-year period. Items concerning theft, rape, murder, assault and so forth were compared to FBI crime reports for the period and to public opinion concerning criminal activity. There was no relationship between changes in actual rates of crimes and amount of coverage of the particular type of crime. Public opinion concerning certain types of crime--theft and violent crimes except rape--was more similar to newspaper coverage than to actual occurrence.

342. Day, Richard C. and Maryam Ghandour. "The Effect of Television-Mediated Aggression and Real-life Aggression on the Behavior of Lebanese Children." Journal of Experimental Child Psychology, Vol. 38, No. 1, 1984, pp. 7-18.

Investigates the effect of TV-mediated aggression on behavior of children aged 6-8 years in a Beirut elementary school. Controlling for pre- experimental aggression, subjects were assigned to a viewing of human- film aggression, cartoon-film aggression, neutral film or real-life (act of war) aggression. Post film play behaviors were observed. Results indicate that boys as a group were more aggressive than girls, and exhibited more imitative aggression after viewing both violent film and real-life violence. Girls were not more violent after viewing filmed aggression, but were affected by the real-life violence. Results suggest that one effect of war on children is to increase their acts of antisocial, aggressive behaviors.

343. Dee, Juliet Lushbough. "Media Accountability for Real-Life Violence: A Case of Negligence or Free Speech?" Journal of Communication, Vol. 7, No. 2, 1987, (in press).

A review of the U.S. court decisions on cases in which a child or young adult was the victim of violence that was said to have been induced by the media - from films to television to rock music - suggests that the courts have in general hesitated to hold media organizations accountable for inciting the violent acts of individuals.

344. deKoning, T. L., D. P. Conradie, and E. M. Nel. The Effect of Different Kinds of Television Programming on the Youth. Pretoria, South Africa: Institute for Communication Research, Human Sciences Research Council, 1980.

A long term field experiment designed to investigate the relative effect of different kinds of television programs on certain aggressive and pro-social behavior and attitudes of school-going and pre-school children in South Africa. Groups of randomly selected television-naive subjects were shown a series of either aggressive, pro-social, or neutral television programs. A control group saw no programs. Using a test-retest design, pre- and post-exposure data were generated on a number of measuring instruments. In regard to the Berkowitz Arousal Theory, some evidence indicates that watching certain television content (eg., humor) may lower the excitatory potential and lead to a reduction of aggressive behavior. Variables such as age, sex, home language, and program interest, however, modified the effect of the programs. The results reveal that a single simple explanation or theory is probably inadequate to explain the relative effects of different kinds of television content.

345. Deleon, Dennis L. and Robert L. Naon. "The Regulation of Televised Violence." Stanford Law Review, Vol. 26, No. 6, 1974, pp. 1291-1325.

A concise review of laboratory and field studies centering on the issue of the impact of television violence prefaces this outline of the sources of regulation. The author discusses the potential and limitations of the industry and the Federal Communications Commission to control violent content and proposes new legislation, especially in regard to programming for children, which would involve scheduling and censorship. The author argues that such legislation, if carefully drawn by Congress and carefully administered by the Federal Communications Commission, could be consistent with First Amendment freedoms.

346. Diener, Ed and Darlene DeFour. "Does Television Violence Enhance Program Popularity?". Journal of Personality and Social Psychology, Vol. 36, No. 3, 1978, pp. 333-341.

Two studies were conducted to explore the effects of fictional television violence on adventure show popularity. In Study 1, the amount of violence within 62 episodes of 11 programs was correlated with the national Nielsen viewer index. A very low and nonsignificant relationship emerged. In study 2 an adventure program was presented to subjects either uncut or with the violence deleted. Although the uncut version was preceived as significantly more violent, it was not liked significantly more. The violence condition accounted for approximately one percent of the variance in reported liking. There is presently little evidence that violence enhances program popularity.

347. Doerken, Maurine. Classroom Combat; Teaching and Television. Englewood Cliffs, NJ: Educational Technology Publications, 1983.

This book is based on the premise that war is being waged between the classroom and the living room for greater impact on children's learning and information sources. In chapter 2, the author provides a brief review and some study details of research supporting widely divergent points of view in regard to effects of TV violence on children. Also cited are examples of legal action resulting from children's alleged imitation of TV in committing violent crimes. TV industry attitudes toward violence and areas of social and educational concern are also discussed.

348. Dominick, Joseph R. "Children's Viewing of Crime Shows and
Attitudes of Law Enforcement." Journalism Quarterly, Vol. 51, No. 1,
1974, pp. 5-12.

   371 fifth grade children in 4 New York City schools (2 in
   blue-collar areas and 2 in white-collar areas) completed
   questionnaires in May, 1972. The amount of time a child spent
   watching crime and police shows was unrelated to the judged
   importance of television as an information source. For boys and
   girls, viewing crime shows was positively correlated with (1)
   identification with a TV character associated with law
   enforcement; (2) belief that criminals usually get caught; and (3)
   knowledge of civil rights when arrested. For both boys and girls
   the strongest predictors of general evaluation of police were the
   perceived attitude of friends and family. For boys only, more
   personal contact with police was associated with negative
   evaluation. Legal terms and processes frequently seen on TV were
   better known than those things not commonly portrayed.

349. Dominick, Joseph R. "Crime and Law Enforcement in the Mass
Media." In Charles Winick (ed.), Deviance and Mass Media, Beverly
Hills, CA: Sage, 1978, pp. 105-128.

   A review of content analyses examining the portrayal of crime and
   law enforcement in newspapers, broadcast news, and broadcast
   entertainment. Also discusses the special problems of media
   coverage of terrorism because in many of these episodes the medium
   itself is manipulated by the individuals or terrorist group
   involved.

350. Dominick, Joseph R. "Videogames, Television Violence and
Aggression in Teenagers." Journal of Communication, Vol. 34, No. 2,
1984, pp. 136-147.

   250 high school students received questionnaires in which they
   estimated the amount of time per week that they spent playing
   video games. They were also asked if they usually went to the
   arcades alone, or with friends. Additional data were gathered on
   aggression and self-esteem. Videogame playing is neither the
   menace it is purported to be nor free of possible negative
   consequences. Heavy videogame players were not necessarily more
   aggressive; but boys who frequently played arcade videogames had
   significantly lower self-esteem.

351. Dominick, Joseph R. and Bradley S. Greenberg. "Attitudes Toward
Violence: The Interaction of Television Exposure, Family Attitudes, and
Social Class." In George A. Comstock and Eli A. Rubinstein (eds.),
Television and Social Behavior, Vol. 3, Television and Adolescent
Aggressiveness. Washington DC: U.S. Government Printing Office, 1972,
pp. 314-335.

This study assessed the impact of televised violence on the aggressive attitudes of a sample of 434 boys and 404 girls between the ages of 9 and 11. Children who perceived that their parents clearly disapproved of violence were less likely to approve of aggression or to believe that violence was an effective means of solving problems. They also expressed less willingness to use violence. Children exposed to a higher level of TV violence indicated more willingness to use it and to suggest it as a means of resolving conflict, particularly among the boys. The most positive attitudes toward violence and aggression were found among heavy violence viewers who perceived no definite parental stand on aggressive behavior.

352. Donnerstein, Edward and Daniel Linz. "Mass Media, Sexual Violence and Male Viewers." American Behavioral Scientist, Vol. 29, No. 5, 1986, pp. 601-618.

The authors examine the research on aggressive pornography and the research that examines nonpornographic media images of violence against women, the major focus of recent research and the material that provokes negative reactions. The final section examines the research on nonviolent pornography. There is no evidence for any harm related effects from sexually explicit materials, but the research does support potential harm effects from aggressive materials.

353. Donnerstein, Edward and Leonard Berkowitz. "Victim Reactions in Aggressive Erotic Films as a Factor in Violence Against Women." Journal of Personality and Social Psychology, Vol. 41, No. 4, 1981, pp. 710-724.

An investigation of how the behavioral characteristics of the people in erotic films and the nature of the targets available for later aggression can affect subsequent aggression. Eighty male subjects were angered by a male or female confederate. They were then shown a neutral film or one of three erotic films. The erotic films differed in terms of their aggressive content and the reactions of the female victim. Subjects were then allowed to aggress against the confederate via electric shock. Results indicated that the films had no effect on male targets whereas both types of aggressive erotic films increased aggression toward the female.

354. Donnerstein, Edward and Neil Malamuth. "Pornography: Its Consequences On The Observer." In L. Schlesinger and E. Revitch (eds.), Sexual Dynamics of Anti-Social Behavior. Springfield, IL: C. C. Thomas, 1983.

A review of research dealing with the relationship between aggressive erotica and violence against women. The authors find highly consistent data which indicate that exposure to aggressive forms of pornography can change attitudes concerning violence against women and increase the probability that male subjects will overtly aggress against females.

355. Donnerstein, Edward. "Aggressive Erotica and Violence Against Women." Journal of Personality and Social Psychology, Vol. 39, No. 2, 1980, pp. 269-277.

In an examination of the effects of aggressive-erotic stimuli on male aggression toward females, 120 male subjects were angered or treated in a neutral manner by a male or female confederate. Subjects were then shown either a neutral, erotic, or aggressive-erotic film and given an opportunity to aggress against the confederate via the delivery of electric shock. Results indicated that the aggressive-erotic film was effective in increasing aggression overall, and it produced the highest increase in aggression against the female. Even non-angered subjects showed an increase in aggression toward the female after viewing the aggressive-erotic film.

356. Donnerstein, Edward. "Pornography and Violence Against Women: Experimental Studies." Annals of the New York Academy of Sciences, Vol. 347, 1980, pp. 277-288.

A review of experimental research on pornography and violence against women. While research has been directed at the effects of erotic media presentations on behavior, the issue of whether such presentations can in some manner be related to increased aggressive attacks against women has been only recently of concern. It is generally believed by a large proportion of the population that many sexual materials can precipitate violent sexual crimes.

357. Donnerstein, Edward. "Aggressive Pornography: Can It Influence Aggression toward Women?" In C. Albee, S. Gordon, and H. Leitenberg (eds.), Promoting Sexual Responsibility and Preventing Sexual Problems. Hanover, NH:, 1983.

This paper examines recent research on the effects of aggressive pornography and subsequent aggression toward women. The author suggests that nonaggressive erotic or pornographic images have really no measurable effect on aggression toward women; it is only the aggressive forms that seem to produce negative effects.

358. Donnerstein, Edward. "Pornography: Its Effect on Violence Against Women." In Neil M. Malamuth and Edward Donnerstein (eds.), Pornography and Sexual Aggression. Orlando, FL: Academic Press, 1984, pp. 53-81.

Overview of research reveals that it is difficult to make a straightforward definitive conclusion about the relationship between pornography and aggression toward women. Certain types of pornography can influence aggression and other asocial attitudes and behaviors toward women; others, especially nonaggressive pornography, do not. The aggressive content of pornography is the main contributor to violence against women.

359. Donnerstein, Edward, Marcia Donnerstein, and Gary Barrett. "Where Is The Facilitation of Media Violence: The Effects of Nonexposure and Placement of Anger Arousal." Journal of Research in Personality, Vol. 10, 1976, pp. 386-398.

This study examined the conditions under which media violence would facilitate aggression in angered individuals. It was predicted that increased aggression would occur only under the condition of viewing an aggressive film prior to anger arousal (compared to a no-film control). When subjects were angered prior to film exposure, neutral films reduced aggression; but aggressive films did not differ from the no-film control.

360. Doob, Anthony H. and Robert J. Climie. "Delay of Measurement and Effects of Film Violence." Journal of Experimental Social Psychology, Vol. 8, No. 2, 1972, pp. 136-142.

College students who viewed a violent film segment displayed a greater degree of aggression than subjects who viewed a neutral segment when measured immediately after exposure. This difference was not found for subjects who performed an unrelated task during a 20-minute period after viewing, which was determined to be the result of a decrease in arousal.

361. Doob, Anthony N. and Glenn E. Macdonald. "The News Media and Perceptions of Violence." Report of the Royal Commission on Violence in the Communications Industry, Vol. 5, Learning from the Media. Toronto, Canada: The Royal Commission 1977, pp. 171-226.

In Toronto, the public overestimates the incidence of violence. Public anxiety is lower in response to media violence when background information is provided or when violent events are identified as rare. Complex socio- economic, geographic, and cultural factors are involved in establishing these perceptions, along with media exposure.

362. Doob, Anthony N. and Glenn E. Macdonald. "Television Viewing and Fear of Victimization: Is the Relationship Causal?" Journal of Personality and Social Psychology, Vol. 37, No. 2, 1979, pp. 170-179.

A test of cultivation of fear via TV exposure to violence using a Toronto sample of 300 adults (70 percent female) based on responses to 25 questions. The questions related to the nature and frequency of crime and violence and chances of personal involvement in crime. Responses to some of the questions were related more strongly to area of residence--that is, high-crime urban area versus low-crime urban or suburban area--than to TV viewing.

363. Dorr Leifer, Aimee and Donald F. Roberts. "Children's Responses to Television Violence." In John P. Murray, Eli A. Rubinstein, and George A. Comstock (eds.), Television and Social Behavior, Vol. 2, Television and Social Learning. Washington, DC: U.S. Government Printing Office, 1972, pp. 43-180.

Report of a series of studies that explored the role of motivation for, and consequences of, aggressive acts in modifying the effects of exposure to such acts. Children, as they grow up, understand more and more about the television programs they view. There is rather clear evidence that exposure to television programs that include aggressive acts produces greater subsequent aggression than one would find without such exposure.

364. Dorr, Aimee and Peter Kovaric. "Some of the People Some of the Time--But Which People? Televised Violence and Its Effects." In Edward L. Palmer and Aimee Dorr (eds.), Children and the Faces of Television: Teaching, Violence, Selling. New York: Academic Press, 1981, pp. 183-199.

A brief review of results of studies dealing with the effects of televised violence on individuals grouped according to age, cognitive ability, sex, ethnicity, social class, personality characteristics, and propensity for aggression. Evidence of a direct relationship between TV violence and aggressive behavior is mixed in each case, although certain groups are more likely to be heavier viewers of violence. The authors conclude with consideration of alternatives for policy and action, including responsibilities of parents, teachers, creators of programs, and viewers themselves.

365. Drabman, Ronald S. and Margaret Hanratty Thomas. "Does Media Violence Increase Children's Toleration of Real-Life Aggression?" Developmental Psychology, Vol. 10, No. 3, 1974, pp. 418-421.

Children aged 8-9 who viewed a violent film took longer to seek adult assistance when confronted with increasingly violent behavior of younger children (visible on a videotape monitor) than did children in a control group.

366. Drabman, Ronald S. and Margaret Hanratty Thomas. "Children's Imitation of Aggressive and Prosocial Behavior When Viewing Alone and In Pairs." Journal of Communication, Vol. 27, No. 3, 1977, pp. 199-205.

Male preschoolers observed either an aggressive modeling film or a prosocial modeling film. The impact of the exposure was assessed by observing the behavior of the boys in a free-play session with the same clown as in the movie. Half of the boys viewed and played in pairs, half individually. The results suggest that the likelihood of children imitating modeled aggressive behavior may be increased when viewing and performance take place in the presence of peers. Imitation of prosocial behavior was not

101

enhanced when the boys viewed in pairs. The boys in this condition, however, exhibited relatively high prosocial scores.

367. Dunand, Muriel, Leonard Berkowitz, and Jacques-Philippe Leyens. "Audience Effects with Viewing Aggressive Movies." British Journal of Social Psychology, Vol. 21, 1984, pp. 69-76.

A study of 54 male college students in Brussels demonstrated the influence of a group setting on tendencies toward violence in response to violent movie content. The presence of another, actively excited spectator served to reduce inhibitions against aggressiveness, increasing the aggressiveness of subjects' response.

368. Dysinger, Wendell, S. and Christian A. Ruckmick. The Emotional Responses of Children to the Motion Picture Situation. New York: MacMillan, 1933.

Children under the age of 12 demonstrated the most intense reactions to scenes of conflict, danger, and tragedy, with a wide range of cognitive differences in their understanding. The youngest children responded to concrete elements rather than more subtle or comprehensive elements of plot.

369. Dziki, Sylwester, Janina Maczuga and Walery Pisarek (eds.). World Directory of Mass Communication Researchers. Cracow, 1984.

An international listing of mass communication researchers.

370. Edgar, Patricia M. Children and Screen Violence. St.Lucia, Australia: University of Queensland Press, 1977.

A survey on perceptions of three types of film violence using a sample of Australian adolescents. The films portrayed either realistic, fantasy, or emotional intra-family violence. Response varied according to both sex and level of self-esteem of the subjects as well as the type of violence. Realistic and intense intra-family violence elicited stronger reactions. The author concludes that, while realistic violence on television may be upsetting to young people, the promotion of an unattainable lifestyle is a more probable incitement to crime and violence in real life.

371. Edgar, Patricia M. and Donald E. Edgar. "Television Violence and Socialization Theory." Public Opinion Quarterly, Vol. 35, No. 4, 1971, pp. 608-612.

The authors propose a model for the study of television effects upon the attitudes and behavior of children that integrates the major findings of previous research in this field and also applies insights derived from socialization theory. The research model recognizes the need for an interactive view of media influence.

The study based upon this model involved pretesting the social conditions, parental values, teachers' attitudes, children's interests, IQ scores, and attitudes toward violence in the town of Darwin, Australia in 1971 before the introduction of television programming. Post-testing was scheduled to be conducted two years later.

372. Ekman, Paul, Robert M. Liebert, Wallace V. Friesen, Randall Harrison, Carl Zlatchin, Edward J. Malstrom, and Robert A. Baron. "Facial Expressions of Emotion While Watching Televised Violence as Predictors of Subsequent Aggression." In George A. Comstock, Eli A. Rubinstein, and John P. Murray (eds.), Television and Social Behavior, Vol. 5, Television's Effects: Further Explorations. Washington, DC: U.S. Government Printing Office, 1972, pp. 22-58.

The facial expressions of 30 boys and 35 girls, aged 5 or 6, were correlated with their aggressive behavior toward another child. The boys' facial expressions of happiness, pleasantness, and interest during a violent telecast were positively related to subsequent aggression, while expressions of unpleasantness, sadness, anger, disgust, pain, and surprise were negatively related to subsequent aggression. No significant relationships were obtained for girls.

373. Ellis, Glenn T. and Francis Sekyra. "The Effect of Aggressive Cartoons on the Behavior of First-Grade Children." Journal of Psychology, Vol. 81, No. 1, 1972, pp. 37-43.

Violent cartoon viewing by children increases aggressiveness of behavior. Among 51 six-year olds, those who viewed a violent cartoon about a football game demonstrated increased physical aggression in a normal school setting. Those who viewed a nonviolent cartoon or had a discussion instead of viewing showed no increase in aggression.

374. Eron, Leonard D. "Relationship of TV Viewing Habits and Aggressive Behavior in Children." Journal of Abnormal and Social Psychology, Vol. 67, No. 2, 1963, pp. 193-196.

A study of 875 eight-year-olds in New York state correlated peer ratings of aggressive behavior with parental reports of amount of viewing and favorite programs. A strong positive relationship was found for boys between aggression and liking violent programs.

375. Eron, Leonard D. "Parent-Child Interaction, Television Violence, and Aggression of Children." American Psychologist, Vol. 37, No. 2, 1982, pp. 197-211.

Two large-scale longitudinal studies revealed that the relation between television violence and aggression in boys and girls was corroborated in two areas of the United States as well as in Finland, Poland, and Australia. Moreover, it held for both boys and girls. The causal effect was seen as circular, with television violence affecting children's aggression and aggressive children watching a greater amount of televised violence. Important intervening variables were child's identification with aggressive characters and the extent to which television was perceived as an accurate portrayal of life. Parents' role as well as the child's intellectual ability and social relationships also were important variables.

376. Eron, Leonard D., L. Rowell Huesmann, Monroe M. Lefkowitz, and Leopold O. Walder. "Does Television Violence Cause Aggression?" American Psychologist, Vol. 27, No. 4, 1972, pp. 253-263.

A follow-up of Eron's earlier study of 8-year olds, aged 18-19 at the time of this later research. The more violent the program preferences of boys at age 8-9, the more aggressive their behavior at that age and especially at age 18-19. Preference for violence and heavy viewing at age 19 also corresponded with belief that violent programs were realistic and that violent methods are appropriate in real life. Viewing of TV violence was not proposed as a single influencing factor, but it explained more variance than any other single factor analyzed.

377. Eron, Leonard D., L. Rowell Huesmann, Patrick Brice, Paulette Fischer, and Rebecca Mermelstein. "Age Trends in the Development of Aggression, Sex Typing, and Related Television Habits." Developmental Psychology, Vol. 19, No. 1, 1983, pp. 71-77.

A 3-year longitudinal study was conducted with two large samples of elementary school youngsters overlapping in one grade. It was thus possible to trace developmental trends from Grades 1 through 5 on the following variables: aggression; frequency of television viewing; extent of violence viewed on television; judged realism of television programs; and preference for masculine, feminine, or neutral activities. These data support the theory that there is a sensitive period during which the effect of television can be especially influential on children's behavior. Further, since the correlation between violence viewing and aggression tends to increase until age 10-11 years, a cumulative effect beyond the sensitive period is suggested.

378. Eysenck, Hans J. and D. K. B. Nias. Sex, Violence and the Media. New York: Harper and Row, 1978.

A comprehensive review of research relating to the effects of media violence in both the United States and the United Kingdom. Examines the possible influence viewing and reading overtly pornographic and violent material may have on behavior. It examines the methodology used in this area of research and the results of field and experimental field studies, and laboratory experiments. Evidence indicates that media violence increases viewer aggression, and perhaps viewer sexual libido; that effects of pornography, while variable, cannot be disputed; and that the portrayal of violence in media can incite some viewers to violence.

379. Feilitzen, Cecilia von, Leni Filpson, and Ingela Schyller. Open Your Eyes to Children's Viewing: On Children, TV and Radio Now and in the Future. Stockholm: Swedish Broadcasting Corporation (in Swedish and in English), 1977.

A review of fifteen years of research concerning children's use of TV and radio, the influence of television programs imported into Sweden, and the lack of resources for children's broadcasting. The summary, directed to the Swedish Commission on Broadcasting, includes proposals to improve the status of programming for children and adults.

380. Fenigstein, Allan. "Does Aggression Cause a Preference for Viewing Media Violence?" Journal of Personality and Social Psychology, Vol. 37, No. 12, 1979, pp. 2307-2317.

College students were classified according to their expression of aggressive or non-aggressive fantasies and then given a choice of film clips for viewing. Aggressive fantasies in males corresponded with preference for viewing violence, and males chose films that were more violent than those chosen by females. Males given an opportunity to be aggressive were more likely to choose violent content than males not given this opportunity. Results are linked to a bi-directional relationship between aggressive behavior and the viewing of media violence.

381. Ferracuti, Franco and Renato Lazzari. La Violenza nei Mezzi di Comunicazione di Massa. [Violence in the Mass Media]. RAI Radiotelevisione Italiana. Torino: ERI, 1968.

An extensive critical review of mass media effects, concluding that effects are minimized among the normal population.

382. Feshbach, Seymour. "The Stimulating Versus Cathartic Effects of a Vicarious Aggressive Activity." Journal of Abnormal and Social Psychology, Vol. 63, No. 2, 1961, pp. 381-385.

An experimental test of the effect of initial state of arousal on reaction to media violence. Male college students were angered prior to viewing; others were treated neutrally. Subjects then viewed a neutral or an aggressive film of a prize fight. Those who had been angered and saw the aggressive film demonstrated decreased aggressive attitude toward the experimenter. Non-angered subjects did not show increased aggressive attitudes. Catharsis occurs for viewers who are in a state of arousal prior to viewing violent material.

383. Feshbach, Seymour. "Reality and Fantasy in Filmed Violence." In John P. Murray, Eli A. Rubinstein, and George A. Comstock (eds.), Television and Social Behavior, Vol. 2, Television and Social Learning. Washington, DC: U.S. Government Printing Office, 1972, pp. 318-345.

Following up on experiments designed to measure the cathartic effect of film and TV violence, primary school children viewed either neutral (baseball or circus films), fantasy aggression (war films), or real aggression (police/college student riots). Results of this series of experiments were inconclusive.

384. Feshbach, Seymour, and Robert D. Singer. Television and Aggression: An Experimental Field Study. San Francisco: Jossey-Bass, 1971.

A field experiment analyzing the relationship between televised violence and imitative behavior. Boys in residential schools (academies and care facilities) were assigned to either violent or non-violent television fare for a six-week period. Personality and attitude measures were taken before, during, and after the viewing period. In three schools, those who were in the non-violent content group were significantly more aggressive with peers and with school authorities than boys in the other schools. Viewing of violence corresponded with a lower level of aggression among boys in the care facilities only. The role of fantasized aggression was also examined by the authors and was incorporated in their interpretation of the results as the effect of catharsis.

385. Foulkes, David, Edward Belvedere, and Terry Brubaker. "Televised Violence and Dream Content." In George A. Comstock, Eli A. Rubinstein, and John P. Murray (eds.), Television and Social Behavior, Vol. 5, Television's Effects: Further Explorations. Washington, DC: U.S. Government Printing Office, 1972, pp. 59-119.

Dream content was used to assess effects of television fantasy violence on 40 ten to eleven year old boys. Half of the subjects were heavy viewers of TV violence and the other half seldom watched these types of shows. On one night they viewed a relatively violent episode from a children's Western series and on another night they saw a non-violent episode. Subjects slept in the laboratory and their REM periods were monitored. The results showed that exposure to a violent film before sleeping did not have any systematic effect on dream hostility, anxiety, guilt, hedonic tone, or overall vividness and intensity.

386. Fouts, Gregory T. "Effects of Television on Children and Youth: A Developmental Approach." Report of the Royal Commission on Violence in the Communications Industry, Vol. 6. Toronto, Canada: The Royal Commission, 1977, pp. 1-123.

Examination of the influence of variables which mediate the effects of viewing televised violence among children. Interviews conducted in the homes of 300 children and their parents and at the time of viewing specific programs provided information about viewer characteristics (age, birth order, personality traits, motives for viewing) and perceptions of televised and real-life violence; about family characteristics (family size, choice of programs, comments about programs); and program type.

387. Fraczek, A. "Age and Gender Related Trends in Patterns of TV Violence Viewing and Interpersonal Aggression in Children." Polish Psychological Bulletin, Vol. 14, No. 1, 1983, pp. 25-38.

A sample of 237 children in Warsaw were studied in each of three years (1979, 1980, 1981) in a longitudinal design covering grades one to five. Data analysis showed boys watch more tv in general, and more violent programs than girls. Boys have stronger identification than girls with aggressive tv characters, and they fantasize more frequently about tv shows. With increasing age, boys watch more, girls watch less tv. Both have increasing opportunities for viewing violence. Boys have higher behavioral aggression than girls, but are only slightly higher in self-rated aggression. Positive correlations have been obtained between preferences for violent television programs and the behavioral aggression level, as well as between the latter and identification with aggressive television characters.

388. Freedman, Jonathan L. "Effect of Television Violence on Aggressiveness." Psychological Bulletin, Vol. 96, No. 2, 1984, pp. 227-246.

Reviews and evaluates the design and results of field experiments and correlational surveys dealing with the relationship between TV violence and real-life aggression. The marginal relationships documented by these studies cannot be interpreted as causal. Nor is there clear evidence that those individuals labeled "predisposed to violence" are more likely than other individuals to respond to televised violence with aggressive or violent behavior.

389. Friedman, Herbert L. and Raymond L. Johnson. "Mass Media Use and Aggression: A Pilot Study." In George A. Comstock and Eli A. Rubinstein (eds.), Television and Social Behavior, Vol. 3, Television and Adolescent Aggressiveness. Washington DC: U.S. Government Printing Office, 1972, pp. 336-360.

A comparison of aggressive and nonaggressive adolescents revealed heavier viewing and preference for somewhat more violent programs among the more aggressive adolescents.

390. Friedrich, Lynette Kohn and Aletha Huston-Stein. "Aggressive and Prosocial Television Programs and the Natural Behavior of Preschool Children." Monographs of the Society for Research in Child Development, Vol. 38, No. 4, 1973.

97 children (52 boys and 45 girls) were used as subjects in an experiment conducted during a 9-week nursery school program. Observations of aggressive and prosocial behavior were made during free play periods. During the middle 4 weeks the children saw either 12 aggressive television programs, 12 prosocial programs, or 12 neutral films. The aggressive programs produced more aggressive behavior during the free play periods. Aggressive programs also influenced inter-personal aggression, but only for

those children who were initially above the group average in aggression. By contrast, prosocial programs produced a number of positive changes in the children's behavior -- they showed increased task persistence, role obedience, and tolerance of delay, especially among the more intelligent children.

391. Furnham, Adrian F. and Barrie Gunter. "Sex, Presentation Mode and Memory for Violent and Nonviolent News." Journal of Educational Television, Vol. 11, No. 2, 1985, pp. 99-105.

In this study, 68 undergraduates were presented with violent and nonviolent news stories, either audio-visually, audio only, or in print, and then immediately tested for cued recall of story content. Presentation mode was shown to be significant: recall of news was best from print and worst from audio-visual. Males recalled violent news better than nonviolent, while for females the reverse was true. Males also recalled violent news much better than females in the audio-visual mode, but no such difference occurred in any other mode. Furthermore, the presentation of violent news stories audiovisually can produce especially impaired memory performance among female viewers.

392. Gadow, Kenneth D., Joyce Sprafkin and Thomas J. Ficarrotto. "Effects of Viewing Aggression-Laden Cartoons on Preschool-Aged Emotionally Disturbed Children." Journal of Child Psychiatry and Human Development, (in press), c. 1987.

In two separate studies, three classes of preschool-aged emotionally disturbed (ED) children were exposed to both aggressive and control cartoons. Treatment effects were assessed using direct observations of classroom behaviors. The findings from the first experiment with one class of ED youngsters failed to confirm the existence of a media effect. The two classes in Experiment II, however, showed a clear pattern of media reactivity. Their level of nonphysical aggression increased following both aggressive and control cartoons, which corroborates Sawin's (1975) earlier research on preschoolers in an inner city day care center. Contrary to expectation, the ED children became less noncompliant and exhibited less play aggression following exposure to the cartoons. Both ED classes exhibited this same reaction pattern.

393. Garofalo, James. "Crime and the Mass Media: A Selective Review of Research." Journal of Research in Crime and Delinquency, July, 1981, pp. 319-350.

Documents amount of newspaper and television coverage of crime, including entertainment programs, by reviewing studies from the earliest periods available. Newspaper coverage of crime-related topics has been consistent from the 1930s to 1980 (about 5 to 10 percent of news space), but with variations from area to area and newspaper to newspaper. There is no relationship between amount of crime coverage and number of actual crimes. News media in several countries over-represent violent crimes by individuals,

especially murder. Studies dealing with effects of media
violence, including effects on behavior and attitudes, indicate
that early exposure to TV violence, especially by aggressive
males, is related to aggressive behavior later in life.

394. Geen, Russell G. "The Meaning of Observed Violence: Real Versus
Fictional Violence and Consequent Effects on Aggression and Emotional
Arousal." Journal of Research in Personality, Vol. 9, 1975,
pp. 270-281.

   Sixty male subjects were either attacked or treated neutrally by a
   confederate, after which each saw a videotape of two men fighting.
   Subjects were informed that the fight was either real or
   fictitious or were given no explanation of it. Subjects who had
   previously been attacked and had observed the fight under a set to
   perceive it as real were subsequently more punitive in their
   treatment of the confederate than subjects in all other
   conditions. The combination of prior attack and observation of
   real violence also sustained blood pressure at near the level
   produced by the attack, whereas the blood pressure of attacked
   subjects in the other conditions declined during the time the
   fight was observed. Palmar sweat measures revealed that
   observation of real violence was more arousing than observation of
   fictitious fighting. The results are discussed in terms of the
   effects that the reality of observed violence has on emotional
   arousal.

395. Geen, Russell G. and David Stonner. "Context Effects in Observed
Violence." Journal of Personality and Social Psychology, Vol. 25,
No. 1, 1973, pp. 145-150.

   Sixty male subjects watched a movie of a prize fight, having first
   been attached (via electric shock) or neutrally treated by a
   confederate. One-third of the subjects were told that the fight
   was motivated by revenge; one-third understood it to be purely
   professional; one-third were shown the film without prior comment.
   Findings of the study suggest that aggression following the
   observation of violence depends partly upon the degree to which
   the subjects motive state compares with that of actors in the film
   viewed. Interpretations of observed violence apparently play a
   role in raising or lowering inhibitions against aggression on the
   part of the observer.

396. Geen, Russell G. and Leonard Berkowitz. "Some Conditions
Facilitating the Occurrence of Aggression After the Observation of
Violence." Journal of Personality, Vol. 35, No. 4, 1967, pp. 666-676.

   An experiment in which male college students viewed a film about
   boxing. Subjects then were introduced to a confederate in the
   experiment having the same name as one of the boxers. Subjects
   angered by a confederate who assumed the name of the filmed victim
   were more aggressive than those angered by a confederate who
   assumed the name of the victor.

397. Gerbner, George and Larry Gross. "Living With Television: The
Violence Profile." Journal of Communication, Vol. 26, No. 2, 1976,
pp. 173-199.

   Description of Cultural Indicators research project, including
   findings from Violence Profile No. 7. Findings from the message
   system analysis of week-long annual samples of prime-time and
   weekend-daytime network drama revealed that there has been no
   significant reduction in the overall Violence Index despite some
   fluctuations in the specific measures and a definite drop in early
   evening violence in the 1975 season. Findings from the
   cultivation analyses revealed that those who view four or more
   hours of television each day were more likely to give "televison
   answers" to questions about the proportion of people employed in
   law enforcement, whether or not most people can be trusted, and
   one's chances of being involved in violence during any given week.

398. Gerbner, George and Larry Gross. "The Scary World of TV's Heavy
Viewer." Psychology Today, Vol. 9, No. 11, 1976, pp. 41-45, 89.

   Report of ongoing Cultural Indicators research reveals that
   television dramatically demonstrates the power of authority in
   society. Violence-filled programs show who gets away with what,
   and against whom. It teaches the role of victim, and the
   acceptance of violence as a social reality. Research shows that
   people who watch a lot of television see the real world as more
   dangerous and frightening than those who watch very little. Heavy
   viewers are less trustful of their fellow citizens and more
   fearful of the real world.

399. Gerbner, George and Larry Gross. "The Violent Face of Television
and its Lessons." In Edward L. Palmer and Aimee Dorr (eds.), Children
and the Faces of Television: Teaching, Violence, and Selling. New
York: Academic Press 1981, pp. 149-162.

   The presentation of findings and the implications of the
   long-range research project, Cultural Indicators. Suggests that
   what children and other viewers learn about violence from
   television is not necessarily learned from just seeing acts of
   violence. Violence presents a scenario of power -- it tells who
   will come out on top instead of on the bottom. The results of
   surveys of both adults and children indicate that violence-laden
   television not only cultivates aggressive tendencies in a minority
   but, perhaps more importantly, also generates a pervasive and
   exaggerated sense of danger and mistrust. Findings from numerous
   analyses provide considerable support for the conclusion that
   heavy television viewers perceive social reality different from
   light television viewers, even when other factors are held
   constant.

400. Gerbner, George. "Scenario for Violence." Human Behavior, October, pp. 91-96. Also in Robert Atwin, Barry Orton, and William Verterman (eds.) American Mass Media: Industry and Issues, New York: Random House, 1975, pp. 102-107.

A discussion of some of the political issues surrounding the study of violence on television. Notes how the chief social function of symbolic violence is in what it teaches about types of people and power.

401. Gerbner, George. "The Real Threat of Television Violence." In Judy Fireman (ed.), TV Book: The Ultimate Television Book. New York: Workman Publishing Company, 1977, pp. 358-359.

Television presents a distorted picture of its violence. The leading causes of injury and violent death are highway and industrial accidents, but we rarely see those on television. Rather, television presents such violence as can best serve its dramatic and social functions: to demonstrate how power works in society and show who can get away with what. Notions of fear, prejudice, and power are enhanced by television violence. Evidence from ongoing research shows that heavy viewing of television, independent of other facts of life, induces an exaggerated sense of danger, mistrust, and vulnerability. Symbolic violence achieves the purposes of real violence in setting up a scenario of domination and control through the manipulation of our fears.

402. Gerbner, George. "Death in Prime Time: Notes on the Symbolic Functions of Dying in the Mass Media." The Annals of the American Academy of Political and Social Science, Vol. 447, 1980, pp. 64-70.

The cultural (and media) significance of dying rests in the symbolic context in which representations of dying are embedded. An examination of that context of mostly violent representations suggests that portrayals of death and dying serve symbolic functions of social typing and control and tend, on the whole, to conceal the reality and inevitability of the event.

403. Gerbner, George, Larry Gross, Marilyn Jackson-Beeck, Suzanne Jeffries-Fox, and Nancy Signorielli. "Cultural Indicators: Violence Profile No. 9." Journal of Communication, Vol. 28, No. 3, 1978, pp. 176-207.

A discussion of the diversification of the Cultural Indicators project and findings from Violence Profile No. 9. Detailed content analyses of annual week-long samples of prime-time and weekend-daytime network dramatic programs revealed that the amount of violence decreased in the fall 1977 season. Nevertheless, violence still appeared in more than two-thirds of all prime-time programs and in 9 out of 10 weekend-daytime (children's) programs. Between 1969 and 1977 63 percent of all major characters were involved in violence with victims outnumbering those who commit violence. Women, minorities, and older women are especially

111

likely to be victimized. Those who commit violence are usually
white, middle-class men in the prime of life. Cultivation
analyses revealed that more heavy viewers tend to respond in terms
of the world of television than do light viewers in the same
demographic groups, in regard to questions about violence and
mistrust. Analyses of data from a sample of New Jersey school
children and the 1975 and 1977 NORC General Social Surveys are
presented.

404. Gerbner, George, Larry Gross, Michael F. Eleey, Marilyn
Jackson-Beeck, Suzanne Jeffries-Fox and Nancy Signorielli. "TV
Violence Profile No. 8: The Highlights." Journal of Communication,
Vol. 27, No. 2, 1977, pp. 171-180.

Summary of the annual report of the Cultural Indicators project
shows increases in the amount of violence on television, including
early evening and weekend-daytime (children's) programs. The
profile also reveals the unequal structure of power and risk in
the world of television drama, and showed children's particular
vulnerability to the effects of television. Heavy viewers
revealed a significantly higher sense of personal risk, mistrust,
and suspicion than did light viewers in the same demographic
groups, exposed to the same real risks of life. The results also
showed that television's independent contributions to the
cultivation of these conceptions of a "mean world" and other
aspects of social reality are not significantly altered by sex,
age, education, income, newspaper reading, and church attendance.

405. Gerbner, George, Larry Gross, Michael Morgan and Nancy
Signorielli. "The 'Mainstreaming' of America: Violence Profile
No. 11." Journal of Communication, Vol. 30, No. 3, 1980, pp. 10-29.

Findings of the Cultural Indicators project research support the
hypothesis that television makes specific and measurable
contributions to viewers' conceptions of social reality. Violence
continued as an important thematic element and as a demonstration
of power in the television world. Cultivation analyses revealed
that many differences between groups of viewers could be explained
in terms of one of two systematic processes -- mainstreaming (the
sharing of a relative commonality of outlooks) or resonnance (the
congruence of aspects of one's social environment with
television's messages).

406. Gerbner, George, Larry Gross, Michael Morgan and Nancy
Signorielli. "Charting the Mainstream: Television's Contributions to
Political Orientations." Journal of Communication, Vol. 32, No. 2,
1982, pp. 100-127.

Report of the team's ongoing Cultural Indicators project. The
results from the message analysis of annual week-long samples of
prime-time and weekend-daytime network dramatic programming
revealed that enforcing the law on TV takes nearly three times as
many characters as the number of characters in all blue-collar and
service worker roles. The average viewer sees over 30 police

officers each week. Threats abound and crime, in prime-time, is
at least ten times as rampant as in the real world. An average of
5 to 6 acts of overt physical violence involve over half of all
major characters. Symbolic violence demonstrates power; it shows
victimization, not just aggression, hurt but not therapy; it shows
who can get away with what against whom. Results of cultivation
analyses focusing upon political orientations reveal that although
television brings conservatives, moderates, and liberals closer
together on numerous issues, the liberal position is the weakest
among heavy viewer. On issues dealing with minorities and
personal rights viewing tends to blur traditional differences and
blends them into a more homogeneous mainstream.

407. Gerbner, George, Larry Gross, Michael Morgan, and Nancy
Signorielli. "Television's Mean World: Violence Profile, No. 14-15."
The Annenberg School of Communications, University of Pennsylvania,
1986.

This update revealed that the Violence Index for 1984-85 was the
higheset and for 1985-1986 the fourth highest on record. The
Violence Index for the last two seasons was considerably above the
average of Cultural Indicators monitoring since 1967. In
addition, in the 1984-85 and 1985-86 seasons, the early evening
"family hour" (when most children are in the audience) had the
second and third highest Violence Indices ever recorded. Violence
continued to reflect the structure of power in society with women,
young and old people, and some minorities ranking as the most
vulnerable to victimization. Heavy viewers were more likely than
comparable groups of light viewers to express the feeling of
living in a self-reinforcing cycle of a mean and gloomy world.

408. Gerbner, George, Larry Gross, Nancy Signorielli, and Michael
Morgan. "Television Violence, Victimization, and Power." American
Behavioral Scientist, Vol. 23, No. 5, 1980, pp. 705-716.

Research conducted as part of the group's ongoing Cultural
Indicators project has revealed that violence plays an important
role in television's portrayal of the social order. It provides a
calculus of life chances in conflict and shows the rules by which
the game is played. It demonstrates the relative distributions of
power and of the fear of power. In generating among the many a
fear of the power of the few, television violence may achieve its
greatest effect. The results of adult and child surveys show
consistent learning and children's particular vulnerability to
television. These results also confirm that violence-laden
television not only cultivates aggressive tendencies in a
minority, but also generates a pervasive and exaggerated sense of
danger and mistrust. Heavy viewers revealed a significantly
higher sense of personal risk and suspicion than did light viewers
in the same demographic groups.

409. Gerbner, George, Larry Gross, Nancy Signorielli, Michael Morgan, and Marilyn Jackson-Beeck. "The Demonstration of Power: Violence Profile No. 10." Journal of Communication, Vol. 29, No. 3, 1979, pp. 177-196.

Annual progress report sums up findings suggesting that fear and inequity may be television's most pervasive lessons. Message system analyses of week-long samples of prime-time and weekend-daytime network dramatic programs reveal that violence in weekend-daytime children's and late evening programs on all three networks rose to near record levels in the fall of 1978. Violence is the simplist and cheapest dramatic means to demonstrate who wins in the game of life and the rules by which the game is played. It demonstrates who has the power and who must acquiesce to that power. Cultivation analyses revealed that in samples of adolescents in suburban New Jersey and New York City heavy viewers were more likely than light viewers to overestimate the number of people involved in violence, the proportion of people who commit serious crimes, and to express more fear.

410. Gerson, Walter M. "Violence as an American Value Theme." In Otto N. Larsen (ed.), Violence and the Mass Media. New York: Harper and Row, 1968, pp. 151-162.

A discussion of media violence in a socio-cultural context, citing the reciprocal relationship between mass media and public opinion in a democratic society. The dimensions of violence are outlined, along with qualities that distinguish legitimate and non-legitimate forms. Violent real-world events and circumstances contribute to media themes of speed, force, and violence.

411. Ginpil, Stephen. "Violent and Dangerous Acts on New Zealand Television." New Zealand Journal of Educational Studies, Vol. 11, No. 2, 1976, pp. 152-157.

A content analysis of one week of afternoon and evening programs broadcast in New Zealand in 1975. Violent actions were classified to determine the number and type of actions that were most likely to be imitated by children, considering such factors as actual availability of weapons and effectiveness of the dramatic act. The average hourly rate was about 7 violent acts, the majority of which were assaults. About one or two acts during each evening of viewing had an increased probability of being imitated. This study also documented the impact of imported television programs. Of the 99 programs surveyed almost two-thirds were produced in the U.S. (these were above average in violence). Only 5 programs originated in New Zealand.

412. Glucksmann, Andre. "Rapport sur les Recherches Concernant les Effets sur la Jeunesse des Scenes de Violence au Cinema et a la Television." Communications, t. 7, pp. 74-119. Published in English as Violence on the Screen: A Report on Research into the Effects on Young People of Scenes of Violence in Films and Television. London: British Film Institute, 1971, 1966.

A review and evaluation of early research in several countries
concerning the impact of film/television violence on young people.
The author posits different levels of effects of media violence
and concludes that the direct, immediate behavioral effects
hypothesized in much of the research had not been substantiated
among the general viewing public in contrast to effects on
adolescents' values, particularly relative to age.

413. Goddard, Peter. "Violence and Popular Music." Report of the
Royal Commission on Violence in the Communications Industry, Vol. 4,
Violence in Print and Music. Toronto, Canada: The Royal Commission,
1977, pp. 223-239.

Elements of music performance prone to violent effect are
examined: the sound of certain music, lyrics, stage presentation,
packaging and marketing styles. The evolution of rock music
during successive counter-cultural movements in the 1950s and
1960s is discussed. While the countercultural value of certain
music and performance style can be accepted, such values and
techniques have also been used to manipulate audiences without
concern for social consequences.

414. Goranson, Richard E. "Media Violence and Aggressive Behavior: A
Review of Experimental Research." In Leonard Berkowitz (ed.), Advances
in Experimental Social Psychology, Vol. 5. New York: Academic Press,
pp. 1-31. See also, Robert K. Baker and Sandra J. Ball, Mass Media and
Violence, Vol. 9. Washington, DC: U.S. Government Printing Office,
1969, 1970, pp. 395-413..

Examines research on media violence in regard to four
issues: learning effects, emotional effects, catharsis, and
impulsive aggression. Aggression in the mass media is often
presented as a highly effective form of behavior. Children learn
novel, aggressive behavior sequences through exposure to realistic
portrayals of aggression on television or in films. Behavior may
be retained, especially if practiced at least once. Frequent
exposure also produces emotional habituation to media violence.
The symbolic aggressive catharsis hypothesis has not proved
tenable.

415. Goranson, Richard E. "Observed Violence and Aggressive
Behavior: The Effects of Negative Outcomes to the Observed Violence."
Dissertation, University of Wisconsin, 1970.

This laboratory study involved the participation of 48 male
introductory psychology students, with two variations in the
experimental design. In the context of a learning experiment, all
subjects were first angered, then shown a brief, highly violent
film sequence. Each subject then viewed one of three alternative
film endings -- the outcome of the violence, a positive outcome,
and a control version. The experimental hypothesis -- that the
level of aggression following the observation of aggressive action

will be reduced if that action is followed by a depiction of its tragic outcome -- was upheld.

416. Goranson, Richard E. "Television Violence Effects: Issues and Evidence." Report of the Royal Commission on Violence in the Communications Industry, Vol. 5, Learning from the Media. Toronto, Canada: The Royal Commission 1977, pp. 1-29.

A review of research on various effects of televised violence organized around twelve issues. These include influence on imitative behavior, desensitization, cultivation of attitudes, limiting circumstances such as the portrayal of consequences, and parental influence. The bibliography is organized in sections relating to each issue.

417. Gordon, Margaret T. and Linda Heath. "The News Business, Crime, and Fear." Reactions to Crime, Vol. 16, 1981, pp. 227-251.

A content analysis of 8015 articles about crime in newspapers published in Philadelphia, Chicago, and San Francisco between Nov. 1977 and May 1978 revealed that crime news is easy news. Crime stories permit the police to function as gatekeepers. Circulation figures for these newspapers revealed that crime is competitive news. Telephone interviews with a random sample of residents in each city (N=1,389) revealed that the fear of crime among readers of newspapers that exploit crime as easy, competitive news is higher than among readers of newspapers that give less prominence to crime coverage. Data also revealed that more readers of newspapers that present a lot of crime consider crime to be the major problem facing their neighborhoods than do readers of newspapers that present less crime news.

418. Graber, Doris A. "Evaluating Crime-Fighting Policies: Media Images and Public Perspective." In Ralph Baker and Fred A. Meyer, Jr. (eds.), Evaluating Alternative Law-Enforcement Policies, Lexington, MA: Heath Lexington Books, 1979, pp. 179-199.

Comparison of amount of coverage of types of crime in several Midwestern United States newspapers and television newscasts with public perceptions concerning the frequency of these crimes during 1976-1977. Reports of political terrorism accounted for 5 percent of press reports and 8 percent of television news reports and ranked fourth out of eight news topics. Respondents' daily viewing diaries, in which summaries of news items were recorded, revealed a similar pattern.

419. Graber, Doris A. Crime News and The Public. New York: Praeger, 1980.

Knowledge about the nature of crime news and its impact on the images that people form about crime were the focus of this study. Through field interviews and content analyses of major print and electronic news sources during a one-year period, several hypotheses about learning about politically significant news from the mass media were tested. Results confirmed the hypothesis that exceptionally large amounts of crime information desensitize audiences to the extent that significant amounts are ignored. The opposite was true for the hypothesis that personal images of crime are more strongly influenced by media images than by official crime data.

420. Granzberg, Gary and J. Steinbring. Television and the Canadian Indian. Technical Report. Department of Anthropology, University of Winnipeg (Canada), 1980.

Analysis of the effect of the introduction of television in a Cree community indicated increased aggressiveness among heavy viewers.

421. Greenberg, Bradley S. "Televised Violence: Further Explorations (Overview)." In George A. Comstock, Eli A. Rubinstein, and John P. Murray (eds.), Television and Social Behavior, Vol. 5, Television's Effects: Further Explorations. Washington, DC: U.S. Government Printing Office, 1972, pp.1-21.

This overview presents statements of the principal questions raised by the investigators, a description of the variables and methods used in these studies, and a summary of the major findings and limitations of each of these studies.

422. Greenberg, Bradley S. "British Children and Televised Violence." Public Opinion Quarterly, Vol. 38, No. 4, 1974, pp. 531-547.

Research was conducted in 1972 to assess the relationship between viewing violent television content and aggressive behavior among London schoolchildren aged 9-15. Sampled children indicated that they regularly watched half of the listed programs with frequent violent incidents (they watched about half of the listed non-violent programs, also). Older children were more likely to concentrate their viewing on particular program types. The correlations between exposure to violent material and attitudes concerning the effectiveness and likelihood of use of violence were low (.15 to .17) and vary by age and social class. These figures are similar to those reported in comparable correlational studies conducted in the United States.

423. Greenberg, Bradley S. and Thomas F. Gordon. "Social Class and Racial Differences in Children's Perceptions of Television Violence." In George A. Comstock, Eli A. Rubinstein, and John P. Murray (eds.), Television and Social Behavior, Vol. 5, Television's Effects: Further Explorations. Washington, DC: U.S. Government Printing Office, 1971, pp. 185-230.

Ten year old children were exposed to different versions of a
45-minute film. There was more acceptance of television violence
and greater perception of such violence as realistic among lower
class boys and among black boys.

424. Grixti, Joe. Mass Media Violence' and the Study of Behavior"
Educational Studies, Vol. 11, No. 1, 1985, pp. 61-76.

Discusses the relationship between the depiction of violence in
the mass media and subsequent motivation and behavior. The
behaviorist and neobehaviorist models of learned aggressiveness
are rejected, and it is argued that the notion of innate
aggressiveness has not been disproven. Methodological flaws in
the behaviorist and social learning approaches render their
findings inconclusive. It is further argued that the behaviorist
and neobehaviorist explanations of human behavior are
reductionistic and attempt to account for violence in falsely
assuring ways.

425. Groebel, Jo and Dagmar Krebs. "A Study of the Effects of
Television on Anxiety." In C. D. Spielberger and R. Diaz-Guerrero
(eds.), Cross-Cultural Anxiety, Vol. 2. New
York: Hemisphere-Mcgraw-Hill, 1983.

A self-report scale was constructed to measure the probability of
occurence of anxiety in two situations -- interpersonal ego threat
and physical threat. These categories were compared with ratings
of a number of fear-evoking situations in television programs by
more than 1200 eleven-to-fifteen-year-old children. Relatively
high correlations were found between physical threat factors of
the programs and viewer characteristic variables such as
neuroticism, extraversion, and self-concept.

426. Groebel, Jo. "Cognitive Dimensions of Environmental Threat."
Paper presented to the International Council of Psychologists,
University of California at Los Angeles (UCLA), 1981.

Data from a longitudinal field study on TV, aggression, and
anxiety were used to test the dimensionality of environmental
threat items. Personal experience with threatful situations was
rated by 405 11-to-15 year olds. No cognitive distinction was
made by boys between personally experienced threat and imagined
threat. However, threat elements were a common category and
independent of personal environment for girls.

427. Groebel, Jo. "Vielseher und Angst." [Fear and the Heavy Viewer].
Fernsehen und Bildung, Vol. 15, 1981, pp. 136-144.

A longitudinal study of the influences of television on children
and youth, with major focus on attitudes toward aggression.
Questionnaires designed to assess daily viewing habits, anxiety
levels, and other personal and environmental variables were
distributed among pupils aged 11-15. The author suggests that the

relationship between fear and heavy viewing results from an interaction of cognitive discrimination, neuroticism, media-socialization, and prior learning. The findings of the study showed that while personality traits and situational factors have a greater influence on fear than does amount of television viewing, information conveyed by television plays a central role by reinforcing fear and developing mechanisms to cope with it.

428. Groebel, Jo. "Federal Republic of Germany: Aggression and Aggression Research." In Arnold1983, P. Goldstein and Marshall H. Segall (eds.), Aggression in Global Perspective. New York: Pergamon Press.

One major world-wide stereotype of the German is that of an aggressive human being. Different periods in German history contributed to this picture, especially the Third Reich and the holocaust. Aggression is considered in two ways, one that describes the different forms of actual aggressive or aggression-related acts, and one that primarily deals with the variety of scientific approaches to the problem.

429. Groebel, Jo. "Mass Communication and Personal Communication." International Psychologist, Vol. 1, 1984, pp. 17-18.

A summary of West German research on the individual compatibility of mass communication and personal communication. Short-term effects versus long-term effects of personal communication's influence on media use are addressed. In a longitudinal field study, the author investigated the long-term relationship between social anxiety and television use. It was found that, while physical anxiety in general decreased over time, for heavy viewers with higher anxiety, TV reinforced physical activity. This result confirms the hypothesis that electronic media may serve as a substitute for personal contacts.

430. Groebel, Jo. "Determinants of Science Reporting In Europe." In J. H. Goldstein (ed.), Reporting Science: The Case of Aggression. Hillsdale, NJ: Lawrence Erlbaum Associates, 1985.

Aggression research must deal with complex phenomena and the interaction of many different factors (biological, psychological, sociological, etc.). Aggression researchers must also make a distinction between the different kinds of media they are dealing with. The more mass-oriented a specific medium, the more likely that it will select spectacular aspects of reported research that fit into a given formula or context and meet specific news values.

431. Gunter, Barrie and Adrian Furnham. "Personality and the Perception of TV Violence." Journal of Personality and Individual Differences, Vol. 4, No. 3, 1983, pp. 315-321.

An experiment to investigate relationships between individuals'
personality characteristics and their perceptions of violent TV
portrayals. A panel of 40 viewers rated brief violent episodes
from 5 categories of programming, contemporary British
crime-detective series, American police series, westerns,
science-fiction series, and cartoons on eight scales. These
responses were then related to viewers' scores on the Neuroticism
(N), Extraversion (E), and Psychoticism (P) dimensions of the
Eysenck Personality Questionaire (EPQ). Results showed that
violent scores from contemporary settings were rated as more
serious than scores from non-contemporary and fantastic settings.
In addition, viewers exhibited individual differences in ratings
of TV violence which were related to certain of their EPQ scores.
In particular high N scores tended to perceive violence generally,
but especially that from contemporary British drama, as more
serious than did low N scorers. This study indicates the need to
include personality measures in the analysis of audience reactions
to TV violence.

432. Gunter, Barrie and Adrian Furnham. "Perceptions of Television
Violence: Effects of Programme Genre and Type of Violence on Viewers'
Judgments of Violent Portrayals." British Journal of Social
Psychology, Vol. 23, 1984, pp. 155-164.

This paper reports two studies which examined the mediating
effects of programme genre and physical form of violence on
viewers' perceptions of violent TV portrayals. In the first
experiment, a panel of British portrayals from five program
genres: British crime-drama series, U.S. crime-drama series,
westerns, science-fiction series, and cartoons which feature
either fights or shootings. In the second experiment, the same
viewers rated portrayals from British crime-drama and westerns
which featured four types of violence (fist-fights, shootings,
stabbings, and explosions). All scenes were rated along eight
unipolar scales. Panel members also completed four subscales of a
personality hostility inventory. Results showed that both
fictional setting and physical form had significant effects on
viewers' perceptions of televised violence. British crime-drama
portrayals, and portrayals that featured shootings and stabbings,
were rated as most violent and disturbing. Individuals who were
more physically aggressive tended to perceive unarmed, physical
violence as less violent than did individuals who were more
verbally aggressive.

433. Gunter, Barrie and Mallory Wober. "Television Viewing and Public
Perceptions of Hazards to Life." Journal of Environmental Psychology,
Vol. 3, 1983, pp. 325-335.

A representative sample of viewers from one region of Britain was
asked to estimate the likelihood of personal risk from a number of
hazards, which were then related to how much television they
watched--particularly news programs and documentaries. In the
presence of controls for sex, age, and socioeconomic status, the
overall amount of viewing--but not of news or documentary viewing
in particular--was related to perceptions of personal risk on four

out of twelve hazards of life. Heavy television viewers more
often perceived higher risks from lightning, flooding and
terrorist bomb attacks than did light television viewers; medium
viewers most often perceived higher risk from cancer.

434. Gunter, Barrie and Mallory Wober. "Television Viewing and Public
Trust." British Journal of Social Psychology, Vol. 22, 1983,
pp. 174-176.

Data were collected from a large British sample on TV viewing
behaviors and levels of personal fearfulness, impersonal mistrust,
anomie, and belief that the world is a just place. Program
appreciation diaries with attached opinion questionnaires were
sent out to 800 members of IBA's London region panel during one
week of November, 1980. Results showed that viewing of
action-adventure programs and of U.S. programs was related to
belief in a just world. This relationship suggests that the
message assimilated by viewers from action-drama programs relates
to the triumph of justice rather than the harm inflicted by
criminals on innocent people.

435. Gunter, Barrie. "Personality and Perceptions of Harmful and
Harmless TV Violence." Personality and Individual Differences, Vol. 4,
No. 6, 1983, pp. 665-670.

Examined viewers' perceptions of violent TV portrayals
characterized by different degrees of observable harm to victims
and by different program settings, and related these perceptions
to subjects' scores on the Eysenck Personality Questionnaire
(EPQ). Subjects aged 15-55 years rated brief TV scenes depicting
violence in American crime detective or science fiction settings
that resulted in fatal or nonfatal injury, or in no observable
harm to victims. Harmful violence was rated as significantly more
serious than harmless violence in American crime detective
settings, but was less salient in science fiction settings. Older
subjects and those with lower Psychoticism scores tended to
perceive harmful violence as more violent, frightening and likely
to disturb others than were younger subjects with higher P scores.

436. Gunter, Barrie. Dimensions of Television Violence. New
York: St. Martin's Press, 1984.

This research project examines certain methods of classifying and
weighting the seriousness of violence portrayed in fictional TV
drama. An experimental approach investigates the ways in which
ordinary viewers perceptually differentiate and evaluate a wide
range of violence extracted from current TV drama. Violent
episodes were taken from British made crime-detective shows,
American made crime-detective shows, westerns, sci-fi and
cartoons. Effects on viewers' perceptions of TV violence on the
types of characters involved, types of weapons used, the physical
setting, and the consequences of violent incidences were
systematically explored. They indicate that ordinary viewers can
and do use many different attributes or features of aggressive TV

portrayals when judging how seriously violent they are. This research demonstrates the complexity and variety of violent forms on TV, and viewers' appraisals of them.

437. Halloran, James D. "Studying Violence and the Mass Media: A Sociological Approach." In Charles Winick (ed.), Deviance and Mass Media, Beverly Hills, CA: Sage, 1978, pp. 287-305.

The portrayal of violence by the media, especially television, is seen as a major social problem in North America and Western Europe. The process of media influence is more complex and probably more far-reaching than commonly realized. It also cannot be adequately assessed by most conventional research designs. Suggests some of the social and political consequencees that may result from the ways the media deal with violence and related phenomenon.

438. Halloran, James D., Roger L. Brown, and David Chaney. Television and Delinquency. Leicester: Leicester University Press, 1970.

Report of a study conducted in Great Britain on television viewing behavior of juvenile delinquents. Most of the significant differences were found in regard to the uses of television by these children (mostly boys). Data were not sufficient either to offer proof of or to disprove any suggested causal relationship between media content and deviant or law breaking behavior. Research points to the mass media as playing a contributory role rather than being the sole cause of delinquent behavior.

439. Haney, Craig and John Manzolati. "Television Criminology: Network Illusions of Criminal Justice Realities." In Elliot Aronson (ed.), Readings About the Social Animal. San Francisco: W. H. Freeman, 1980.

Common themes in television drama are not representative of criminal justice realities such as frequency of types of crime and underlying causes of crime. Examples of such themes are: criminality as a result of personality traits rather than as a response to social conditions such as unemployment; emphasis on street crime rather than offenses related to intoxication or white-collar crime; and police violations of law as justified in the apprehending of criminals. A cultivation study of several hundred viewers revealed that heavy viewers were more likely to express attitudes reflecting these themes, such as automatic presumption of guilt of a suspect; belief that legal rights protect the guilty rather than the innocent; and the belief that police are not restricted by law in their efforts to apprehend suspected criminals.

440. Hapkiewicz, Walter C. and Aubrey H. Roden. "The Effect of Aggressive Cartoons on Children's Interpersonal Play." Child Development, Vol. 42, 1971, pp. 1583-1585.

60 second-grade children were randomly assigned to same sex pairs, and each pair was randomly assigned to one of three treatment groups: aggressive cartoon, nonaggressive cartoon, and no cartoon. Results indicate no difference among the groups on measures of interpersonal aggression, although boys exhibited significantly more aggression than girls. Although boys also demonstrated more prosocial behavior (sharing) than girls, boys who viewed the aggressive cartoon performed this response at a reduced rate.

441. Hart, Henry O. "Emergent Collective Opinion and Upheaval in East Europe and the Role of Radio Communication: A Further Extension of Basic Models." Munich, 1980.

Theoretical analysis of models of communication in relation to the role of interpersonal and mass media channels in organizing and maintaining political dissent, using five Eastern European communist bloc countries as examples and with particular reference to events in Poland from 1956 to 1977. The author outlines the contribution of Radio Free Europe in the containment of civil violence in conjunction with reinforcement of traditional values at odds with a new socio-political system.

442. Hartnagel, Timothy F., James J. Teevan, Jr., and Jennie J. McIntyre. "Television Violence and Violent Behavior." Social Forces, Vol. 54, No. 2, 1975, pp. 341-351.

The relationship between exposure to television violence and violent behavior was examined with questionnaire data obtained from adolescents. Respondents' sex and school performance accounted for more of the variance in aggressive behavior than did amount of violent TV viewing. Those who perceived violence in their favorite program as an effective means to a goal were more violent than others, indicating an indirect relationship between viewing and behavior.

443. Haskins, Jack B. "'Cloud with a Silver Lining' Approach to Violent News." Journalism Quarterly, Vol. 50, No. 3, 1973, pp. 549-552.

An experiment testing level of reader interest in crime- and violence- related news items altered to provide a constructive treatment--that is, news about violence supplemented by information that provided greater understanding or suggested improvement in the situation. Constructive treatment was found more interesting than straight news treatment on two test topics, more so for one concerning a high-school riot than for one about rates of violence and crime.

444. Hawkins, Robert P. and Suzanne Pingree. "Some Processes in the Cultivation Effect." Communication Research, Vol. 7, No. 2, 1980, pp. 193-226.

Cultivation data for a 1977 study of Australian school children is used to analyze the influence of perceived reality of television, real-world sources of confirmation of beliefs, developmental differences, and variations in program content. Older children, while more able to discriminate between fantasy and reality in programs, appear to be more susceptible to complex, subtle messages about the world delivered via dramatic characters and events. Viewing is discussed as a relatively low-level experience, with effects determined by salience and repetition of content and short-term memory processes of the viewer.

445. Hawkins, Robert P. and Suzanne Pingree. "Uniform Content and Habitual Viewing: Unnecessary Assumptions in Social Reality Effects." Human Communication Research, Vol. 7. No. 4, 1981, pp. 291-301.

Analysis of television's cultivation effect on Australian primary-school children and teenagers in 1977 revealed many differences related to program type, particularly in regard to beliefs about the level of violence in society. Among ten types of program content, viewing of crime programs was most strongly related to belief in a more violent world and lack of trust. Viewing may be more selective than previously thought. These findings, while challenging the hypothesis that messages are consistent across all television programs, supports the cultivation hypothesis and may account for cultivation of different beliefs and attitudes in different segments of a population.

446. Hawkins, Robert P. and Suzanne Pingree. "Television's Influence on Social Reality." In David Pearl, Lorraine Bouthilet, and Joyce Lazar (eds.), Television and Behavior, Vol. 2, Technical Reviews. Rockville, MD: National Institute of Mental Health, 1982, pp. 224-247.

A thorough review of cultivation effects research, synthesizing the common findings and explaining the disagreements--with particular attention to methodology, such as use of sequential versus simultaneous controls. The article includes an overview of the cognitive/experimental processes that may influence the extent of cultivation of beliefs and values by television. The authors conclude that the cultivation effect is most strongly supported in regard to perceptions about demographics of content (such as amount of violence and crime, and number of policemen). Analysis of value systems is considerably more complex.

447. Haynes, Richard B. "Children's Perceptions of 'Comic' and 'Authentic' Cartoon Violence." Journal of Broadcasting, Vol. 22, No. 1, 1978, pp. 63-70.

Schoolchildren aged 10-11 were randomly placed in one of two experimental groups. The respondents perceived the actions of comic and authentic cartoons as being significantly different. The comic cartoon was perceived as more violent and less acceptable than the authentic. Violent content in comic cartoons is recognized as violent by children. The findings also point to the possibility that comic violence is seen as more violent, possibly more feared by the child viewer, and less acceptable than violence occurring in authentic cartoon programs.

448. Heinrich, Karl. "Filmerleben, Filmwirkung, Filmerziehung: der Einfluss des Films auf die Aggressivitaet bei Jugendlichen." [Film Experience, Film Effects, Film Education: The Influence of Films on Aggressiveness of Youth]. Berlin: H. Schroedel, 1961.

Three types of films were shown to 2,000 German children aged 12 to 16: aggression-arousing, appeasing (featuring pleasant action), and ambivalent (with no dominant aggression theme and characters not easily identified with). A Thurstone measure of aggressive attitudes indicated that aggressive attitudes were stimulated by aggressive films that were dynamic and realistic, featuring characters with whom viewers easily identified. One of the appeasing films reduced aggressive attitudes. The ambivalent films had no influence on viewers' aggressive attitudes.

449. Heller, Melvin S. and Samuel Polsky. Studies in Violence and Television. New York: American Broadcasting Company, 1976.

Presentation of the results of a number of studies examining the responses of disturbed children (e.g. emotionally vulnerable children, young male offenders, children from broken or unstable homes) to television viewing. The results revealed that television-depicted violence was correlated more with aggressive fantasy than with aggressive behavior. Television was also found to be highly effective in suggesting technique but not actually causing or aggravating antisocial behavior. Finally, studies revealed that the most disturbed children were more attuned to the prosocial elements of whatever kind of television program they were shown.

450. Hennigan, Karen M., Marlyn L. DelRosario, Linda Heath, Thomas D. Cook, J. D. Wharton, and Bobby J. Calder. "Impact of the Introduction of Television on Crime in the United States: Empirical Findings and Theoretical Implications." Journal of Personality and Social Psychology, Vol. 42, No. 3, 1982, pp. 461-477.

An analysis of Federal Bureau of Investigation statistics on homicide and aggravated assault during the years 1949-1952 in 34 U.S. cities in which television had been introduced and 34 comparable cities in which TV licenses were restricted during that period. All geographical areas of the country were represented in the sample. No consistent effect of television on violent crime was found in four independent tests. These results may not be generalizeable to later periods, since the nature of depicted violence may have changed over time.

451. Hicks, David J. "Imitation and Retention of Film-Mediated Aggressive Peer and Adult Models." Journal of Personality and Social Psychology, Vol. 2, No. 1, 1965, pp. 97-100.

The relative effect of peer and adult models as transmitters of novel aggressive responses was investigated. Children viewed either male or female adult or male or female peer models presented on film and a test for imitative aggression was made. Six months after seeing the films the same children were reobserved in order to assess the long-term influence of the models. In addition, a test of retention was made after the six month interval. It was found that the male peer had the most immediate influence in shaping children's aggressive behaviors while the adult male had the most lasting effect. A significantly greater number of the models' behaviors were retained after six months than were performed.

452. Hicks, David J. "Effects of Co-observer's Sanctions and Adult Presence on Imitative Aggression." Child Development, Vol. 39, No. 1, 1968, pp. 303-309.

The effects of film-mediated aggression of a co-observer's positive, negative, or nonsanctions and his subsequent presence or absence during performance opportunities were investigated. It was found that positive and negative sanctions produced corresponding disinhibition and inhibition effects only when the experimenter remained with the children during a postexposure test of imitative performance. The results seemed related to social-learning theory in that the children's expectations for receiving various consequences appeared to determine the amount of imitation.

453. Himmelweit, Hilde T., A. N. Oppenheim, and Pamela Vince. Television and the Child: An Empirical Study of the Effect of Television on the Young. London: Oxford University Press, 1958.

Content analysis of 20 western and crime programs in Britain revealed stylized presentation of weapons, with infrequent portrayal of moral consquences. These consequences were most remote in westerns, but realistic and personal in crime shows. Crime shows were a preferred program type among children aged 10-14. Children younger than age six often were frightened by violence on television, according to reports by mothers. Beyond that age, media violence was accepted as fantasy. Children were most upset by violence that was similar to their real-life situation. Analysis of ratings of aggressive behavior of children, personality inventories, and viewing habits revealed no relationship between TV viewing and aggressive behavior. While media violence may affect emotionally-disburbed or already aggressive children, a more general effect may be a limitation of children's awareness of consequences of aggression and acceptance of aggression as a means of conflict resolution.

454. Hirsch, Kenneth William. "Research Findings and Theoretical Trends: Mass Media Violence." Sacramento, CA: The California Commission on Crime Control and Violence Prevention, 1982.

The bulk of this report examines research findings concerning the effects of media content containing violence on audience members.

455. Holz, Josephine, Eric Cardinal, and Dennis Kerr. "The Achille Lauro: A Study in Terror." Paper prepared for the 42nd annual conference of the American Association for Public Opinion Research, Hershey, PA, May 14-17, 1987.

Study based on the June 17, 1986 NBC News Special examining the events surrounding the hijacking of the Achille Lauro cruise ship in October, 1985. This broadcast was unique in terrorist media coverage in affording considerable coverage of the hijackers' political goals and beliefs. A national sample of adults was recruited for a panel study. Prior to the broadcast, two hundred and eleven respondents were interviewed about their beliefs and opinions regarding terrorism and the news media, and then reinterviewed subsequent to the broadcast. Findings show no support for the argument that terrorists are humanized by news coverage, or that legitimacy is lent to their cause. Regarding the claim that news coverage of terrorism may increase the viewers' sense of personal risk and fear, findings were mixed and inconclusive. Some support was found for the hypothesis that coverage results in viewer identification with the victims rather than with the terrorists.

456. Hoult, Thomas F. "Comic Books and Juvenile Delinquency." Sociology and Social Research, Vol. 33, No. 4, 1949, pp. 279-284.

This survey of groups of delinquent and nondelinquent boys and girls in the Los Angeles area revealed that both groups read about the same number of "harmless" comic books (romance and animal cartoons). The delinquent children, however, read many more "harmful" (crime and gangster) and "questionable" (jungle adventure, cowboy and indian) comics than the nondelinquents.

457. Howe, Michael J. A. Television and Children. London: New University Education, 1977.

Chapter four of this book examines available evidence about the ways TV violence can affect children and adolescents. Alternative research methods suggested include laboratory experiments, surveys and field studies, and each are considered in light of characteristic advantages and limitations. Different ways in which children can be influenced by violence are considered. Evidence points to certain conclusions in this regard, it is noted, and their implications are discussed.

458. Howitt, Dennis and Guy Cumberbatch. "Audience Perceptions of Violent Television Content." Communication Research, Vol. 1, No. 2, 1974, pp. 204-223.

Viewers stratified by social class provided ratings on several descriptive variables for a number of television programs, including violent content, fantasy-reality orientation, and justification of violence. It was hypothesized that these variables might influence the effect of televised violence. Certain types of programs were perceived as less violent than others, despite the actual amount of physical violence depicted. Fictional and humorous violent sequences were rated less violent than violence with a realistic orientation. Viewers also distinguished between justified and unjustified violence.

459. Howitt, Dennis and Guy Cumberbatch. Mass Media, Violence and Society. New York: Wiley and Sons, 1975.

Review of media violence/effects research generally reveals that effects are limited to a very small segment of a given population.

460. Howitt, Dennis. The Mass Media and Social Problems. Oxford: Pergamon Press, 1982.

Posits that mass media research has been social problem oriented (role of the mass media in causing crime, violence, civil disturbances, etc.) rather than academic and theoretical. Looking at research in Great Britain and the United States, the author emphasizes the "no effects" point of view. Likewise the review of research on sex, eroticism, and pornography suggests that evidence is not really available to support a link between pornography and sexual deviance or sexual crime. Finally, the review of research on crime and the mass media revealed no simple relationship between amount of exposure to crime in the media and criminal behavior and no simple link between coverage of crime in the news media and the audience's perception of the amount of crime in society.

461. Howitt, Dennis, and Guy Cumberbatch. "Affective Feeling for a Film Character and Evaluation of an Anti-Social Act." British Journal of Social and Clinical Psychology, Vol. 11, 1972, pp. 102-108.

Adolescents viewed a 20-minute film edited to portray a likeable character (a street-corner boy) or another character as having performed a violent act. Liking a media character does not influence a child to accept more easily the violent behavior of that character.

462. Huesmann, L. Rowell. "Television Violence and Aggressive Behavior." In David Pearl, Lorraine Bouthilet, and Joyce Lazar (eds.), Television and Behavior, Vol. 2, Technical Reviews. Rockville, MD: National Institute of Mental Health, 1982, pp. 126-137.

Outlines the uses of cognitive psychology in studying and
explaining the relationship between televised violence and
aggressive behavior. Summarizes much of the research conducted in
the fields of psychology and child development since the 1972
Surgeon General's Report. Of five hypothesized psychological
processes, recent longitudinal field studies lent increased
support to imitation of observed behavior and attitude change as
processes that influence response to televised violence.
Emotional/physiological arousal and justification of pre-existing
aggressiveness (selective exposure to violent programs) are also
supported by research, but their role is not yet clearly defined.
Catharsis (discharge of aggression through vicarious experience)
has not been convincingly supported.

463. Huesmann, L. Rowell, Kirsti M. J. Lagerspetz, and Leonard Eron.
"Intervening Variables in the Television Violence-Aggression
Relation: Evidence from Two Countries." Developmental Psychology,
Vol. 20, 1984, pp. 746-775.

A cross-cultural study of the complex relationship between media
violence and aggression. Children aged 6 to 8 were observed over
a three-year period in the United Staties and in Finland.
Information was provided by children's self-reports as well as by
peers, parents, and schools. In the U.S., a positive correlation
was observed for boys (r=+.25) and for girls (r=+.29) over a
three-year period, with stronger correlations among older
children. In the smaller Finnish sample, a significant positive
correlation between viewing and aggression was found only for boys
(r=+.22).

464. Huesmann, L. Rowell, Leonard D. Eron, Monroe M. Lefkowitz, and
Leopold O. Walder. "Stability of Aggression Over Time and
Generations." Developmental Psychology, Vol. 20, No. 6, 1984,
pp. 1120-1134.

Demonstrates the stability of level of aggression over time and
generation within a family in relation to the role of situational
variables such as the viewing of televised violence. The authors
recapitulate the findings of the 22-year research project begun by
Eron in 1960, when the subjects were approximately eight years
old. The latest data on aggression was gathered in 1981 when the
subjects were about age 30 and utilized interviews with spouses
and children as well as information from police records.

465. Huesmann,L. Rowell, Leonard D. Eron, Rosemary Klein, Patrick
Brice, and Paulette Fischer. "Mitigating the Imitation of Aggressive
Behaviors by Changing Children's Attitude About Media Violence."
Journal of Personality and Social Psychology, Vol. 44, 1983,
pp. 899-910.

A sample of 169 first and third grade children, selected because of their high exposure to television violence, was randomly divided into experimental and control groups. Over the course of two years the experimental subjects were exposed to two treatments designed to reduce the likelihood of their imitating the aggressive behaviors they observed on television. The control group received comparable neutral treatments. By the end of the second year, the experimental subjects were rated as significantly less aggressive by their peers, and the relation between violence viewing and aggressiveness was diminished.

466. Huston-Stein, Aletha. "Televised Aggression and Prosocial Behavior." In Psychology: From Research to Practice. New York: Plenum, 1978.

A review of research funded by Congress after the 1968 hearings held by the National Commission on the Causes and Prevention of Violence.

467. Huston-Stein, Aletha, and Lynette Kohn Friedrich with Fred Vondracek. "Television Content and Young Children's Behavior." In John P. Murray, Eli A. Rubinstein, and George A. Comstock (eds.), Television and Social Behavior, Vol. 2, Television and Social Learning. Washington, DC: U.S. Government Printing Office, 1972, pp. 202-317.

A naturalistic experiment testing the effects of both aggressive and prosocial television programs on the social behavior of 97 preschool children in a nursery school over a nine-week period. Overall results indicated that children who were adjudged to be initially somewhat more aggressive became significantly more aggressive as a result of viewing Batman and Superman cartoons. Children who viewed 12 episodes of Mister Rogers' Neighborhood became significantly more cooperative, willing to share toys, and to help other children. Children who were initially below average in aggression did not respond differentially to the three television conditions.

468. Huston-Stein, Aletha, Sandra Fox, Douglas Greer, Bruce A. Watkins, and Jane Whitaker. "The Effects of TV Action and Violence on Children's Social Behavior." Journal of Genetic Psychology, Vol. 138, 1981, pp. 183-191.

Experimental test of the independent contributions of TV action (rapid movement by characters) and violence (physical aggression by characters) on the attention and social behavior of 66 preschool children. Children who viewed high-action programs gave greater visual attention; visual attention was not affected by amount of violence. When children's free play before and after viewing was compared, fantasy play increased for children who viewed low action-low violence or who did not watch TV; fantasy play decreased for those who viewed high action-high violence. Aggressive behavior was greater for children viewing high action regardless of amount of violence.

469. Independent Broadcasting Authority. "Experience of Television, and of the World at Large: Some Scottish Evidence." IBA, Audience Research Department, 1979.

   Research conducted in Central Scotland which challenges the theory of cultivation in regard to televised violence. It is suggested on the basis of audience surveys that what people knew about real levels of violent crime in their locality was what actually kept them indoors; consequently in violent cities or neighborhoods people stay in and see more television.

470. Independent Broadcasting Authority. "'Death Wish' -- Can Violence Defeat Violence?" IBA, Audience Research Department, 1981.

   An audience study of ITV's "Death Wish" in Great Britain. The results suggest that when people are aroused in a particular way, these emotions can be counteracted by viewing a particular film. Subjects in this study, for example, exhibited a switch from fear to anger after viewing "Death Wish."

471. Indian Institute of Mass Communication. "Audience Reactions to Six Films on Violence: A Study in Delhi." Dept. of Communication Research, Indian Institute of Mass Communication, D-13, South Extension Part II, New Delhi, India, 1974.

   A survey of audience reactions by the Indian Institute of Mass Communication to six films produced to indicate that violence and strikes are bad in themselves and against the larger interests of the country (India). The study found that the overwhelming majority of the respondents believed these films would be effective in influencing the views of the common man favourably, and would help in weaning them away from violence, strike, and anti-social activities.

472. Israel, Harold, W. R. Simmons and Associates, and John P. Robinson. "Demographic Characteristics of Viewers of Television Violence and News Programs." In George A. Comstock and Eli A. Rubinstein (eds.), Television and Social Behavior, Vol. 4, Television in Day-to-Day Life: Patterns of Use. Washington, DC: U.S. Government Printing Office, 1972, pp. 87-128.

   Male heavy viewers of violence are disproportionately from lower income groups and have less education. They also tend to be over 50 and black. Males between 18 and 24 who are high school dropouts are especially heavy viewers of violence. Race seems to be the major determinant of violence viewing among women; education, income, and age play less important roles. Most viewers of news programs are older, regardless of their educational level or overall television viewing.

473. Jackson, Robert J., Michael J. Kelly, and Thomas H. Mitchell. "Collective Conflict, Violence and the Media." Report of the Royal Commission on Violence in the Communications Industry, Vol. 5, Learning from the Media. Toronto, Canada: The Royal Commission, 1977, pp. 227-314.

   A review of U.S. Government-sponsored research on the relationship between media coverage of conflict and violence in society prefaces this analysis data for 19 countries, including Canada. The U.S. finding of no direct relationship is supported by the cross-cultural data. Newspaper coverage in Ontario of 129 incidents of collective violence and 9 incidents involving individuals during 1965-1975 was examined to determine amount of emphasis given these events. Violence- and crime-related items accounted for 20 percent of first-page coverage, including 8 percent relating to political violence. Initial coverage of individual violence was three times as extensive as that of collective violence. The authors recommended policies and practices by which media and law enforcement agencies could limit the potential for aggravating conflict situations.

474. Jaehnig, Walter B., David H. Weaver, and Fred Fico. "Reporting Crime and Fearing Crime in Three Communities." Journal of Communication, Vol. 31, No. 1, 1981, pp. 88-96.

   A panel of 45 adults in each of three communities of different sizes and in different regions was recruited in January, 1976. Data on fear of crime was supplemented by content analyses conducted from January-August, 1976, of each community's major newspaper. The rankings of concern over crime were identical to the rankings of both newspaper emphasis on crime and the number of violent crimes per person in the three communities, suggesting that both fear of crime and newspaper coverage of crime may be more a consequence of the frequencies of all kinds of crime. The percentages also indicate that the level of fear is associated more strongly with newspaper emphasis on violent crime than with the actual frequency of violent crime in the community.

475. Johnson, Raymond L., Herbert L. Friedman, and Herbert S. Gross. "Four Masculine Styles in Television Programming: A Study of the Viewing Preferences of Adolescent Males." In George A. Comstock and Eli A. Rubinstein (eds.), Television and Social Behavior, Vol. 3, Television and Adolescent Aggressiveness. Washington DC: U.S. Government Printing Office, 1972, pp. 361-371.

   This study of the program preferences and viewing habits of a racially mixed group of 80 adolescent males examined the role of television violence in delinquent behavior. Half of the boys were labeled by school officials as aggressive, and they spent about 20 percent more time viewing television than their non-aggressive peers. The aggressive young men more frequently named violent programs as their favorites, and tended to dislike family comedy shows.

476. Joy, Leslie A., M. Kimball, and Merle L. Zabrack. "Television
Exposure and Children's Aggressive Behavior." In Tannis MacBeth
Williams (ed.), The Impact of Television: A Natural Experiment
Involving Three Towns. New York: Academic Press, 1986.

A Canadian field experiment that examined aggressive behavior of
children living in three towns with and without television (Notel,
Unitel, and Multitel) and reassessment of the children in Notel
two years after the introduction of television. Results of the
longitudinal study of 44 children observed at time 1 and time 2
indicated that there were no differences across the three towns at
time 1 but, at time 2, the children in the former Notel were
significantly more aggressive, both physically and verbally than
the children in Unitel or Multitel. Only children in Notel showed
any significant increase in physical and verbal aggression from
time 1 to time 2.

477. Kaplan, Robert M. and Robert D. Singer. "Television Violence and
Viewer Aggression: A Re-examination of the Evidence." Journal of
Social Issues, Vol. 32, No. 4, 1976, pp. 35-70.

Evaluates the existing body of research on the effect of
television violence on aggressive behavior and raises questions
about external validity in relation to particular elements of
methodology such as setting, composition of samples of viewers,
and measures of aggression. Summaries of studies which support
three general effects of media violence--imitation, catharsis, and
no effect--are provided. The authors consider the evidence
supporting the null hypothesis the most acceptable.

478. Katzman, Natan I. "Violence and Color Television: What Children
of Different Ages Learn." In George A. Comstock, Eli A. Rubinstein,
and John P. Murray (eds.), Television and Social Behavior, Vol. 5,
Television's Effects: Further Explorations. Washington,
DC: U.S. Government Printing Office, 1972, pp. 253-308.

Boys in the 4th, 5th, and 6th grades served as subjects in this
study using 4 versions of a detective program (high-low violence
and color-black and white presentation) as the stimulus materials.
Overall, the high violence presentation was perceived as
significantly more violent than the low violence presentation.
Moreover, the color format had no significant effect on perceived
violence or on measures of liking the program. After a two-week
period the high violence version was rated as significantly more
violent than it was rated immediately after presentation. The low
violence version was rated at the same level both times. In
general, color does not improve the learning of visual material
that is central to a presentation.

479. Kessler, Ronald C. and Horst Stipp. "The Impact of Fictional
Television Suicide Stories on U.S. Fatalities: A Replication."
American Journal of Sociology, Vol. 90, No. 1, 1984, pp. 151-167.

In a recent issue of this journal, Phillips reported evidence that fictional suicide stories on daytime television serials trigger real-life suicides and motor vehicle fatalities. This paper calls attention to a serious error in the data which invalidates reported results. The authors describe a more precise approach which contradicts Phillips' findings, producing evidence that suicides and single-vehicle motor fatalities actually decreased slightly following the showing of a suicide on a daytime serial television drama.

480. Killias, Martin. "Mass Medias, Peur du Crime et Politique Criminelle: Une Revue Selective de la Litterature Recente." [Mass Media, Fear of Crime, and Criminal Policy: A Selective Review of Recent Literature]. Revue Internationale de Criminologie et de Police Technique, Vol. 36, No. 4, 1983, pp. 60-71.

Proposes a model that permits the integration of attitudes on cognitive, semi-specific and diffuse levels, that each partially explain the fear of crime. Research is reviewed on the representation of crime in the media and its relation to public perceptions of the incidence of violent crime, the fear of crime and punitiveness. It is concluded that the mass media are not the cause of the discrepancy between the objective risk of victimization and the fear of criminality, and that there is little relationship between attitudes, particularly punitiveness, and descriptions of crime in the media.

481. Klapper, Joseph T. "Effects of Crime and Violence in the Media." In Joseph T. Klapper, Effects of Mass Communication. New York: Free Press, 1960.

Research has shown that crime and violence are depicted in virtually all mass media. Research also suggests that crime and violence in the media are not likely to be prime movers toward delinquency, but that such fare is likely to reinforce existing good and evil behavioral tendencies of individuals.

482. Klapper, Joseph T. "The Impact of Viewing 'Aggression': Studies and Problems of Extrapolation." In Otto N. Larsen (ed.), Violence and the Mass Media. New York: Harper and Row, 1968, pp. 131-139.

A review of media-stimulated aggression studies by Columbia Broadcasting System's research staff. The author raises questions about validity arising from definitions and measures employed in this research, and from the generalizability of results. Specific studies are outlined as examples of these methodological issues.

483. Koelle, B. S. "Primary Children's Stories as a Function of Exposure to Violence and Cruelty in the Folk Fairy Tale." Dissertation, University of Pennsylvania. Dissertation Abstracts International, Vol. 42, 1981, pp. 1203b.

Primary-age school children heard four Grimm fairy stories which were similar in structure but different in amount and quality of violence depicted. They then donated stories of their own which were analyzed for structure. Subsidiary measures included a structured interview, a checklist of amount and kind of TV watched, and a parents' questionnaire. Results were analyzed from three theoretical viewpoints: developmental/cathartic, learning theory and anxiety-reaction. Significant differences in content supported the anxiety-reaction hypothesis. Differences in story structure and length, and those attributable to gender or TV watching were not significant. Conclusions, limited by size and the high SES level of the sample, suggest that unexpurgated tales should be told only with caution to young children.

484. Krattenmaker, Thomas G., and L. A. Powe, Jr. "Televised Violence: First Amendment Principles and Social Science Theory." Virginia Law Review, Vol. 64, 1978, pp. 1123-1297.

Review of research on television and violence from a legal perspective. Concludes that available research does not warrant, from a legal or constitutional perspective, the implementation of a regulatory program to inhibit violent programming.

485. Lamberti, Amato. Camorra: Analisi e Stereotipi - Televisione radio e giornali in Campania. [Organized Crime: Analysis and Stereotypes - Television, Radio and Press in Campania]. Rome: RAI Radiotelevisione Italiana, Verifica Programmi Trasmessi, 1985.

An examination of the ways in which the criminal activities of the "Camorra" have been presented in radio, television, and the press. Coverage of these events and the institutional reaction to them in each communications medium resembled that of general crime stories: reports were stereotyped and sensational and failed to consider underlying social, political, economic, and cultural factors which generate organized crime. Challenged institutions were portrayed as sound. Media focus on the judiciary and law enforcement agencies served to legitimize these institutions rather than to mobilize community action against organized crime.

486. Lang, Gladys Engel and Kurt Lang. "Some Pertinent Questions on Collective Violence and News Media." Journal of Social Issues, Vol. 28, No. 1, 1972, pp. 93-110.

News coverage that focuses on the violence of confrontations has been considered inflammatory; yet this has not been documented by communications research. Some specific effects of media presence, practices, and coverage in relation to potentially violent situations are discussed. Examples drawn from civil protests during the 1960s are employed to demonstrate ways in which media can inhibit as well as incite or aggravate political violence. A more significant effect may be the impact on public attitudes and responses relating to organized protest.

487. Langham, J. and W. Stewart. "Television Viewing Habits and Other Aggressive Characteristics of Normally Aggressive and Non-Aggressive Children." Australian Psychologist, Vol. 16, No. 1, 1981, pp. 123-133.

Among 7-11 year-olds in this Australian study, those identified as aggressive by teachers preferred more aggressive television programs.

488. Larsen, Otto N. (ed.). Violence and the Mass Media. New York: Harper and Row, 1968.

An overview of the issue of violent content in media, containing perspectives and reports of research. Most of the articles examine the question of how the nature and incidence of real violence might be affected by exposure to mass media violence.

489. Larsen, Otto N. "Controversies About the Mass Communication of Violence." Annals of the American Academy of Political and Social Science, Vol. 364, 1966, pp. 37-49.

Few would dispute that American mass communication dispenses large doses of violence to ever growing audiences. Two related controversies stem from this fact. One concerns the question of effects and the other the problem of control. An inventory of relevant research is inconclusive about effects, partly because of varying conceptions of what constitutes evidence. A dynamic opinion process leads to control efforts. Critics play a vital part in defining discontent. A reciprocal relationship emerges between the public, the critic, and the media. American media respond to controversy and threat of censorship with systems of self-regulation. These grow out of public opinion and are sustained by it in a delicate balance dependent somewhat on developing knowledge of the effects of violence.

490. Lavin, Michael, and Deborah A. Hanson. "Desensitization and Television Violence: Does It Generalize to Non-Media Situations?" Thesis, Department of Psychology, Saint Bonaventure University, Saint Bonaventure, New York, 1984.

The results of this experiment using 54 undergraduates as subjects indicate that emotional desensitization (measured by physiological responses) generalizes to neutral and real violence settings. The finding of no desensitization effect in the fantasy violence condition limits, however, the ability to state with confidence that desensitization generalizes to non-media situations.

491. Lee, Margaret Ann. "The Effects of Observed Television Violence on the Aggressive Behavior of Abused and Non-Abused Children." Dissertation Abstracts International, Vol. 45, No. 3,1983, p. 997B.

Study to determine whether abused children exposed to aggressive TV cartoons exhibit significantly more aggressive behavior than non-abused children. Also to determine differences between the two groups in comprehending story content, motivation of main characters and consequences of aggressive actions. 64 children, aged 3-6, 32 classified as abused, 32 non-abused, were subjects. Hypothesis 1, that abused children, after viewing aggression on film, would "hurt" a fictitious child longer than a non-abused child would - and Hypothesis 3, that after viewing, an abused child would have better comprehension of content/motivation consequences, were not supported. Hypothesis 2, that following viewing filmed aggression, the total group of abused children would be willing to "hurt" a fictitious child for significantly longer than the non-abused group, was supported.

492. Lefkowitz, Monroe M., Leonard D. Eron, Leopold O. Walder, and L. Rowell Huesmann. "Television Violence and Child Aggression: A Follow-Up Study." In George A. Comstock and Eli A. Rubinstein (eds.), Television and Social Behavior, Vol. 3, Television and Adolescent Aggressiveness. Washington DC: U.S. Government Printing Office, 1972, pp. 35-135.

This correlational field study of long-term effects of television violence over a ten-year period began in 1955. It employed measures of aggressive behavior and subjects' preferences for violent media content at age 8 and again at age 18. Among boys, the correlation coefficient for preference for violent material and aggression was .21 at age 8-9, and .31 at age 18-19. The significant predictor of aggression was preference for violent content at the earlier age. Such preference at the later age, of itself, did not correspond to aggressive behavior at that age.

493. Lefkowitz, Monroe M., Leonard D. Eron, Leopold O. Walder, and L. Rowell Huesmann. Growing Up To Be Violent: A Longitudinal Study of the Development of Aggression. New York: Pergamon Press, 1977.

Summarizes findings on the relationship between viewing television violence and aggressive behavior using a large sample of eight-year-olds in 1960, about half of whom were studied in a follow-up ten years later.

494. Lefkowitz, Monroe M., Leopold O. Walder, Leonard D. Eron, and L. Rowell Huesmann. "Preferences for Televised Contact Sports as Related to Sex Differences in Aggression." Developmental Psychology, Vol. 9, No. 3, 1973, pp. 417-420.

As part of a study of 8-year-olds and media, authors tested the hypothesis that preference for viewing aggressive contact sports would correspond to aggressive behavior in real life. The analysis revealed a significant relationship for girls, but not for boys.

495. Lefkowitz, Monroe M. and L. Rowell Huesmann. "Concomitants of Television Violence Viewing in Children." In Edward L. Palmer and Aimee Dorr (eds.), Children and the Faces of Television: Teaching, Violence, Selling. New York: Academic Press, 1981, pp. 165-182.

Author suggests that findings of the Surgeon General's report and subsequent empirical and observational studies have demonstrated the contribution of television portrayals to the escalation of violence within American society. Four concomitant categories of violence-viewing effect -- aggression, socialization and values, physiological responses, and mood -- are discussed. So far none of this evidence has lead to a significant decrease in television violence. Suggests three possible strategies for regulation: parents' regulation of children's exposure to television, self-regulation of the industry in regard to amount and type of violence presented, and government regulation of violent television programming.

496. Leyens, Jacques-Philippe, Ross D. Parke, Leoncio Camino, and Leonard Berkowitz. "Effects of Movie Violence on Aggression in a Field Setting as a Function of Group Dominance and Cohesion." Journal of Personality and Social Psychology, Vol. 32, No. 2, 1975, pp. 346-360.

A Belgian study using groups of boys at a residential secondary school. The groups saw either a violent or a neutral film every evening for a one week period and behavior was observed before, during, and after exposure to these films. There was an immediate short-term increase in aggressive behavior among boys in the groups who viewed violent films.

497. Liebert, Robert M., John M. Neale, and Emily S. Davidson. The Early Window: Effects of Television on Children and Youth. New York: Pergamon Press, 1973.

This book provides a comprehensive account of contemporary theory and research concerning television and children's attitudes, development, and behavior. It also explores the political and social questions that surround these issues and the implications of research findings for social policy. Laboratory and field studies pertaining to television and aggression as well as studies focusing on the ability of the medium to foster prosocial behavior are reviewed.

498. Liebert, Robert M. "Television and Social Learning: Some Relationships Between Viewing Violence and Behaving Aggressively (Overview)." In John P. Murray, Eli A. Rubinstein, and George A. Comstock (eds.), Television and Social Behavior, Vol. 2, Television and Social Learning. Washington, DC: U.S. Government Printing Office, 1972, pp. 1-42.

Review of research on the relationship between children's viewing of television violence and their aggressive behavior. The data suggest consistently that children are exposed to a heavy dose of violence on television. It is also clear that they can and do retain some of the aggressive behaviors which they see, and are often able to reproduce them. Studies show better recall with increasing age. Violent content appears to be learned and remembered at least as well as nonviolent fare.

499. Liebert, Robert M., Joyce N. Sprafkin, and Emily S. Davidson. The Early Window: Effects of Television on Children and Youth. (2nd Edition). New York: Pergamon Press, 1982.

The second edition of this book presents a history of research conducted on the effects of television violence both prior to and subsequent to the Surgeon General's Report. The commercial structure of television and the impact of television advertising are also discussed.

500. Liebert, Robert M. and Robert A. Baron. "Short-Term Effects of Television Aggression on Children's Aggressive Behavior." In John P. Murray, Eli A. Rubinstein, and George A. Comstock (eds.), Television and Social Behavior, Vol. 2, Television and Social Learning. Washington, DC: U.S. Government Printing Office, 1972, pp. 181-201.

As a follow-up to Bandura's studies of media-induced aggressive behavior in children, the authors employed a real person as a target of anticipated aggression and real television programs rather than experimental ones. In this experiment, children viewed a brief segment of a crime/violence-oriented program or a taped sports competition (races, hurdles). Those who viewed the violent dramatic segment were more likely than the other subjects to choose to "hurt" an unseen child. The effect was stronger for younger children.

501. Linne, Olga. "Reactions of Children to Violence on TV." Stockholm: Swedish Broadcasting Corporation, Audience and Program Research Department, 1971.

An examination of the influence that fictional violence has on children. A distinction is drawn between short-term effects (measured in an experimental stimulus-response situation) and long-term effects (studied via an analysis of children's reactions to violence.) Data on media habits, aggression, and reactions to a popular TV western were collected for 34 five- and six-year-olds and their mothers. Results indicated that there were no significant differences in aggression between children who were shown the film and those who were not. Hence the film caused no short-term effects regarding aggressiveness. A larger proportion of high-exposed children than low-exposed children, however, chose aggressive behavior in a conflict situation regardless of whether they had seen the test film.

139

502. Linne, Olga. "The Viewer's Aggression as a Function of a Variously Edited Film." Stockholm: Swedish Broadcasting Corporation, Audience and Programming Research Department, 1974.

A sample of Stockholm viewers who saw a violent film edited to be more exciting demonstrated more aggressive behavior after seeing the film than subjects who saw a less exciting version of the same film (with the same amount of violence). Depiction of physical harm as a result of violence did not appear to influence the level of viewer aggression.

503. Linz, Daniel Gerard. "Sexual Violence in the Media: Effects on Male Viewers and Implications for Society." Dissertation Abstracts International, Vol. 46, No. 4,1985, p. 1382B.

Four studies were conducted to investigate effects of exposure to filmed sexual violence. Study 1: Men viewing 5 movies depicting violence against women have fewer negative reactions to films, perceive them as less violent, and consider them significantly less degrading to women than a control group who saw no films. The exposed group judged the victim of violent assault and rape as less injured, and evaluated her as less worthy than control group. Study 2: Examined exposure to R-rated slasher films, R-rated teenage sex films, and X-rated sexually explicit non-violent films, across two exposure periods (2 or 5 films). Found no difference in desensitization between exposure groups. Study 3: Examines relationship between individual differences in psychoticism and hostility, and exposure to movies with sexual violence and rape. Those subjects high in psychoticism and exposed to rape films were more likely to endorse force in sexual relations, and have lower esteem for victims. Study 4: Measured effectiveness of debriefings in Studies 2 & 3. Results indicate that even after 7 months, debriefed subjects' attitudes about sexual violence showed significant positive change.

504. Linz, Daniel, Charles W. Turner, Bradford W. Hesse, and Steven Penrod. "Bases of Liability for Injuries Produced by Media Portrayals of Violent Pornography." In Neil M. Malamuth and Edward Donnerstein (eds.), Pornography and Sexual Aggression. Orlando, FL: Academic Press, 1984, pp. 277-304.

This article explores the possibility for a plaintiff to claim injury through a third party as a result of exposure to violent pornography. An overview of tort law is provided highlighting cases dealing with the effect of television violence and subsequent injury. The means by which current psychological research on violent pornography might be incorporated within a civil trial is explored. Greater reliance by the courts upon researchers working on the relationship between exposure to violent pornographic material and behaviors is predicted. A successful civil suit of this nature might have important ramifications in limiting the proliferation of violent pornographic matter at a broad social level.

505. Linz, Daniel, Edward Donnerstein, and Steven Penrod. "The Effects of Multiple Exposures to Filmed Violence Against Women." Journal of Communication, Vol. 34, No. 3, 1984, pp. 130-147.

A continuation of research on pornography and attitudes toward women. Five commercially-released, feature-length R-rated movies depicting violence against women were shown to 52 men. The impact of this exposure on judgments about the victim of a violent sexual assault was measured. As predicted, subjects' perceptions of the violence portrayed in the films changed over the five days of the study. The films were perceived to be significantly less violent by the last day of viewing; ratings of how degrading the films were to women and of offensiveness also were significantly lower by the last day.

506. Lovaas, O. Ivar. "Effect of Exposure to Symbolic Aggression on Aggressive Behavior." Child Development, Vol. 32, 1961, pp. 37-44.

An experimental test of the effect of viewing filmed violence on a small sample of five-year-old children. Children viewed either a 5-minute cartoon depicting a significant amount of aggression or a non-aggressive nature film. In two experiments measuring the children's later aggression in the use of a particular toy, there were no significant results. A third experiment involving choice of a ball or dolls that could hit showed a positive relationship between viewing violence and aggressive behavior within the acceptable probability range.

507. Lovibond, S. H. "The Effect of Media Stressing Crime and Violence upon Children's Attitudes." Social Problems, Vol. 15, No. 1, 1967, pp. 91-100.

Comic book use and film attendance by 354 Australian adolescents in the days before television showed positive correlation with scores measuring negative humanitarian goals such as belief in the necessity of preventive war, and perception of Army life as "fun" and crime as acceptable under certain circumstances. Comic books were more blatant in portrayal of such themes. A similar procedure then was used to investigate the relationship between these values and television use. Heavy viewing and preference for crime/violent programs also correlated positively with acceptance of violence. High exposure to such values could reinforce acceptance of delinquency by others in real life for most children.

508. Loye, David, Roderic Gorney, and Gary Steele. "An Experimental Field Study." Journal of Communications, Vol. 27, No. 3, 1977,, pp. 206-216. See also American Journal of Psychiatry, Vol. 134, No. 2 1977, pp. 170-174.

This 1974 study was designed to test the hypothesis that
measurable psycho-social effects result from viewing specific
types of program content. Subjects were 183 men assigned to 20
hours of a particular TV diet for one week--provided in their
homes via cable TV in Los Angeles. The diets were: prosocial,
violent, neutral (light entertainment), mixed (prosocial and
violent), and natural (free choice). Subjects' moods and behavior
were recorded during the week by their female partners. While
positive mood (social affection) significantly decreased for both
the prosocial- and violence-viewing groups, aggressive mood
increased over the week-long period for the violence-viewing group
and decreased for the prosocial-viewing group. High levels of
hurtful behavior were found among subjects assigned to the violent
and especially to the natural TV diets. There were no significant
differences in amount of helpful behavior.

509. Maccoby, Eleanor E., Harry Levin, and Bruce M. Selya. "The
Effects of Emotional Arousal on the Retention of Aggressive and
Nonaggressive Movie Content." American Psychologist, Vol. 10, 1955,
pp. 359.

Each of five classes of 5th and 6th grade children was divided
into two teams for a spelling bee, shown a chapter in a serial
movie featuring the Dead-End Kids and Junior G-Men, and a week
later tested for recall of four types of content. The "red" team
(discriminated against in the spelling bee by being given very
difficult words to spell) recalled significantly more aggressive
central content than the "blue" team (consistently given easy
words). The "blue" team recalled significantly more neutral
central, detailed neutral, and detailed aggressive material than
did the "red" team.

510. Maccoby, Eleanor E. and William C. Wilson. "Identification and
Observational Learning from Films." Journal of Abnormal and Social
Psychology, Vol. 55, 1957, pp. 76-87.

This research analyzed the relationship between children's
identification with particular media characters and recollection
of violent content. Adolescents viewed movies with various types
of characters and later were interviewed. Recollection depended
on subjects' identification choice and the relevance of the
content to their needs. The adolescents tended to identify with
characters of the same sex and of the social class to which they
aspired. Overall, boys remembered aggressive action in the
portrayals more than girls did; aggression by female characters
appeared to be less salient than other forms of portrayed
interaction for adolescent girls.

511. Malamuth, Neil M. "Aggression Against Women: Cultural and
Individual Causes." In Neil M. Malamuth and Edward Donnerstein (eds.),
Pornography and Sexual Aggression. Orlando, FL: Academic Press, 1984,
pp. 19-52.

Analysis of the causes of male violence against women requires
consideration of the interaction among three types of factors:
cultural factors, the psychological makeup of individuals more
likely to commit such acts of violence, and situational factors
that may suppress or trigger the actual expression of aggressive
responses. The author describes data from a research program
designed to investigate cultural and individual causes of
aggression against women. The primary focus is on the general
population rather than on individuals arrested for crimes such as
rape.

512. Malamuth, Neil M., and Edward Donnerstein. "The Effects of
Aggressive-Pornographic Mass Media Stimuli." In Leonard Berkowitz
(ed.), Advances in Experimental Social Psychology, Vol. 15. New
York: Academic Press, 1982, pp. 103-136.

A review of the literature on "aggressive" pornography (depictions
in which physical force is used or threatened to coerce a woman to
engage in physical acts).

513. Malamuth, Neil M., and Edward Donnerstein. Pornography and Sexual
Aggression. Orlando, FL: Academic Press, 1984.

A collection of articles focusing upon pornography and sexual
aggression. Includes experimental, correlational, and
cross-cultural studies. Implications for men and women and the
role of the mass media are also explored.

514. Malamuth, Neil M., and James V. P. Check. "The Effects of Mass
Media Exposure on Acceptance of Violence Against Women: A Field
Experiment." Journal of Research in Personality, Vol. 15, No. 4, 1981,
pp. 436-446.

An experiment on the effects of exposure to films portraying
sexual violence as having positive consequences employed 271
students as subjects. The subjects were randomly assigned to
view, on two different evenings, either violent-sexual or control
feature-length films. Results indicated that exposure to films
portraying violent sexuality increases male subjects' acceptance
of interpersonal violence against women. For females, there were
nonsignificant tendencies in the opposite direction--women exposed
to the violent-sexual films tended to be less accepting of
interpersonal violence and of rape myths than control subjects.

515. Malamuth, Neil M. and Victoria Billings. "The Functions & Effects
of Pornography: Sexual Communication versus the Feminist Models in
Light of Research Findings." In Jennings Bryant and Dolf Zillman
(eds.), Perspectives on Media Effects, Hillsdale, NJ: Lawrence Erlbaum
Associates, 1986.

Discusses problems of defining pornography, and presents two
theoretical models proposed to describe functions and effects of
pornography, followed by consideration of empirical research
findings relevant to the theoretical models.

516. Manning, Sidney A. and Dalmas A. Taylor. "The Effects of Viewing
Violence and Aggression: Stimulation and Catharsis." Journal of
Personality and Social Psychology, Vol. 31, 1975, pp. 180-188.

Inconsistencies in the results of tests of the catharsis
hypothesis may be due to the use of two types of response measures
-- aggressive and hostile. This study involved a direct
comparison of the two types of responses under conditions of
instigation versus no instigation and aggressive versus neutral
film. A main effect of instigation was found with subjects in the
instigation condition having higher scores than those in the
non-instigation condition. A main effect of film was found with
subjects having lower scores in the aggressive film condition than
in the neutral film condition. A significant film-response outlet
interaction was found which offered support for the predicted
catharsis effect on the hostility measure. There was no support
for the predicted stimulation effect on the aggression measure.
Results offer support for the main thesis that in examining the
effects of viewed violence, separation of hostile responses and
aggressive responses is necessary for full understanding.

517. Mattern, Kimberly K. and Bryon W. Lindholm. "Effect of Maternal
Commentary in Reducing Aggressive Impact of Televised Violence on
Preschool Children." The Journal of Genetic Psychology, Vol. 146,
No. 1, 1985, pp. 133-135.

In an experiment, the authors subjected two groups of children and
their mothers to viewing a television segment with numerous
expressions of violence. In the treatment group, mothers made
anti-violence comments during viewing. In the non-treatment
condition the mothers made no commments. Data were gathered in
two settings following the viewing. Data analysis revealed that
treatment condition subjects did not differ significantly in
help-hinder behavior, although sex differences were indicated.

518. McCarthy, Elizabeth D., Thomas S. Langner, Joanne C. Gersten,
Jeanne G. Eisenberg, and Lida Orzeck. "Violence and Behavior
Disorders." Journal of Communication, Vol. 25, No. 4, 1975, pp. 71-85.

This five year follow-up study of children (N=732) in New York
City found heavy viewing related to disasdvantaged social and
cultural backgrounds and to "behavior disorders," including
aggression. The study supplies potential support for the
hypothesis of a causal relationship between exposure to television
violence and aggression.

519. McIntyre, Jennie J., James J. Teeven, Jr., with Timothy Hartnagel. "Television Violence and Deviant Behavior." In George A. Comstock and Eli A. Rubinstein (eds.), Television and Social Behavior, Vol. 3, Television and Adolescent Aggressiveness. Washington DC: U.S. Government Printing Office, 1972, pp. 383-435.

This study examined the relationship between amount of violence in four favorite TV programs and self-report measures of deviant behavior and approval of aggression in a sample of 2270 teenagers. There was a significant positive correlation between preference for TV violence and indices for petty delinquency, fighting with parents, and aggressive deviance such as fighting with peers (r=+.11), and serious delinquency involving contact with the police (r=+.16). These associations remained after the implementation of statistical controls. There were similar correlations between violent favorites and approval of adult violence, teenage violence, and police violence. Those who preferred violent programming also tended to perceive a higher incidence of serious crimes in real life.

520. McLeod, Jack M., Charles K. Atkin, and Steven H. Chaffee. "Adolescents, Parents, and Television Use: Adolescent Self-Report Measures from Maryland and Wisconsin Samples." In George A. Comstock and Eli A. Rubinstein (eds.), Television and Social Behavior, Vol. 3, Television and Adolescent Aggressiveness. Washington DC: U.S. Government Printing Office, 1972, pp. 173-313.

There was a clear, if moderate, positive association between adolescents' level of violence viewing and their level of self-reported aggression -- the correlation between self-reports of frequency of viewing violence and an index of aggresion was +.31.

521. Menard, Bernard S. and Thibodeau-Gervais. "Suicide et Mass Media." L'Union Medicale du Canada, 1974.

The authors compared monthly suicide rates for a six-year period with newspaper accounts of suicides during the same months. Although there was a significant overall relationship, month-to-month variation made generalization difficult. Results for certain types of suicide--by means of firearms and hanging--yielded more conclusive results.

522. Messner, Steven F. "Television Violence and Violent Crime: An Aggregate Analysis." Social Problems, Vol. 33, No. 3, 1986, pp. 218-235.

The relationship between levels of exposure to TV violence and rates of violent crime is examined for samples of population aggregates. The primary hypothesis is that aggregates with high levels of exposure to violent TV content will exhibit high rates of criminal violence. The results of a series of multivariate, cross-sectional analyses fail to provide any support for this hypothesis. Contrary to expectations, aggregate levels of exposure are consistently related to rates of violent crime in an inverse direction. It is suggested that the theory of "criminal subcultures" and the "routine activities" approach offer possible explanations of these seemingly anomalous findings.

523. Meyer, Timothy P. "Some Effects of Real Newsfilm Violence on the Behavior of Viewers." Journal of Broadcasting, Vol. 15, No. 3, 1971, pp. 275-285.

Male college students were angered experimentally by means of electric shocks before viewing a 1969 network news report from South Vietnam in which a South Vietnamese soldier executed a North Vietnamese prisoner of war. The violent action was described as either justified or unjustified. Other groups of subjects viewed a non-violent film or no film. Those who viewed the justified violence behaved more violently, returning a greater number of shocks and more intense shocks than did other subjects.

524. Meyer, Timothy P. "Effects of Viewing Justified and Unjustified Real Film Violence on Aggressive Behavior." Journal of Personality and Social Psychology, Vol. 23, 1972, pp. 21-29.

Study tested the effects of viewing justified and unjustified film violence on aggressive behavior. Subjects were angered by an accomplice by means of electric shocks; the subjects saw a nonviolent film segment, a violent film segment, or no film; the subjects then were allowed to return shocks to the accomplice. Measures of the subjects' aggressive behavior included number of shocks returned and shock intensity. Results showed that angered college students who viewed justified real film violence returned significantly more shocks and more intense shocks than angered subjects viewing unjustified real or fictional film violence, a nonviolent film, or no film. The findings suggest that the effects of increased aggression demonstrated for angered viewers of justified fictional violence are also applicable to angered viewers of real film violence.

525. Meyer, Timothy P. "Children's Perceptions of Justified/Unjustified and Fictional/Real Film Violence." Journal of Broadcasting, Vol. 17, No. 3, 1973, pp. 321-332.

A test of age as a factor in discriminating between justified and unjustified motives depicted in media violence. Seven- and eight-year-old children were more likely than six-year-olds to distinguish correctly between justified and unjustified violence. Boys who viewed justified realistic violence (war scene) were considerably more likely to report that they would act the same way in a similar situation than were boys who viewed unrealistic fictional violence. About one-third of the boys said they would act similarly when the violence was depicted as unjustified.

526. Meyerson, Leonard J. "The Effects of Filmed Aggression on the Aggressive Responses of High and Low Aggressive Subjects." Dissertation, University of Iowa. Dissertation Abstracts International, Vol. 27, No. 9B,1967, p. 3291.

Eight-year-olds rated by peers as high- or low-aggressive viewed a film portraying aggressive behavior by adults either with another person or with a machine. Low-aggressive subjects were more aggressive after viewing both types of media violence compared to high-aggressive children. The author concludes that increase of aggression following observation of filmed violence requires similarity between the film and real-life settings, which facilitates the learned response.

527. Milavsky, J. Ronald, Ronald Kessler, Horst Stipp, and William S. Rubens. "Television and Aggression: Results of a Panel Study." In David Pearl, Lorraine Bouthilet, and Joyce Lazar (eds.), Television and Behavior, Vol. 2, Technical Reviews. Rockville, MD: National Institute of Mental Health, 1982, pp. 138-157. See also, New York: Academic Press, 1982.

The study is described as a lagged, longitudinal quasi-experiment testing the hypothesized causal relationship between TV violence and increased aggressive behavior in young people. It examines relatively short-term behavior and TV viewing patterns at several intervals ranging from three months to three years (about 10 percent of the subjects were observed over a full three-year period). Subjects were 2400 urban elementary school boys and girls and 800 urban high school boys. The index of aggressiveness for subjects used peer reports for younger children and self-reports of the previous month's behavior for teenaged boys. Exposure to violent TV programs was measured by self-reports of frequency of viewing a list of programs. There were few statistically significant regression coefficients of violent TV viewing predicting increased aggression at a certain interval among the younger children or the teenaged boys or among various subgroups.

528. Milgram, Stanley and R. Lance Shotland. Television and Social Behavior: Field Experiments. New York: Academic Press, 1973.

Discussion of a series of field experiments run in New York, St. Louis, Detroit, and Chicago to determine if the depiction of antisocial behavior on television stimulates imitation among viewers. Specially designed and produced television programs were shown to subjects in preview theaters. Subjects were later tested at a gift distribution center. While the results of most of the experiments were negative, there was a trend (not statistically significant) that one of the anti-social programs engendered imitation. The authors present a number of reasons to explain the negative findings.

529. Miller, N. L. "Media Liability for Injuries That Result from Television Broadcasts to Immature Audiences." San Diego Law Review, Vol. 22, No. 1, 1985, pp. 377-400.

The author argues that, when a child or a third party is injured as a result of the child's imitative act of television violence, the broadcaster should be held subject to liability. As with parents, teachers and neighbors who might contribute to a child's ability to commit an act of violence, the issue of whether the broadcaster exercised reasonable care in the particular case should be presented to a jury for determination.

530. Morcellini, Mario. "L'Informazione Periodica in Televisione" and "L'Attualita' Televisiva: Struttura Dell'Offerta Informativa Sul Territorio." In RAI Radiotelevisione Italiana, Terrorismo e TV, Vol. 1, Italia. Immagini del Terrorismo nel Rotocalco Televisivo. Rome: RAI, Verifica dei Programmi Trasmessi, 1982.

Results of content analysis on terrorism in evening information and cultural programs on Italian television networks during November 1980 - August 1981. Terrorism accounted for slightly more than 2 percent of the thematic content. Terrorism in other countries (particularly Ireland and Germany) was given wide coverage.

531. Morgan, Michael. "Symbolic Victimization and Real World Fear." Human Communication Research, Vol. 9, No. 2, 1983, pp. 146-157.

This study examines the relationship between relative victimization in television drama and variations in susceptibility to the cultivation of a sense of personal risk in the real world. Over 300 demographic subgroups defined by all combinations of age, sex, race, marital status, and class categories were constructed from data gathered in a 1979 national probability survey. Viewers whose fictional counterparts were more likely to be shown as victims showed stronger associations between viewing and perceived vulnerability. Moreover, the relative power hierarchy of television drama (derived from the "risk ratio" of committing violence to being victimized) strongly matches the real-world hierarchy of susceptibility to violence.

532. Motto, Jerome. "Newspaper Influence on Suicide." Archives of General Psychiatry, Vol. 23, 1970.

Analysis of the suicide rate in Detroit during a period of 268 days in 1967-68 during which there were no newspapers. This rate was compared to rates for the preceding four years and the following year. The period in which newspapers were not available had a significantly lower suicide rate for females under age 35, but not for males.

533. Mueller, Charles W., Edward Donnerstein, and John Hallam. "Violent Films and Prosocial Behavior." Personality and Social Psychology Bulletin, Vol. 9, No. 1, 1983, pp. 83-89.

Forty-two female college students were treated in either a positive or neutral manner by a confederate and then watched a violent, arousing film, a neutral non-arousing film, or no film. Following this, participants were given the opportunity both to aggress against or reward the confederate. As predicted, individuals treated in a positive manner and shown the violent film were more generous in administering reward to the confederate than were similarly treated individuals exposed to the neutral film or no film.

534. Murray John P. and Susan Kippax. "From the Early Window to the Late Night Show: International Trends in the Study of Television's Impact on Children and Adults." In Leonard Berkowitz (ed.), Advances in Experimental Social Psychology, Vol. 12. New York: Academic Press, 1979, pp. 253-320.

Review of research on television conducted in 16 countries. Television has made a world-wide impact upon daily life activities as well as viewers' behavior, attitudes, and values. Television acts as a socializing agent; it is a source of information and attitudes for both children and adults. Numerous experiments clearly document that viewing televised violence causes increased aggressive behavior as well as anxiety and fear. Despite controversies surrounding interpretation of the results of specific studies, the pattern of results from this extensive body of literature is sufficiently robust to suggest that television content can and does influence the viewer at various levels from changing attitudes and values to modifying interpersonal behavior.

535. Murray, John P. "Television and Violence: Implications of The Surgeon General's Research Program." American Psychologist, Vol. 28, 1973, pp. 472-478.

Discussion of the many research projects conducted as part of the Surgeon General's Research Program. The major implication of the results of these studies is the clear need for a reduction in the level of violence portrayed on television. It is also equally important to modify programming to reflect more prosocial content.

536. Murray, John P. Television and Youth: 25 Years of Research and Controversy. Boys Town, NE: Boys Town Center for the Study of Youth Development, 1980.

A review of much of the research on television and children, including that dealing with violence, aggression, and prosocial behavior. Included is an extensive bibliography.

537. Murray, John P. "Children and Television Violence." In The Future of Children's Television: Results of the Markle Foundation/Boys Town Conference, New York: Markle Foundation, 1982.

A discussion of the history of research addressing the impact of televised violence on children. The author defends criticisms directed at the validity and accuracy of these reports, stating that the almost 1,000 field and laboratory studies conducted provide enough evidence that TV violence can cause aggression.

538. Murray, John P. "A Soft Response to Hard Attacks on Research." Media Information Australia, No. 33, August, 1984, pp. 11-16.

This article is in response to an article by Bear that precedes it, arguing that the causal relationship between media violence and violent behavior is a myth. This author provides point-by-point refutation of each of Bear's seven reasons for rejecting this causal link. The author argues that Bear represents a community of scholars who approach the study of society critically rather than empirically, and that the major differences in style and substance of these two approaches accounts for Bear's disagreement with the conclusions of several decades of empirical research.

539. Murray, John P. "Impact of Televised Violence On Children." Testimony on behalf of the American Psychological Association before the U.S. Senate Subcommittee on Juvenile Justice, 1984.

A brief summary of thirty years of research on TV violence. Murray presents evidence of a correlation between televised attitudes, values, and behaviors. He also cites several longitudinal studies that suggest that watching televised violence can cause an increase in viewers' aggressive behavior, whereas watching pro-social programs can foster cooperative behaviors. Included is a description of several Federal policy initiatives aimed at increasing the number of educational and pro-social childrens' TV programs and countering the possible negative impact of violent programs. The proposed policies include tax incentives for corporations, regulations for the networks to encourage pro-social children's programs, and mandatory public service announcements to warn viewers about the potential negative impact of violent programs.

540. Murray, John P. "Children and Television--What Do We Know?" In A. Burns, J. Goodnow, R. Chisolm, and J. P. Murray (eds.), Children and Families in Australia: Contemporary Issues and Problems. Sydney, Australia: Allen & Unwin, 1985.

An overview of various aspects of television and its effects on child viewers, with particular reference to televised violence. Summarizes results of research in several countries, including Australia and the U.S., concerning levels of TV violence and the relationship between viewing and aggressive attitudes and behaviors. The author points to the important influence of

150

individual personality and environmental factors on response to media content.

541. Murray, John P., Oguz B. Nayman, and Charles K. Atkin. "Television and the Child: A Comprehensive Research Bibliography." Journal of Broadcasting, Vol. 16, No. 1, 1972, pp. 3-20.

A bibliography based on work completed for the surgeon general's scientific advisory committee on television and social behavior. Includes sections on content and programming, viewing patterns and general effects, impact of televised and filmed violence.

542. Mussen, Paul and Eldred Rutherford. "Effects of Aggressive Cartoons on Children's Aggressive Play." Journal of Abnormal and Social Psychology, Vol. 62, No. 2, 1961, pp. 461-464.

This study tested the hypothesis that exposure to aggressive fantasy in an animated cartoon may intensify children's impulses to aggression. Subjects were 36 first grade children of middle class origin. The intensity of the child's aggressive impulses was inferred from his/her responses to questions concerning desire to "play with" or "pop" a large yellow balloon held by a tester. The experimental findings clearly supported this hypothesis. Two possible explanations for these results were discussed: that intensification of instigation to aggression may have resulted from the child's identification with the aggressive cartoon characters, with accompanying assumption of their motives; and that the relaxed "fun" context of animated cartoons may lead to a reduction of inhibitions against aggressive expression in a permissive play situation.

543. National Coalition on Television Violence. NCTV News. Champaign, IL: NCTV, 1980 to date.

This newsletter reports on many aspects of violence in society: research on media content and effects, ratings and reviews of programs, scholarly and popular commentary, citizen and governmental action relating to media, industry viewpoints, and crime statistics vis-a-vis TV portrayal. Monitoring results of violent content--classified by network, program, and sponsor--are a regular feature, along with reviews of current theatre films. NCTV also expresses concern about other aspects of violence and aggression in society, including violence-related toys and games, sports, pornography, and interpersonal aggression.

544. Nias, David K. B. "The Effects of Televised Sex and Pornography." In Michael J. A. Howe (ed.), Learning From Television: Psychological and Educational Research, London: Academic Press, 1983.

Based on the theory that the portrayal of violence is almost
always potentially harmful, but that the portrayal of sex is not
necessarily so, the author suggests that a case for sex on
television can be made on the grounds of entertainment and
education, pointing out that most commercially available
pornographic films at present are antilove and antiwomen.
Discusses widely differing research results on effects of erotica
and pornography regarding imitation, disinhibition,
desensitisation, treatment procedures, sex-aggression link, ethics
and censorship.

545. Noble, Grant. "Effects of Different Forms of Filmed Aggression on
Constructive and Destructive Play." Journal of Personality and Social
Psychology, Vol. 26, No. 1, 1973, pp. 54-59.

This study employed two measures of behavioral effect of filmed
violence. Children aged 6-7 played less constructively (a measure
of anxiety) after viewing film segments depicting realistic
violence and violence filmed with sight of the victim than after
viewing unrealistic fictional violence and violence filmed at a
distance. Children's play also was more destructive after
realistic than after unrealistic fictional violence, although this
variable did not appear to be affected by distance of camera from
the violent action.

546. Osborn, D. K. and R. C. Endsley. "Emotional Reactions of Young
Children to TV Violence." Child Development, Vol. 42, No. 1, 1971,
pp. 321-331.

Short televised films were viewed by 25 four- and five-year old
children. The films were either violent (with a realistic
aggressor or a fantasy-character aggressor) or nonviolent (images
of children on a farm or a nonviolent cartoon). Measurement of
Galvanic Skin Response indicated that violent programs increased
emotional/physiological reaction. Nonviolent programs did not
have this effect.

547. Paletz, David L. and Robert Dunn. "Press Coverage of Civil
Disorders: A Case Study of Winston-Salem." Public Opinion Quarterly,
Vol. 33, No. 3, 1969, pp. 328-345.

The civil unrest on which this study centers occurred two years
after major racial disturbance in Los Angeles. The authors
present the view that guidelines designed to restrict sensational
coverage of urban riots may have unexpected and possibly negative
consequences and outline details of the 1967 Winston-Salem riot as
a case study. Coverage of the four-day riot by one local,
racially-progressive newspaper was analyzed and compared to
coverage by two other newspapers, including the New York Times,
and to interview data provided by press personnel and participants
in the riots. The role of local media in maintaining a
sociocultural consensus, in delaying rather than inciting violent
conflict, is revealed in this analysis. However, the authors
interpret such a role as a subtle, possibly inadvertant form of

hostility in that it fails to contribute to better understanding of the black community.

548. Palmer, Edward L., A. B. Hockett and W. W. Dean. "The Television Family and Children's Fright Reactions." Journal of Family Issues, Vol. 4, No. 2, 1983, pp. 279-292.

This study was designed to examine the question of children's fright reactions to television violence; whether potential for fright increases or decreases with the child's age. Elementary school children in grades two and six responded to questions regarding frequency of fear reaction, popularity of frightening programs, frequency of program avoidance and general viewing patterns. Program related fear was significant;y more frequent among second grade children, with more frequent fear response from girls than boys. Heavy adult program viewing and a prevalence of nonregulation by parents was evident in both groups.

549. Palmer, Edward L. and Aimee Dorr (eds.). Children and the Faces of Television: Teaching, Violence, Selling. New York: Academic Press, 1981.

Violence, one of three "faces" of television, is examined in one section of this book. Included is a historical perspective, examination of research on violence and television, and issues relating to social policy.

550. Parke, Ross D., Leonard Berkowitz, Jacques-Philippe Leyens, Stephen G. West, and Richard J. Sebastian. "Some Effects of Violent and Nonviolent Movies on the Behavior of Juvenile Delinquents." In Leonard Berkowitz (ed.), Advances in Experimental Social Psychology, Vol. 10. New York: Academic Press, 1977, pp. 135-172.

A study involving two groups of American boys in residential schools. During a five-day period, one group of boys viewed violent films and the other viewed nonviolent films. There was a short term (one-week) increase in aggressive behavior (verbal and physical) for the boys exposed to violent films. There was a longer term effect for boys initially more aggressive and for low-aggressive boys who viewed non-violent films.

551. Pearl, David. "Violence and Aggression: Television at the Crossroads." Society, Vol. 21, No. 6, 1984.

This paper surveys and discusses the research on effects of televised violence. Results from 1952 through the 1970s suggest a relation between viewing televised violence and aggressive behavior. Four processes have been suggested as responsible for the relation: observational learning, attitude changes, physiological arousal, and justification processes. It is noted that the catharsis theory, which predicts that aggression will be reduced after watching violence on television, is contradicted by the data.

552. Pearl, David, Lorraine Bouthilet, and Joyce Lazar (eds.).
Television and Behavior: Ten Years of Scientific Progress and
Implications for the Eighties, Vol. 2, Technical Reviews. Rockville,
MD: National Institute of Mental Health, 1982.

These technical reviews form the documentation for the update of
the Surgeon General's Report. A perspective by Eli A.Rubinstein
prefaces major studies relating to televised violence--its forms
and its contributions to the socialization process. The projects
address past problems and differences in research design and
indicate the direction of the most current research.

553. Pfuhl, Erdwin H., Jr. "Mass Media and Reported Delinquent
Behavior: A Negative Case." In Maravin E. Wolfgang, Leonard Savitz,
and Norman Johnston (eds), The Sociology of Crime and Delinquency. New
York: Wiley, 1970, pp. 509-523.

Data do not substantiate the notion that mass media dealing with
crime and violence are an inducement to criminal and delinquent
behavior, or that techniques of criminal behavior displayed in the
media will be adopted by youth, thus promoting a delinquent
career. There was also no consistently significant difference
between the more and less delinquent in patterns of interest in,
or exposure to, crime themes in the mass media.

554. Phillips, David P. "The Influence of Suggestion on Suicide:
Substantive and Theoretical Implications of the Warner Effect."
American Sociological Review, Vol. 39, June, 1974, pp. 340-354.

Data from national postwar suicide statistics, The New York Daily
News, the Chicago Tribune, and the London Daily Mirror for each
month during the period 1946 to 1968 were used in an investigation
of the impact of front page suicides on suicide trends. The
number of suicides increased proportionately with the amount of
publicity devoted to a suicide story.

555. Phillips, David P. "Suicide, Motor Vehicle Fatalities, and the
Mass Media: Evidence Toward a Theory of Suggestion." American Journal
of Sociology, Vol. 84, No. 5, 1979, pp. 1150-1173.

Daily motor vehicle fatalities in California, from 1966 to 1973,
and front page suicide stories from five major California
newspapers were examined to test the sociological theories of
suggestion and imitation. The author found that three days after
a publicized suicide, mobile fatalities increased by thirty-one
percent. The more the suicide was publicized, the more the
automobile fatalities increased.

556. Phillips, David P. "Airplane Accidents, Murder, and the Mass
Media: Towards a Theory of Imitation and Suggestion." Social Forces,
Vol. 58, No. 4, 1980, pp. 1001-1023.

A selected number of eighteen noncommercial plane accidents between 1968 and 1973 (provided by the U.S. National Transportation Safety Board) were investigated to identify a link between publicizing murder-suicides disguised as plane crashes (intentionally caused by the pilot) and ensuing increases of fatal airplane accidents. The largest newspaper from each of nine states containing operative civilian aircraft were additionally examined following the occurence of a murder-suicide plane crash. Results showed that after murder-suicide stories there is an increase in noncommercial and airline crashes. This increase persists for approximately nine days, and then the level of crashes returns to normal.

557. Phillips, David P. "The Deterrent Effect of Capital Punishment: New Evidence on an Old Controversy." American Journal of Sociology, Vol. 86, No. 1, 1980, pp. 139-147.

Weekly homicide statistics in London between 1858 and 1921 and The London Times during this period were analyzed to test for a relationship between publicizing executions and subsequent homicides. On the average, homicides decreased by 36 percent immediately following a publicized execution. The more publicity devoted to the execution, the more homicides decreased thereafter.

558. Phillips, David P. "Strong and Weak Research Designs for Detecting the Impact of Capital Punishment on Homicide." Rutgers Law Review, Vol. 33, No. 3, 1981, pp. 790-798.

A discussion of some methodological shortcomings of many studies in the deterrent effect of capital punishment. The author suggests that, to determine whether capital punishment influences the homicide rate, the effect of capital punishment must be disentangled from the effect of other variables on homicide. This can be accomplished by using a controlled experiment.

559. Phillips, David P. "The Impact of Fictional Television Stories on U.S. Adult Fatalities: New Evidence on the Effect of the Mass Media on Violence." American Journal of Sociology, Vol. 87, No.6, 1982, pp. 1340-1359.

Evidence that fictional violent television stories trigger imitative deaths and near-fatal accidents is provided in this study which compared National Center for Health Statistics on Suicides with occurence of fictional suicide on television. In 1977, suicides, motor vehicle deaths, and non-fatal accidents all rose immediately following soap opera suicide stories. Female suicides increased proportionately more than male suicides.

560. Phillips, David P. "The Impact of Mass Media Violence on U.S. Homicides." American Sociological Review, Vol. 48, No. 4, 1983, pp. 560-568.

The author attempts to apply behavior modeling theory, as related
to media-aggression studies, to real life. This "found
experiment" time series regression analysis is applied to
U.S. homicide statistics and 18 heavyweight prizefights betwteen
1973 and 1978. Championship fights occurring outside the U.S. and
publicized in network newscasts accompanied increases in the
homicide rate within 10 days of the broadcast, and particularly on
the third day. Other aggressive events linked to gambling, such
as football championships, do not appear to have a similar effect
on violent behavior.

561. Phillips, David P. "The Found Experiment: A New Technique for
Assessing the Impact of Mass Media Violence in Real World Aggressive
Behavior." Public Communication and Behavior, Vol. 1, 1985.

A detailed discussion of the strengths and limitations of "found
experiments," in which nature, rather than the researcher, creates
the experimental and control groups. Thus instead of creating the
experiment, the researcher has "found" it. Also, a review of
Phillip's research on the effects of publicized violence.

562. Phillips, David P. and John E. Hensley. "When Violence is
Rewarded or Punished: The Impact of Mass Media Stories on Homicide."
Journal of Communication, Vol. 34, No. 3, 1984, pp. 101-116.

An examination of the media-coverage of more than 140,000 United
States daily homicides before and after prizefights, innocent
verdicts, life sentences, death sentences, and execution. The
authors found evidence that publicized punishments have a
short-term deterrent effect on the homicides of white victims.

563. Piepe, Anthony J., Joyce Crouch, and Miles Emerson. "Violence and
Television." New Society, Vol. 41, September, 1977, pp. 536-538.

A test of TV cultivation effect in Great Britain analyzed data for
a representative sample of 842 men and women. Fear of crime and
suspicion were related more strongly to location of respondents'
home than to TV viewing. Cultivation effect appeared to influence
liberal-conservative attitude, leading authors to hypothesize
socio-cultural differences in the specific attitudes influenced by
exposure to television.

564. Pierce, Chester M. "Television and Violence: Social Psychiatric
Perspectives"." American Journal of Social Psychiatry, Vol. 4, No. 3,
1984, pp. 41-44.

Reviews the current data supporting the position that TV can
socialize individuals toward violent behavior. Some possible
medical implications of this research are discussed. It is
suggested that the research effort can help dilute some of the
negative impact of TV, promote health and prevent illness.
Guidelines that have particular clinical relevance for parents and

children are offered for helping patients when TV is thought to be
an actual or potential problem.

565. Pietila, V. "Some Notes About Violence in Our Mass Media --
Especially in Fictitious TV Programmes." Research on Peace and
Violence, Vol. 4, 1976.

Violence is associated with crimes against property among those
who watch American and English detective and crime series, while
violence is associated with crimes against the society or state
among those who watch Russian programs.

566. Pingree, Suzanne and Robert Hawkins. "U.S. Programs on Australian
Television: The Cultivation Effect." Journal of Communication,
Vol. 31, No. 1, 1981, pp. 97-105.

Questionnaires addressing media beliefs, habits, opinions, and
knowledge were administered to 1,385 public school children in
Western Australia. Included were measures of beliefs about
violence in society and general "meanness" in the world. Results
of the study indicated that the Mean-World and Violence-in-Society
scores correlated significantly with viewing U.S. programs, but
not with viewing non-U.S. programs. Contrary to expectations, the
Australian children seemed to accept the biases of U.S. television
as relevant to Australia. The authors conclude that cultivation
of beliefs about the world--at least beliefs about violence and
crime--occurs even when the messages are imported from another
country.

567. Potts, Richard, Aletha C. Huston and John C. Wright. "The Effects
of Television Form and Violent Content on Boys' Attention and Social
Behavior." Journal of Experimental Child Psychology, Vol. 4, No. 1,
1986, pp. 1-17.

Investigated the independent effects of TV violence and action
level on children's attention to programs and their postviewing
social behavior. 32 pairs of 39-75 month old boys participated in
2 experimental sessions in which they saw animated and live TV
programs varying in violence and action levels. They then played
with toys containing cues for either aggressive or prosocial
interaction. Results show that rapid character action facilitated
visual attention to programs; violent TV content did not
facilitate attention. Strong effects of toy cues were found
independently of TV treatment effects; aggressive and prosocial
toys produced aggressive and prosocial behavior, respectively.
Violent TV content led to changes in subjects' style of
interaction and was also associated with increases in some
prosocial behavior. Results are discussed within the theoretical
frameworks of observational learning and general arousal.
Implications for children's TV programming are also discussed.

568. Pourtois, Jean-Pierre. "La Violence a la Television Influence-t-elle le Comportement Agressif des Enfants?" [Does Television Violence Affect Aggressive Behavior in Children?]. Reseaux, 1978, pp. 32-34, 95-102.

Asserts that the ambiguous concept of violence is not necessarily the same as brutality. Questions necessity to censor all forms of brutality from programming. Omnipresent effects of brutality viewing vary dependent upon the child's predisposition. Interviews with children reflect their disturbed, anguished and intimidated responses to such programming. Two educational policy proposals are made: 1)the encouragement of pre- programming discussion and 2)to stimulate the production of more audiovisual documentaries that would focus greater attention on the subject.

569. Rabinovitch, Martin S., Malcolm S. McLean, Jr., James W. Markham, and Albert D. Talbott. "Children's Violence Perception as a Function of Television Violence." In George A. Comstock, Eli A. Rubinstein, and John P. Murray (eds.), Television and Social Behavior, Vol. 5, Television's Effects: Further Explorations. Washington, DC: U.S. Government Printing Office, 1972, pp. 231-252.

57 sixth grade children observed violent or nonviolent slides after viewing a violent or nonviolent television program. Those who viewed a detective program tended to perceive less violence in the slide presentations than those who viewed a situation comedy. Children in the control group that saw no film were most likely to perceive violence. The findings contradicted the hypothesis that children who had been exposed to violence portrayals would perceive more violence in slides than those in the nonviolence or control groups.

570. Randall, Murray L., Richard R. Cole, and Fred Fedler. "Teenagers and TV Violence: How They Rate and View It." Journalism Quarterly, Vol. 47, No. 2, 1970, pp. 247-255.

Teenagers categorized violence into three types (physical, mental, and verbal) and defined it as senseless and occurring without good reason. High and low users of violent content were identified to determine which variables best predict the use of violent television content and differentiate between them. Sex was the best predictor of violence viewing. Alienation and viewing of violent content, however, bore little relationship to each other. Telephone interviews revealed that few of the teens in this sample spent a lot of time watching television.

571. Rarick, David L., James E. Townsend, and Douglas A. Boyd. "Adolescent Perceptions of Police: Actual and as Depicted in Television Dramas." Journalism Quarterly, Vol. 50, No. 3, 1973, pp. 438-446.

A Q analysis revealed that adolescents' image of television police is not correlated with their image of actual police. Perceptions of actual police are diverse, ranging from highly favorable to openly hostile. Perceptions of television police are relatively homogeneous and positive. Adolescents adjudicated delinquent perceive television police in much the same way as non-delinquents. They also do not have more negative impressions of actual police.

572. Rehman, S. N. and Reilly, S. S. "Music Videos: A New Dimension of Television Violence." The Pennsylvania Speech Communication Annual, Vol. 41, 1985, pp. 61-65.

Music videos were rated for violent content and arranged in two different orders -either ascending or descending order of violence- and then shown to groups of college students to see if their perception of the violent content of the videos rose and declined as the actual level of violent content rose and declined. Two-tailed t-tests revealed that the violence was rated higher by women than by men. In descending exposed group, as violence decreased so did the subjects' violence ratings. In the ascending exposed group, however, ratings did not increase along with violent content. The authors accepted an alternative hypothesis that desensitization to violence does occur.

573. Reisman, Judith A. "Mass Media and Civil Rights." In Ann Wolbert Burgess (ed.), Rape and Sexual Assault, NY:Garland Publishing, Inc., 1985, pp. 365-373.

Suggests evidence is surfacing which links certain sex/violent media with possible murder and mutilation of women and children, as well as citing use of sexually explicit media in entrapment of children in sex and pornography rings. Advocates serious investigation into components of mass media which may be facilitating an increase in rape and sexual assault of women and children, citing evidence which supports the relationship between some mass media and seduction/abduction/murder of women and children.

574. Research and Forecasts. The Figgie Report on Crime: America Afraid. Willoughby, Ohio: A-T-O, Inc., 1980.

This report is based upon telephone interviews with more than 1000 randomly selected people. Findings reveal that those who report exposure to violence both on television and in newspapers on a daily basis are likely to be fearful. Almost half of the respondents who say they read about violent crime in daily newspapers express high levels of fear compared with only about a third who read about crime less often. Similarly, 43 percent of those who see such reports on television daily exhibit a high level of fear compared with only 35 percent of those who see violent televised news reports less often.

575. Roberts, Churchill. "Children's and Parent's Television Viewing and Perceptions of Violence." Journalism Quarterly, Vol. 58, No. 4, 1981, pp. 556-564, 581.

> 415 children in the fourth, fifth, and sixth grades in northwest Florida served as the subjects in this study. Results suggest that to a limited extent parents' viewing behavior and attitude toward violence are related to those of their children. The best predictor of the amount of time children spent watching television each week was parental viewing. Likewise, children's expressions of fear of walking alone at night seemed to some degree to reflect their parents' fear. But for the most part, children's perceptions of violence were explained by their age and sex. Younger children were more likely than older ones to think it is all right to hit someone when you are mad at them, and girls were more likely than boys to be afraid to walk alone near their home at night.

576. Robinson, Deanna Campbell. "Young Adults' Assessment of Dramatic Television Violence." Manuscript based on 1980 presentation to the International Communication Association, Acapulco, Mexico, 1981.

> A study designed to assess what viewers, rather than researchers or activist groups, consider to be television violence. 258 young adults rated the violence of edited television program segments. Questionnaires provided data on subjects' demographic characteristics, media habits, and attitudes. Segment ratings indicated that response to TV action as violent is greater when viewers identify with the plight of the characters involved. In additon, viewers regard some shows generally considered violent as silly and unreal.

577. Robinson, John P. and Jerald G. Bachman. "Television Viewing Habits and Aggression." In George A. Comstock and Eli A. Rubinstein (eds.), Television and Social Behavior, Vol. 3, Television and Adolescent Aggressiveness. Washington DC: U.S. Government Printing Office, 1972, pp. 372-383.

> A comparison of teenaged boys grouped according to the amount of violence in their favorite TV programs indicated that those who preferred programs with the most violence tended to be more aggressive.

578. Rosenfeld, Erica, Susan Maloney, L. Rowell Huesmann, Leonard D. Eron, Paulette Fisher, Vita Musonis, and Ann Washington. "The Effect of Fantasy Behaviors and Fantasy-Reality Discriminations on the Observational Learning of Aggression." Aggressive Behavior, Vol. 5, No. 2, 1979, pp. 216-217.

> Aggression and television violence viewing profiles of primary school children were correlated with measures of fantasy orientation and of perceived reality of television programs. Negative-aggressive fantasy orientation corresponded to levels of overt aggression for girls and boys. Degree of perceived realism

appeared to mediate the positive relationship between viewing TV
violence and aggressive behavior, particularly for girls. A
supplementary experiment explored the effect of training on
fantasy-reality discrimination.

579. Rosengren, Karl Erik. "Media Panel." In School Research
Newsletter, Stockholm, Sweden: National Board of Education, November,
1984.

A review of the Media Panel's longitudinal research exploring
children's uses of the mass media. The Media Panel comprises two
groups of schoolchildren, on whom data was collected on four
occasions concerning mass media habits. The Panel has attempted
to combine two research traditions -- effects and utilization
research. Although the final data on these children has not been
reported yet, certain results have emerged from data analyses.
Children watch more television between the ages of 10 and 12 and
less between the ages of 15 and 16. Also, the use of mass media
by children and young persons is very dependent upon the social
position of the family and the situation of the individual child.

580. Rothenberg, Michael B. "Effect of Television Violence on Children
and Youth." American Medical Association Journal, Vol. 234, No. 10,
1975, pp. 1043-1046.

146 articles in behavioral science journals, representing 50
studies involving 10,000 children and adolescents from every
conceivable background, all showed that violence viewing produces
increased aggressive behavior in the young and that immediate
remedial action in terms of television programming is warranted.

581. Rowland, Willard D. The Politics of TV Violence. Beverly Hills,
CA: Sage Publications, 1983.

Examination of violence effects research focusing upon the roles
and contributions of researchers, politicians, reformers, and the
industry.

582. Rubins, William. "Sex and Violence on TV." Journal of
Advertising Research, Vol. 21, No. 6, 1981, pp. 13-20.

Bias and superficiality of many polls of attitudes concerning
television violence are cited by the author, who reports results
of a Roper Organization survey supplemented by two follow-up
studies of 2400 adult viewers. Attitudes about violence in 17 TV
entertainment programs were solicited. Only two programs were
associated with positive or negative attitudes of more than 5
percent of the sampled viewers, and considerably larger
percentages of viewers rated the programs very favorably. Three
percent or fewer of the respondents felt that certain programs
should be taken off the air for either violent or sexual content.
The follow-up surveys revealed some differences in results caused
by variation in the format of the questions posed to viewers.

583. Rubinstein, Eli A. "Television Violence: A Historical Perspective." In Edward C. Palmer and Aimee Dorr (eds.), Children and the Faces of Television: Teaching, Violence, Selling. New York: Academic Press, 1980, pp. 113-128.

An historical overview of research on television violence conducted since the early 1950's. Discusses numerous Senate hearings, the Eisenhower Commission, the Surgeon General's Program of Research, as well as some of the public campaigns against television violence. Notes that most of the research has indicated that television violence is harmful to viewers and that television is both an important positive and negative influence upon children.

584. Rubinstein, Eli A. "Television and Behavior: Research Conclusions of the 1982 NIMH Report and Their Policy Implications." American Psychologist, Vol. 38, No. 7, 1983, pp. 820-825.

Research on television and behavior in the 1970s has recently been reviewed and evaluated in a report from the National Institute of Mental Health (NIMH). The general conclusion is that TV is an important influence on child development in ways well beyond earlier findings which focused on violence and aggression. Media focus and public emphasis on violence as the major issue has masked an even larger issue. Rather than concern with violent content, there is a need to see the totality of TV viewing as a continuing form of informal education. Government regulation is undesirable and more industry creativity unlikely, so the need is for a continuing process to facilitate the translation of research knowledge into policy-making actions.

585. Rushton, J. Philippe. "Effects of Prosocial Television and Film Material on the Behavior of Viewer." In Leonard Berkowitz (ed.), Advances in Experimental Social Psychology, Vol. 12. New York: Academic Press, 1979, pp. 321-351.

Review of 35 experimental studies from both laboratory and naturalistic settings. Findings reveal that television programs and films can modify viewers' social behavior in a prosocial direction. These conclusions lend "construction validation" to the findings of research suggesting a relationship between television and antisocial behavior and/or violence.

586. Sapolsky, Barry S. "Arousal, Affect, and the Aggression-Moderating Effect of Erotica." In Neil M. Malamuth and Edward Donnerstein (eds.), Pornography and Sexual Aggression. Orlando, FL: Academic Press, 1984, pp. 85-113.

A review of research on the consequences of exposure to both nonaggressive and aggressive sexual stimuli. A two-component model, incorporating both arousal capacity and affect-eliciting qualities of an erotic stimulus, is proposed as a means of examining the impact of nonaggressive sexual stimuli on aggression. The affective component of responses to erotica emerges as the primary determinant of a stimulus's aggression-moderating effects. The major influences upon the affective responsiveness of the individual to such stimuli are also explored.

587. Savitsky, Jeffrey C., Ronald W. Rogers, Carroll E. Izard, and Robert M. Liebert. "The Role of Frustration and Anger in the Imitation of Filmed Aggression Against a Human Victim." Psychological Reports, Vol. 29, No. 3, 1971, pp. 807-810.

Boys aged 6-7 who viewed a brief film of a boy behaving aggressively against a human clown displayed more imitative aggression in free play than did boys who did not see the film. Frustration induced by denial of a toy had no significant effect on overt aggression; pre-existing anger appeared to be associated with aggression regardless of film viewing.

588. Saxer, U., H. Bonfadelli, and W. Hattenschwiler. "Medienrealitat und Alltagswirklichkeit." In U. Saxer, H. Bonfadelli, and W. Hattenschwiler (eds.), Die Massenmedien im Leben der Kinder und Jugendlichen. Zug (West Germany), 1980.

A 1976 cultivation analysis with 2750 Swiss children aged 9-15 in Zurich. Four cultivation measures were significantly correlated with controls for age, sex, and socioeconomic status. User gratification was also an important independent variable.

589. Schramm, Wilbur. "The Nature of News." Journalism Quarterly, Vol. 26, 1949, pp. 259-269.

Early research on use/gratifications of newspaper readers indicated two basic interests: stories yielding immediate reward (crime, corruption, accidents, disasters, sports, recreation, social events, and human interest) and those yielding delayed reward (public affairs, economic matters, social problems, science, education, and health). Another factor was the ability to identify one's self or family with subjects of the news story. Interest in delayed reward stories increased with education while interest in immediate reward stories declined.

590. Schramm, Wilbur, Jack Lyle, and Edwin B. Parker. Television in the Lives of our Children. Stanford, CA: Stanford University Press, 1961.

Report of several extensive studies in different areas of the United States and Canada in 1959, including several relating to the effects of televised violence. Questionnaire responses of children and adolescents indicated that adolescents who were frequent television viewers but infrequent readers were more aggressive than other young people. In a study involving two Canadian communities, adolescents with access to television were less aggressive than those in a town without television--there were no differences among the older children. In this research,

163

television is seen as a contributing factor to aggression among some children rather than a primary cause.

591. Searle, Ann. "The Perception of Filmed Violence by Aggressive Individuals with High or Low Self-Concept of Aggression." European Journal of Social Psychology, Vol. 6, No. 2, 1976, pp. 175-190.

The subjects in this experiment were 16 and 17 year olds categorized by self-reports of aggression. They viewed one of two full-length commercial films and then rated the characters. Aggressive characters were rated as more aggressive by subjects with low-aggression self-ratings than by subjects with high-aggression self-ratings. The differences were not related to other variables. The author posits projection theory (viewers project perceptions of aggression onto media characters when appropriate cues are available) to explain these findings.

592. Seasonwein, Roger and Leonard R. Sussman. "Can Extremists Using Television Move an Audience?" Journalism Quarterly, Vol. 49, No. 1, 1972, pp. 61-64.

Gauged effect of abrasiveness of media personalities engaged in debate on political orientation and attitudes of college students. In 1970, members of the "Chicago 7" (political radicals) debated several journalists and a law professor on closed-circuit television. Questionnaire responses before and after the debate indicated that viewers found the abrasiveness of certain members of the Chicago 7 persuasive and that agreement with the radicals increased for certain assertions, particularly among liberal students. However, students generally agreed more with stated goals of the group than with violent methods they may have employed.

593. Shaw, Irene S. and David S. Newell. "Violence on Television: Programme Content and Viewer Perception." London: British Broadcasting Corporation, 1972.

An analysis of the amount and nature of violence in British television programs broadcast between November 1970 and May 1971 revealed that violent behavior was found in films and series. Programs imported from the United States were among the most violent. Cartoons, of which there were relatively few, were also quite violent. The second half of this study was a series of surveys that explored the significance of viewing violence. These surveys examined the extent to which viewers were aware of violence, their emotional responses to the programs, and especially the "uses" to which they put the programs.

594. Sheehan, Peter W. "Age Trends and the Correlates of Children's Television Viewing." Australian Journal of Psychology, Vol. 35, No. 3, 1983, pp. 417-431.

As part of a cross-cultural investigation of TV viewing and its effects in six different countries, 106 children in grades 1, 2 and 3 (cohort 1) and 120 children in grades 3, 4, and 5 (cohort 2) were tested in an overlapping longitudinal design which examined children's television viewing and its correlates during three successive years (1979-1981). Measures were taken of sex-typed behavior, fantasy activity, judged realism, identification with TV characters, and peer-rated aggression. Analysis of age trends revealed consistent sex differences for the older cohort. There were significant relationships between the two viewing variables and aggressive behavior, especially among boys.

595. Siegal, Alberta E. "The Influence of Violence in the Mass Media upon Children's Role Expectations." Child Development, Vol. 29, 1958, pp. 35-56.

This experiment using two classes of second graders tests the hypothesis that children's reality expectations are influenced by the content of dramatic presentations in the mass media. Two radio dramas were used: (A) central character resolved the dramatic conflict by personal physical aggression and (B) another solution was presented for the same conflict. Children were subsequently tested individually via a completion test (presented as an achievement test) for their role expectations. In general, the data support the research hypothesis.

596. Siegel, Alberta E. "Film-Mediated Fantasy Aggression and Strength of Aggressive Drive." Child Development, Vol. 27, 1956, pp. 365-378.

The behavior theory hypothesis of equivalence of forms was tested as it applies to the effects of film-mediated fantasy aggression on strength of aggressive drive in young children. The free play of like-sexed pairs of children in the absence of adults was observed under two conditions: after a highly aggressive cartoon film and after a "matched" nonaggressive film. Play was scored for aggression and for behavioral signs of guilt and anxiety. These scores did not differ significantly for the two conditions. Significant sex differences and session differences were found, and the children's aggression scores correlated significantly with teachers' ratings of habits of aggression in the nursery school.

597. Siegel, Alberta E. "The Effects of Media Violence on Social Learning." In Robert K. Baker and Sandra J. Ball, Mass Media and Violence, Vol. 9. Washington, DC: Government Printing Office, 1969, pp. 261-283.

Discussion of research reveals that films and television teach that the world is a violent and untrustworthy place and demonstrates a variety of violent techniques to cope with this hostile environment.

598. Signorielli, Nancy, Larry Gross and Michael Morgan. "Violence in Television Programs: Ten Years Later." In David Pearl, Lorraine Bouthilet, and Joyce Lazar (eds.), Television and Social Behavior, Vol. 2, Technical Reviews. Rockville, MD: National Institute of Mental Health, 1982, pp. 158-173.

A focus on the methodological aspects of assessing television violence. Content analysis and ratings systems are defined, and examples of research employing these methods are provided. Particular reference is made to the Cultural Indicators Project, which has analyzed trends in television content since 1967. Definition, unitization, and sampling are discussed, with examples given of different approaches. The standardized, reliable statistics on television violence provided by the Cultural Indicators Violence Index from 1967 to 1979 are included. Over the twelve-year period, an average of 71 percent of prime-time programs contained violence; 94 percent of weekend daytime programs contained violence. The hourly rate of violence was 4.8 for prime time and 5.8 for weekend daytime dramatic programs. Finally, cultivation of beliefs and values in subgroups of viewers is discussed, with descriptions of the processes of resonance (attitude reinforcement) and mainstreaming (channeling of attitudes toward the norm emphasized on television).

599. Singer, Benjamin D. "Mass Media and Communication Processes in the Detroit Riot of 1967." Public Opinion Quarterly, Vol. 34, No. 2, 1970, pp. 236-245.

Interviews concerning communication behavior of 500 blacks arrested during the 1967 Detroit riot indicate the relative contributions of various media and personal contacts to perceptions of the event. In recalling what they had witnessed on television, 50 percent of respondents mentioned violent acts and 5 percent mentioned property offenses and attempts at control by authorities. While about half of the respondents reported a negative reaction to the rioting as depicted on television, one-fourth reported resentment of whites and/or authorities. These perceptions were compared to details of actual media coverage, including emphasis on riot activity and location as opposed to emphasis on police action.

600. Singer, Dorothy G. and Jerome L. Singer. "Television Viewing and Aggressive Behavior in Preschool Children: A Field Study." Annals of the New York Academy of Sciences, Vol. 347, 1980, pp. 289-303.

A longitudinal study of the relationship between television viewing within the family setting and possible influences of such viewing on the ongoing patterns of aggression during free-play situations in day care or preschool settings. 200 preschool children were studied for intelligence, capacity for concept information, and receptive listening skills. The children were also observed during their free-play periods, and each family kept television log records for a two-week period three times during the year. The findings suggested that the heavy exposure to aggressive and also to rapid-cut content, or to hysterical behavior by adults, may work together to produce aggression in children.

601. Singer, Dorothy G. and Jerome L. Singer. "TV Violence: What's All the Fuss About?" Television and Children, Spring, 1984, pp. 30-41.

A review of the Yale studies which address the impact of TV viewing on aggression in children. The unique characteristics of televised violence are compared with reading a violent scene: in reading about an event, the creation of the image is in the control of the reader. When one sees a violent image on the screen the image intrudes with greater shock as a literal picture, relatively uncontrolled by one's imagination or values. The authors advise that the control of violence on television and aggression in children is a three-pronged responsibility of the television industry; parents who can control the hours and kinds of programs their children watch as well as discuss the programs with them; and educators who can teach about television and use it in the classroom.

602. Singer, Jerome L. "The Influence of Violence Portrayed in Television or Motion Pictures Upon Overt Aggressive Behavior." In Jerome L. Singer (ed.), The Control of Aggression and Violence: Cognitive and Physiological Factors. New York: Academic Press, 1971, pp. 19-60.

An examination of the scientific evidence regarding the effects of observing violence as depicted on film or TV on child and adult viewers. Finds that evidence is not sufficient to warrant a judgment linking increased violence in the U.S. to the portrayal of violence in fiction or news reporting on TV or in the movies. Research, however, does raise the possibility that specific children or adults strongly aroused by some external frustration immediately after viewing violence on TV or in the movies, could imitate some of the aggression seen in the show or film. Existing research is mostly on a small scale that does not and cannot duplicate actual television viewing conditions in the home. Also measures are usually of aggressive play or simulated aggression, not actual aggressive behavior.

603. Singer, Jerome L., Dorothy G. Singer, and Wanda S. Rapaczynski. "Family Patterns and Television Viewing as Predictors of Children's Beliefs and Aggression." Journal of Communication, Vol. 34, No. 2, 1984, pp. 73-89.

This study reflects an effort to examine the ways in which children's family life and television viewing combine to predict aspects of their social interaction patterns and behavior. Preschool children were observed during play periods in 1977, and scored for aggression. In addition, their parents kept logs of their children's television viewing habits. In 1980, 1981, and 1982, interviews with parents were again carried out to obtain data on children's television environments. The data suggested that later aggression by these children was strongly predicted by

a combination of heavier viewing of violent TV shows, preschool
heavy viewing, and a family that emphasized physical discipline
and the assertion of power.

604. Singer, Jerome L. and Dorothy G. Singer. Television, Imagination,
and Aggression: A Study of Preschoolers. Hillsdale, NJ: Erlbaum, 1981.

This study, analyzing the correlation between viewing televised
violence and aggressive behavior among pre-school children,
employed inter-child aggression during several free play periods
over the course of one year as the measure of aggression.
Children's viewing preferences were assessed by use of logs kept
by parents during four test periods. The correlation coefficient
between viewing violence and aggressive behavior was .31 for boys
and .54 for girls, with an average of .35.

605. Singer, Jerome L. and Dorothy G. Singer. "Psychologists Look at
Television: Cognitive, Developmental, Personality, and Social Policy
Implications." American Psychologist, July, 1983, pp. 826-834.

This article points to some issues concerning the continuing
exposure of children to television. A series of studies are
discussed dealing with the structural format and content of
commercial television and the problems that they pose for the
developing child -- the possible influences on cognitive skills,
imagination, beliefs, motor controls, and aggression. The
relationships between family life-style and television viewing by
the child are also considered. The evidence suggests that heavy
viewing of currently available television fare by children may be
harmful.

606. Slater, Dan and William R. Elliott. "Distinguishing Facts from
Fiction: Television's Influence on Adolescents' Knowledge of Law
Enforcement." Paper presented at Eastern Communication Association
Meeting, Ocean City, MD., 1980.

An examination of the effect of TV police/crime programs on
adolescents' knowledge of real-life law enforcement and their
ability to discern the TV "facts" from the real-life facts. A
sample of adolescents were provided a questionaire on viewing
habits and knowledge of real-life law enforcement. The major
finding of the study is that some types of knowledge questions may
be more effective in determining an audience's social reality.
Those items in which respondents were asked to choose from answers
involving numerical or statistical descriptions were not
significant. Questions for which the answer choices involved
"images" produced significant differences among light and heavy
viewers. The influence of television as an instructor of
statistics about law enforcement may not be significant. But the
influence of television's repetitious portrayal of certain police
methods and behaviors may very well impact on audiences' social
reality.

607. Smith, James R. "Television Violence and Driving Behavior." Educational Broadcasting Review, Vol. 3, No. 4, 1969, pp. 23-28.

Data collected from matched groups of 68 "good" and 68 "bad" drivers supports the hypothesis that "bad" drivers have a greater preference for violent TV programming than "good" drivers.

608. Smith, Susan J. "Crime in the News." British Journal of Criminology, Vol. 24, No. 3, 1984, pp. 289-295.

Interview data from a household survey in Birmingham, England and from seven months' content analysis of a Birmingham daily newspaper are used to examine conclusions about crime news presented by Jason Ditton & James Duffy, namely that: 1)the newspaper is a main agent in revealing crime news; 2)some newspapers distort official data on crime; and 3)distortion may cause unrealistic dimensions of fears about crime. Distortion is found in the percentage of types of crimes which actually occur, versus what is reported, and in the unjustified linking of crimes with ethnic minorities.

609. Snow, Robert P. "How Children Interpret TV Violence in Play Context." Journalism Quarterly, Vol. 51, No. 1, 1974, pp. 13-21.

Interviews were conducted with 50 preadolescent children from 4 middle class school districts in Phoenix, Arizona in the summer of 1971. The data revealed that preadolescent children were primarily play oriented in their response to television. Data also suggest that children associate what they define as make-believe or fantastic TV with their play, prefer make-believe over non-play or more serious programs, and do not seem to take make-believe behavior very seriously. With respect to violence, play and non-play appear to be especially important in that violent behavior as defined by adults does not affect the child viewer adversely when it is interpreted within a play context.

610. Somers, Anne R. "Violence, Television and the Health of American Youth." New England Journal of Medicine, Vol. 294, No. 15, 1976, pp. 811-817.

For a considerable portion of American children and youth, the culture of violence is both a major health threat and a way of life. One contributing factor is television's massive daily diet of symbolic crime and violence in entertainment programs.

611. Sprafkin, Joyce, Kenneth D. Gadow and Patricia Grayson. "Effects of Viewing Aggressive Cartoons on the Behavior of Learning Disabled Children." Journal of Child Psychology and Psychiatry, (in press), c. 1987.

Forty-six learning disabled children ($\underline{M}$ = 7.6 years) were exposed to six aggressive and six control cartoons in school. Treatment effects were assessed using direct observations of five categories of social behavior. There were no main effects for condition, and neither initial aggressiveness nor gender interacted significantly with condition for any of the behaviors. There was a significant interaction of condition with IQ; the low IQ group became significantly more physically aggressive following control compared with aggressive cartoons. The results from the present study are compared with the findings from other field experiments, and their clinical relevance is discussed.

612. Stahl, Brian Neal. "Effects of Long-Term Viewing of Television Violence on Cognitive, Physiological, and Behavioral Responses to Real-Life Violence." Dissertation Abstracts International, Vol. 45, No. 11,1984, p. 3658B.

To assess the relationship between viewing TV violence and expectations of others' physical aggression in conflict situations, 431 4th & 5th graders completed a TV frequency survey and a conflict situation heirarchy. Results showed that heavy viewers expected physical aggression more often. A second study assessed the relationship between violence viewing, latency to seek help in the presence of real-life violence, and physiological responses to real-life violence. 19 high- and 20 low violence viewers from the first study were subjects led to believe they alone were responsible for monitoring younger children in another room via camera and TV monitor. Results suggest that increasing levels of TV violence viewing may be related to increased latency to seek help in real-life aggressive situations, but that the relationship may be modest. Heavy violence viewing may not be associated with physiological desensitization to real-life violence. Author strongly suggests further research before conclusions are warranted.

613. Stanley, Paul R. A. and Brian Riera. "Replications of Media Violence." Report of the Royal Commission on Violence in the Communications Industry, Vol. 5, Learning from the Media. Toronto, Canada: The Royal Commission 1977, pp. 57-88.

The authors requested information from the press and police departments in Canada, the United States, and Europe concerning examples of real-life violence that followed distinctive acts of film or television violence. The information gathered supported the high probability that seven specific films included scenes which caused imitative behavior among viewers. This violence is typically demonstrated by juveniles without any particular malicious intent; by groups accepting violence as a norm and seeking novel outlets for violent activity; and by the emotionally disturbed. Factors that increase likelihood of imitation of media violence are cited, such as similarity of circumstances and a readily-identifiable victim.

614. Steuer, Faye B., James M. Applefield, and Rodney Smith.
"Televised Aggression and the Interpersonal Aggression of Preschool
Children." Journal of Experimental Child Psychology, Vol. 11, No. 3,
1971, pp. 442-447.

Two matched groups of five preschool children were exposed to
either aggressive or nonaggressive television programs for a total
of approximately 110 minutes over a period of 11 days.
Interpersonal aggressive behavior immediately following viewing
was recorded and compared with the same type of behavior during a
prior 10-day baseline period. Subjects who viewed aggressive
television programs showed significantly greater increases in
interpersonal aggression from baseline to treatment than did
subjects who viewed nonaggressive programs. Results extended the
generality of the previous finding that children's
noninterpersonal aggressive behavior increased subsesquent to
viewing filmed aggression.

615. Stroman, Carolyn A. and Richard Seltzer. "Media Use and
Perceptions of Crime." Journalism Quarterly, Vol. 62, No. 2, 1985,
pp. 340-345.

Data from a telephone survey of 610 registered voters in 2
counties outside Washington DC provided some support for the
expectation that different media audiences would differ in their
assessment of the causes of crime and their fear of crime. TV
news viewers were more likely to view flaws in the court system as
a major contributory factor to crime; persons relying on
newspapers were more likely to cite poverty. Fear of crime did
not appear to be related to media usage.

616. Suarez, Audelina Tineo de. El Estereotipo del Delincuente en
Venezuela [The Stereotype of the Delinquent in Venezuela]. Facultad de
Derecho, Instituto de Criminologia, Universidad del Zulia, c.1982.

The ways in which formal and informal social control influences
the process of criminalization and the creation of stereotypes are
the focus of this analysis, which outlines a vertical model of
social control incorporating stereotyped depictions in the
national press.

617. Surette, R. (ed.). Justice and the Media: Issues and Research.
Springfield, IL: Charles C. Thomas, 1984.

Within the context of the media's potential to influence both
attitudes and behavior, four conceptual areas of interaction are
reviewed in the papers of this volume: 1)the media and public
attitudes toward crime and justice, 2)the media and criminal and
violent behavior, 3)the media and crime control, and 4)the media
and case processing.

618. Swift, Carolyn F. . "The Prevention of Rape." In Ann Wolbert Burgess (ed.), Rape and Sexual Assault, NY: Garland Publishing, Inc., 1985, pp. 413-426.

   In outlining guidelines for rape prevention, the author elaborates on the potential of the mass media as an educator in prosocial behavior, with the capabilities to educate in a manner which discourages violence and the glorification of violence against women.

619. Tamborini, Ron, James Stiff, and Dolf Zillmann. "Preference for Graphic Horror Featuring Male Versus Female Victimization: Personality and Past Film Viewing Experiences." Human Communication Research, Vol. 14, No. 4, 1987, pp. 529-552.

   After completing several scales measuring personality and past film viewing experiences, subjects ranked their preference for 13 film descriptions containing different degrees of graphic violence. Two versions of the 13 film descriptions differed in that one featured female victimization in 6 films while the second featured male victimization in the same 6 films. Results of regression analyses demonstrate that both the Machiavellian trait of deceit and past exposure to horror films were good predictors of a general preference for graphic horror. For male subjects only, the enjoyment of pornography was a strong predictor of the preference for graphic horror featuring the victimization of women, but not the victimization of men.

620. Tamborini, Ron, Dolf Zillmann, and Jennings Bryant. "Fear and Victimization: Exposure to Television and Perceptions of Crime and Fear." In Robert H. Bostrum (ed.), Communication Yearbook No. 8. Beverly Hills, CA: Sage Publications, 1984, pp. 492-513.

   The results of an experimental study using 56 male and 59 female subjects revealed that (a) perceptions of crime and safety varied along several dimensions, (b) exposure to a television program dealing with crime has a different effect on these perceptions in different dimensions and (c) the immediate effect of such exposure disappears over time. Exposure to a crime documentary and to the injustice-depicting crime drama led to more exaggerated perceptions of crime and fear of assault in urban environments. In addition, watching the injustice-depicting crime drama increased manifest anxiety, whereas viewing the crime documentary elevated fear for one's mate. No effects were found on personal fear or fear of assault in rural environments.

621. Tan, Alexis S. "Social Learning of Aggression from Television." In Jennings Bryant and Dolf Zillman (eds.), Perspectives on Media Effects, Hillsdale, NJ: Lawrence Erlbaum Assoc., Inc., 1986.

Points to a theoretical model of social learning theory as the
most comprehensive in explaining the relationship between
televised violence and subsequent aggression in viewers, and
discusses recent research theories and results in this light.
Explains why and how TV violence is modeled and learned, but also
why the relationship in the real world between violence exposure
and subsequent aggression, though positive and causal, is small.

622. Tannenbaum, Percy H. "Studies in Film- and Television-Mediated
Arousal and Aggression: A Progress Report." In George A. Comstock, Eli
A. Rubinstein, and John P. Murray (eds.), Television and Social
Behavior, Vol. 5, Television's Effects: Further Explorations.
Washington, DC: U.S. Government Printing Office, 1972, pp. 309-350.

A progress report on a research program examing a theoretical
model which posits that many communication messages, such as
erotic or violent materials, can evoke varying degrees of
generalized emotional arousal. Moreover, this arousal has drive
potential and may increase the degree of subsequent behavior an
individual may perform while still aroused. In experiments,
elicited consequences are attributed more to the level of arousal
elicited by the stimulus materials than to aggressive context cues
in the message.

623. Tannenbaum, Percy H. and Dolf Zillmann. "Emotional Arousal in the
Facilitation of Aggression Through Communication." In Leonard
Berkowitz (ed.), Advances in Experimental Social Psychology, Vol. 8.
New York: Academic Press, 1975, pp. 149-192.

A theoretical review of studies outlining basic assumptions of
research on arousal and aggression. The authors discuss the role
of anger, specifically; variations in media content used as a
stimulus of aggression; variations in the arousal response; and
the relationship between emotional and cognitive factors in the
communication process.

624. Tannenbaum, Percy H. and Eleanor P. Gaer. "Mood Change as a
Function of Stress of Protagonist and Degree of Identification in a
Film-Viewing Situation." Journal of Personality and Social Psychology,
Vol. 2, No. 4, 1965, pp. 612-616.

After a period of initial buildup of stress for the protagonist
the ending of a short film was manipulated to represent different
degrees of stress resolution -- a happy ending in which this
stress is reduced, a sad ending in which it is increased, and an
ambiguous ending. A control group received no ending at all.
Subjects exposed to the respective film endings reported
significant degrees of the corresponding stress state. Subjects
identifying more with the hero experienced significantly more
stress induction than those identifying less. The same tendency
-- more of the corresponding stress state within a condition in
high vs. low identifiers -- existed in the stress resolution
phase, although the difference was significant only in the
happy-ending condition.

173

625. Taylor, Henry and Carol Dozier. "Television Violence, African-Americans, and Social Control: 1950-1976." Journal of Black Studies, Vol. 14, No. 2, 1983, pp. 107-136.

To determine how television might shape audiences' perceptions of violence and the law-enforcement system, television series between 1950 and 1976 with law-enforcement personnel as heroes and/or other violent themes were examined. Violence is systematically presented within a framework which suggests that people have an unquestioned moral and/or legal right to use violence, including deadly force, to protect the status quo. In particular, black characters in violent TV programs are generally portrayed as policemen or collaborators with the law enforcement system who are projected as superheroes and social role models for black youth.

626. Teevan, James J., Jr. and Timothy F. Hartnagel. "The Effect of Television Violence on the Perceptions of Crime by Adolescents." Sociology and Social Research, Vol. 60, No. 3, 1976, pp. 337-348.

Secondary analysis of data reported by McIntyre et al. (1972), testing television's cultivation of perceptions of crime rates and behavior related to these perceptions. Exposure to TV violence did not influence adolescents' perception of the amount of crime in real life. Aggressive behavior was only weakly related to viewing of violence on TV, even among those who perceived TV programs as violent and those who perceived violence in drama as effective in achieving a goal. The authors conclude that television plays only a small part in influencing adolescents' perceptions and behavior related to crime.

627. Thomas, Margaret Hanratty and Ronald S. Drabman. "Toleration of Real-Life Aggression as a Function of Exposure to Televised Violence and Age of Subject." Merrill-Palmer Quarterly, Vol. 21, No. 3, 1975, pp. 227-232.

A replication of the Drabman and Thomas study (1974) incorporating a group of younger children in the sample and employing an excerpt of a television detective series on a TV monitor as a stimulus. The earlier finding was supported among eight-year-old subjects--those who viewed violent action were slower to seek adult assistance in stopping what appeared as real-life violence or made no response at all. The authors propose three explanations for the results: media depictions of violence convey the idea that such behavior is normal; real-life violence is trivial in comparison; and emotional reaction to real violence is reduced as a result of prior media experience.

628. Thomas, Margaret Hanratty, Robert W. Horton, Elaine C. Lippincott, and Ronald S. Drabman. "Desensitization to Portrayals of Real-Life Aggression as a Function of Exposure to Television Violence." Journal of Personality and Social Psychology, Vol. 35, No. 6, 1977, pp. 450-458.

In two separate experiments, the hypothesis that exposure to violence in the context of television drama decreases subjects' emotional responsivity to portrayals of real-life aggression was tested. Subjects were shown either an excerpt from a violent police drama or a segment of an exciting but nonviolent volleyball game before watching a videotaped scene of real aggression. Emotionality was measured continuosuly by changes in skin resistance. In Experiment 1, subjects were 8- to 10-year-old children and the real aggression was a film of an argument and fight between two preschoolers. In Experiment 2, college students participated and reactions to real aggression were measured while subjects watched scenes from news films of the riots at the 1968 Democratic National Convention. With the exception of adult females, subjects who previously had viewed the aggressive drama were less aroused by the scenes of real aggression than were subjects who had seen the control film. Further support for the hypothesis was provided by the finding that for most groups of subjects, the amount of television violence normally viewed was negatively related to responsivity while viewing aggression.

629. Thomson, R. J. Television Crime-Drama: Its Impact on Children and Adolescents. Melbourne, Australia: F. W. Cheshire, 1959.

Australian teenagers viewed two crime dramas. Facial expressions indicated a buildup of tension; but behavioral response afterward revealed no increase in aggression or fear. Constant exposure to media violence is more likely to result in insensitivity or stereotyped reactions than in delinquent or criminal behavior.

630. Thomson, R. J. Television Crime Drama: A Report. Canberra: Australian Broadcasting Control Board, 1972.

Research conducted in 1958-59 on psychological effects of television crime/action drama on Australian teenagers employed pre- and post-exposure measures based on subjects' identification with film characters. The project was designed to assess the degree to which subjects who identify with a protagonist punished for unjustified aggression experience guilt and anxiety; the effect of uncertain perception of a character's motives; and the effect of repeated exposure to such media content. Teenagers with considerable previous experience to "high stress" crime films appeared to experience less anxiety in response to such films than did teenagers with more limited previous exposure. This was explained as a function of "film insight." High-tension films affected anxiety strongly, regardless of film type.

631. Thornton, W. and L. Voigt. "Television and Delinquency: A Neglected Dimension of Social Control." Youth & Society, Vol. 15, No. 4, 1984, pp. 445-468.

Self-report questionnaires were administered to students from
grades four through twelve, to measure delinquency, social control
and media variables. Using correlation and multiple regression,
moderate to strong positive relationships were found between
preference for violent television programming and each type of
delinquency. Negative relationships were found between amount of
weekday viewing and certain types of delinquency, with no
relationship between weekend viewing and any type of delinquency.
Regression analysis indicated, however, that the impact of select
family, school and peer factors exert a stronger influence on
delinquency than do key media variables.

632. Townsend, Richard B. "Investigation into the Relationship Between
Disciplinary Experiences, Television Viewing and Social Violence."
Dissertation Abstracts International, Vol. 45, No. 1,1983, p. 407B.

This study, based on a population of 151 male undergraduates,
looks at the relationship between reported disciplinary
experiences, past & present TV viewing, and the levels of violence
reported in the lives of young adults. The study then looks for
indications of physiological desensitization to scenes of
violence, based on heart rate reactivity to a videotaped boxing
dramatization. Findings indicate that 11 percent of subjects
report bruising or other injuries from parents; 3 percent report
never having been physically punished. All report relatively
similar TV viewing as children. ANOVA indicates groups differing
in severity of discipline, and groups differing in frequency of
discipline, differ in present amount of violence in their lives.
Groups did not differ on heart rate response to the boxing scene.
Regression analysis found that disciplinary effects and TV effects
were largely additive in predicting social violence scores.

633. Tumber, Howard. Television and the Riots. London: British Film
Institute Publishing, 1982.

An investigation of British television's coverage of the 1981
riots in a number of inner-city areas within Mainland Britain.
News bulletins between July 3 and July 16 were content analyzed to
assess systematically the amount and type of news devoted to riot
coverage, the location of the report, how rioters were described,
and causes given for the disturbances. There is no convincing
evidence to support claims that television coverage of acts of
violence such as riots incites further acts of violence.

634. Tyler, Tom R. "Impact of Directly and Indirectly Experienced
Events: The Origin of Crime-Related Judgments and Behaviors." Journal
of Personality and Social Psychology, Vol. 39, No. 1, 1980, pp. 13-28.

Two studies of residents of several urban areas in the United
States measured direct experience with crime, including assault
and forceful robbery, and indirect experience with crime (learned
about through reports by others or through various media).
Attitudes concerning the overall crime rate and perceived personal
vulnerability were measured. Analysis revealed two independent

levels of response to crime--general and personal. Estimates of
overall crime rate were determined solely by indirect experience.
Personal vulnerability appeared to be influenced by both direct
and indirect experience and was strongly related to
crime-prevention behavior.

635. UNESCO. The Effects of Television on Children and Adolescents: An
Annotated Bibliography with an Introductory Overview of Research
Results. Paris: UNESCO, 1964.

This bibliography focuses on several aspects of children and
television, including effects of violent content. The overview
presents the conclusion that television is not the sole cause of
asocial behavior among children generally, and there is no
documentation that it reduces aggression vicariously. At most,
televised violence contributes to delinquent behavior among
maladjusted and other delinquency-prone children.

636. United States Government Hearings. Senate Committee on the
Judiciary, Subcommittee to Investigate Juvenile Delinquency.
Washington, DC, 1964.

Staff studies conducted in 1954, 1961, and 1964 revealed that the
extent to which violence and crime were portrayed on television
was clearly excessive. It was also noted that "in the face of
repeated warnings from officials directly concerned with coping
with juvenile delinquency and from competent researchers that this
kind of television fare can be harmful to the young viewer, the
television industry generally has shown little disposition to
substantially reduce the degree of violence to which it exposes
the American public."

637. United States Government. "Commission Statement on Violence in
Television Entertainment Programs." National Commission on the Causes
and Prevention of Violence (Eisenhower Commission). See also Robert
K. Baker and Sandra J. Ball, Mass Media and Violence Vol. 9 (a Staff
Report to the Commission). Washington, DC: U.S. Government Printing
Office, 1969, 1969.

The Commission's interpretation of the research they sponsored led
to their conclusion that television violence can be imitated by
children to the extent that they identify with characters and that
the portrayed behaviors are perceived as justified and effective
in a situation. Young children, new to the television experience,
are particularly vulnerable to this effect. The Commission
suggested that the industry eliminate violent cartoons and reduce
the time given to violent programs; that the context of portrayed
violence be altered; and that research be conducted on effects.
The Commission also recommended parental supervision of child
viewers and public contacts with television stations.

177

638. United States Government. <u>Television and Growing Up</u>: The Impact of Televised Violence (Report to the Surgeon General), U.S. Public Health Service). See also George A. Comstock, Eli A. Rubinstein, and John P. Murray (eds.) <u>Television and Social Behavior</u> (Technical Reports to the Surgeon General's Scientific Advisory Committee, 5 Vols.) Washington, DC: U.S. Government Printing Office, 1972.

Summary of 23 research projects, including both lab and field studies, funded by the U.S. Government, to examine the effects of televised violence The Surgeon General's Advisory Committee concluded that the majority of findings supported the view that, under certain conditions, television violence causes aggressive behavior among children predisposed to aggressiveness. The number of children so affected remained to be determined.

639. United States Government. "Violence on Television." Report. House of Representatives. Washington, DC: U.S. Government Printing Office, 1977.

Subcommittee findings from hearings regarding the role of mass media in creating a climate which may lead to violent behavior in society. A history of Congressional action in this area is provided, followed by conclusions and recommendations regarding violent portrayal on TV. Dissenting views of some representatives follow, suggesting that the report is too hesitant in its conclusions of adverse effects, and does not place sufficient blame on the television industry.

640. United States Government. <u>Television and Behavior: Ten Years of Scientific Progress and Implications for the Eighties</u>. Vol. 1, <u>Summary Report</u>. See also David Pearl, Lorraine Bouthilet, and Joyce Lazar (eds.), Vol. 2, <u>Technical Reviews</u>. Rockville, MD: National Institute of Mental Health, 1982.

A brief account of the U.S. Government's interest in televised violence and its effects on the public. Summarizes trends in violent content, results of research dealing with effects on behavior and attitudes, and the cultivation of conceptions of violence and mistrust. Methodological issues such as definition and unitization of violence are outlined. A description of the Cultural Indicators Project and a useful bibliography are included.

641. van der Voort, Tom H. A. <u>Kinderen en TV-geweld: Waarneming en beleving</u> [Children and TV Violence: Perception and Experience]. Lisse: Swets & Zeitlinger, 1982.

This study examined the way children between the ages of 9 and 12 perceive and experience violent television drama. The first phase investigated how children perceive violent films, how the perception variables interrelate, and the underlying dimensions. A follow-up study established how the perception dimensions are related to the children's aggressiveness.

642. van der Voort, Tom H. A. "Television Violence: Child's Eye View." Advances in Psychology, Vol. 32, Amsterdam: North-Holland, 1986.

The author discusses TV violence effects with a focus on intervening variables, and proposes a curriculum to intervene and curtail the antisocial influence of television violence. The author discusses perception and experience of real and fanciful programs, and proposes hypotheses then tested and reported, which focus on how children perceive different types of violent programming and the relation of the perception dimension to children's aggressiveness.

643. Viemero, Vappa. Relationships Between Filmed Violence and Aggression. Reports from the Department of Psychology at Abo Akademi, Monograph Supplement 4, 1986.

A total of 220 subjects, originally seven and nine year old boys and girls took part in this eight year longitudinal study on the effects of television and video watching on viewers. The subjects were investigated six times and their parents twice during the course of the study. The study was conducted between 1978 and 1985 in Turku, Finland. There were positive, often statistically significant, relationships between violence viewing and aggression in all phases of the study. The amount of viewing, however, was rather unimportant for viewers' aggression. The analyses supported the assumption that a causal relationship exists between violence viewing and aggression so that extensive violence viewing significantly predicts later aggression. Both boys' and girls' aggression was affected by violence viewing. The effect of violence viewing was most clearly observed in the originally least aggressive subjects.

644. Wakshlag, Jacob J., Leonard Bart, John Dudley, Gary Groth, John McCutcheon, and Cheryl Rolla. "Viewer Apprehension About Victimization and Crime Drama Programs." Communication Research, Vol. 10, No. 2, 1983, pp. 195-217.

Sixty-one college students, assigned to high- or low-apprehension conditions viewed two different versions of a televised crime drama program, one in which the antagonist was shot, the other in which the protagonist was shot. Physiological responses indicated that apprehensive viewers reacted more intensely to the program than their less apprehensive counterparts. Also, apprehensive viewers found the antagonist to be more reprehensible than their less apprehensive counterparts. There were no significant differences in physiological response to noncrime content seen by the same subjects.

645. Walker, Merle R. "The Effects of Video Games and TV/Film Violence on Subsequent Aggression in Male Adolescents." Dissertation Abstracts International, Vol. 46, No. 6,1984, p. 2082B.

Study compared effects on subsequent aggression of viewing a violent TV film, with playing a home video game in 60 late adolescent boys who had been angered. Anger was provoked in these 18-19 year olds by insulting the subjects' performance, and aggression was studied in terms of resistance to interference from stress, expressed feelings of hostility, personality traits of aggressiveness and hostility, and manifestations of aggression. Major study predictions were not supported by the data. The anger manipulation, the neutral film and the measure of aggression were discussed as possible explanation for lack of significant results.

646. Walters, R. and E. Thomas. "Enhancement of Punitiveness by Visual and Audiovisual Displays." Canadian Journal of Psychology, Vol. 17, 1963, pp. 244-255.

A series of experiments in which young adult men and women who were not previously angered or frustrated were shown either a violent clip or neutral film of the same length and were then asked to administer electric shocks to another "subject." The subjects who saw the violent clips administered significantly higher intensity and greater duration shocks to the "subject" than those who did not see the violent stimulus.

647. Warr, Mark. "The Accuracy of Public Beliefs About Crime." Social Forces, Vol. 59, No. 2, 1980, pp. 456-470.

A statistical test is applied to measure the degree and nature of distortion in public opinion concerning amount of specific types of crime. Data from four independent surveys during 1974-1975 on amount of crime and attitudes about personal vulnerability in a southwestern U.S. metropolitan area were compared to official statistics for 1973-1974. Respondents overestimated the official incidence of the least frequent offenses (such as murder and aggravated assault) and underestimated the official incidence of the most frequent offenses (such as theft and simple assault). However, the ranking of crimes in order of frequency of occurrence was generally similar.

648. Warren, Donald I. "Mass Media and Racial Crisis: A Study of the New Bethel Church Incident in Detroit." Journal of Social Issues, Vol. 28, No. 1, 1972, pp. 111-131.

An analysis of immediate and longer-term perceptions of residents in black and white neighborhoods concerning a 1969 racial incident in which a policeman was killed, several people were wounded, and over 100 people were arrested. Different media sources of information were associated with different perceptual processes, moving toward either consensus or polarization. Personal sources of information as well as media sources created polarization of certain perceptions between blacks and whites.

649. Watt, James H., Jr. and Robert Krull. "An Examination of Three Models of Television Viewing and Aggression." Human Communication Research, Vol. 3, No. 2, 1977, pp. 99-112.

Secondary analysis of data collected by McLeod et al. for the 1972 Surgeon General's Report (U.S.) tested three psychological models of response to TV violence: facilitation (leading to imitation of behavior by providing cues), catharsis (release of emotion through vicarious experience), and arousal (physiological changes channeled into some form of behavior). Catharsis was not supported by this analysis. The facilitation model received marginal support among male adolescents. Arousal theory was supported among females. Age was an important factor influencing male response; it was not so important for females.

650. Weaver, James and Jacob Wakshlag. "Perceptions of Personal Vulnerability to Crime, Criminal Victimization Experience, and Television Viewing." Paper presented to the Broadcast Education Association, Las Vegas, Nevada., 1984.

Questionnaires were completed by 108 students at a midwestern U.S. university to assess the relationship between television viewing and perceptions of personal crime. The analysis revealed that the strength and direction of these associations are contingent upon the viewer's level of experientially obtained information about criminal victimization, the type of prime-time television programs viewed, and the nature of the vulnerability to crime being considered.

651. Weigel, Russell H. and Richard Jessor. "Television and Adolescent Conventionality." Public Opinion Quarterly, Vol. 37, No. 1, 1973, pp. 76-90.

Questionnaires were used to assess television involvement and the conventionality of high school and college students, to test the hypothesis that television reinforces the values of a white, upper- middle-class society in the United States. Involvement was an index of variables such as amount of exposure and perceived importance and influence of television. Values and attitudes analyzed included independence of decision-making; attitudes concerning deviance, drug use, and religion; and liberal/conservative orientation. Actual drug use, deviance, and activism also were analyzed. The hypothesis was supported with statistical significance for approximately half of the comparisons, with a stronger relationship among college males and among high school students.

652. Weimann, Gabriel. "The Theater of Terror: Effects of Press Coverage." Journal of Communication, Vol. 33, No. 1,1983, pp. 38-45.

An examination of the effects of press coverage of terrorist events on readers' attitudes regarding the terrorists. Semantic differential scales were used to measure evaluative attitudes before and after 80 students read press clippings describing 2 separate terrorist events. Comparison of the scores before and after exposure shows exposure did tend to enhance the evaluations of the terrorists. Shifts in evaluation were found on several image dimensions, mostly toward a more positive evaluation than before exposure. Thus, the important function of media coverage as the theater of terror is highlighted. Staging a terrorist event that will attract the mass media will, in turn, guarantee worldwide awareness and recognition.

653. Wertham, Fredric C. Seduction of the Innocent. New York: Rinehart, 1954.

The most complete treatise on Wertham's position concerning the effects of comic books on children. He argues that comic books, at their worst, turn children into dangerous juvenile delinquents, and at their best give children a distorted view of the world.

654. Whaley, A. Bennet, Edmund P. Kaminski, William I. Gorden, and D. Ray Heisey. "Docudrama From Different Temporal Perspectives: Reactions to NBC's 'Kent State'." Journal of Broadcasting, Vol. 27, No. 3, 1983, pp. 285-289.

An examination of the reactions of three groups of subjects to the NBC docudrama, "Kent State." The subjects were faculty and staff members who were at the university during the time of the actual events and students currently enrolled at Kent State. Questionnaires were used to assess believability and objectivity of the program. Results indicated correspondence between the faculty and student views of the believability of the docudrama compared to the staff evaluation. Similarity in believability scores existed despite the fact that the students were separated from the event by more than ten years and had no firsthand knowledge of what happened on May 4, 1970.

655. Wiegman, O. "Aanstekelijkheid van gedrag." [Research Study of the Effect of Puppet Film Violence on Young Children]. In Arnold P. Goldstein and Marshall H. Segall (eds.) Aggression in Global Perspective. New York: Pergamon Press, 1975.

Four- and six-year-old Dutch children saw an aggressive, a prosocial, or a neutral puppet show on film. The children could then choose to frighten or to entertain another child by choosing a witch or a rabbit mask. Aggressive behavior increased by one-third after the aggressive film but decreased by two-thirds after viewing the prosocial film.

656. Wiegman, O., M. Kuttschreuter, and B. Baarda. Television Viewing Related to Aggressive and Prosocial Behaviour. The Hague, The Netherlands: Stichting voor onderzoek van het onderwijs, 1986.

A report of the results of a Dutch survey about the effects of viewing violence on television on the behavior of children. Aggressive behavior was found to be positively related to the viewing of violence on television. There was, however, as much evidence for the hypothesis that the viewing of violence leads to aggression, as for the hypothesis that aggression leads to more television violence viewing.

657. Williams, Tannis Macbeth. The Impact of Television: A Natural Experiment in Three Communities. New York: Academic Press, Inc, 1986.

Report of a natural experiment on the impact of television in three communities -- one that started with no television (Notel), one with one station (Unitel), and one with multiple stations (Multitel). A general conclusion was that television affects viewers negatively in a variety of areas via displacement. Television also affects its viewers more directly; the content of television may serve as a teacher, especially in regard to children's beliefs about appropriate behavior for boys and girls. Finally the effects of television have more to do with its presence versus absence than whether one channel of CBHC or four channels, including the three major U.S. networks, are available. The differences between Notel and the other towns were more consistent and tended to be greater than the differences between Unitel and Multitel.

658. Wilson, Bryan. "Mass Media and the Public Attitude to Crime." Criminal Law Review, June, 1961, pp. 376-384.

An examination of the persuasive function of mass media in terms of attention to specific topics, diffusion of ideas, instilling of fantasies, and tolerance of deviance. The author provides examples of hostile acts inspired by the dramatic publicity given to previous, similar incidents, which can act as an incentive. Such publicity can affect public opinion about crime more than the specific crimes.

659. Wilson, Wayne and Randy Hunter. "Movie-inspired Violence." Psychological Reports, Vol. 53(2), Oct. , 1983, pp. 435-441.

A compilation of 58 incidents of alleged movie-inspired violence from 1970 through 1982 produced findings dominated by male victims and handguns. To structure a causal connection between pretend and real violence, authors propose a 3-step standard of identification, perseveration of beliefs and execution of those beliefs.

660. Withey, Stephen B. and Ronald P. Abeles. Television and Social Behavior: Beyond Violence and Children. Hillsdale, NJ: Erlbaum, 1980.

This collection of essays examines a number of issues relating to television that go beyond the obvious focus on violence and children. It presents reports of study groups organized by the Committee on Television and Social Behavior, including one on the need for developing and using indicators of televised violence (a violence profile).

661. Wober, J. Mallory. "Televised Violence and Paranoid Perception: The View From Great Britain." Public Opinion Quarterly, Vol. 42, 1978, pp. 315-321.

This research tested cultivation of viewer fear/mistrust in a representative sample of 1113 adults over the age of 16 in the United Kingdom. Diaries were used to assess viewing during one week in 1976. Interview data provided a two-item index of security (fear of being a victim of violence and interpersonal mistrust). Heavy viewers of violence were not more fearful than light viewers. The author suggests a socio-cultural difference in results of cultivation studies in different countries or the influence of an intervening variable.

662. Wober, J. Mallory,. "Broadcasting and The Conflict In Ireland: Viewers' Opinions Of Two Series, And Their Context." Manuscript, 1981.

A study of viewers' evaluations of two Irish television series, The Troubles, and Ireland: A Television History, both historical and political accounts of Ireland and Northern Ireland. The survey assessed the significance of these two series for the audience, and explored the programs' roles in the formation of impressions of life in Ireland. The two series were both positively evaluated overall. Protestant viewers in Northern Ireland were less likely than Catholics to have considered the series accurate and were more likely to believe that it might encourage violence. Overall, however, the idea that either series might encourage violence was rejected.

663. Wober, Mallory and Barrie Gunter. "Television and Personal Threat: Fact or Artifact? A British Survey." British Journal of Social Psychology, Vol. 21, 1982, pp.239-247.

Analysis of diaries and opinion questionnaires from 322 viewers in the United Kingdom supported the hypothesis that a more general, deep-seated personality factor underlies both TV viewing and attitudes measured by the fear/mistrust variable. This personality factor ("locus of control") relates to subjects' belief in mastery by the self as opposed to belief in fate.

664. Wurtzel, Alan and Guy Lometti. "Researching Television Violence: Television at the Crossroads." Society, Vol. 21, No. 6, 1984, pp. 22-30.

In this paper, two members of the ABC Network's Social Research Unit provide detailed analysis of the 1982 National Institutes of Mental Health (NIMH) report, Television and Behavior: Ten Years of Scientific Progress and Implications for the Future, concerning the relationship between television violence and aggressive behavior and social attitudes. The authors argue that the NIMH findings do not support the conclusion of a causal relationship between tv violence and aggressive behavior, that there is not a clear consensus among most researchers in this regard, that there has been a decrease in the overall amount of television violence in recent years, and that the research does not support the conclusion that TV significantly cultivates viewer attitudes and perceptions of social reality. Also included is a summary of ABC Broadcast standards and practices, policies and procedures, which are the network guidelines to ensure responsible handling when depicting violence in entertainment programming.

665. Wurtzel, Alan. "Television Violence and Aggressive Behavior." Et Cetera, June, 1977, pp. 212-225.

Review of research on television violence and aggression. Touches on definitions and measures, types of studies, and three categories of findings (no effect, catharsis, stimulation).

666. Yaffe, Maurice and Edward C. Nelson (eds.). The Influence of Pornography on Behavior. New York: Academic Press, 1982.

A collection of papers that presents a broad perspective on obscenity and pornography, including chapters focusing upon aggression and pornography.

667. Zillmann, Dolf and Jacob Wakshlag. "Fear of Victimization and the Appeal of Crime Drama." In Dolf Zillman and Jennings Bryant (eds.) Selective Exposure to Communication. Hillsdale, NJ: Erlbaum, 1985.

A review of research addressing the association between fear of crime and viewing crime drama. Overall, it is noted that apprehension can foster increased selective exposure. The most signficant variable in this relationship is portrayal of justice or injustice. Drama that features the restoration of justice after the commission of crime holds great appeal for crime-apprehensive persons. The research provides some evidence that crime-apprehensive viewers find crime drama more exciting than do other viewers; their emotional responses to drama, including enjoyment of favorable resolutions, are more intense.

668. Zillmann, Dolf and Jennings Bryant. "Effects of Massive Exposure to Pornography." In Neil M. Malamuth and Edward Donnerstein (eds.), Pornography and Sexual Aggression. Orlando, FL: Academic Press, 1984, pp. 115-138.

Almost all experimentation to date concerning the consequences of massive exposure to pornography has concentrated on the effects on aggression directly subsequent to erotic stimulation. A two-component model of erotica effects on motivated aggressive behavior is proposed, modified to incorporate behavioral response changes which occur as a result of repeated exposure. The methodology employed in prolonged-exposure work is summarized and the research findings reported. Numerous non-transitory effects of massive exposure on the perception of sexuality and on sex-related dispositions are reported. Further understanding of the nature and consequences of these effects is predicated upon conducting longitudinal investigations.

669. Zillmann, Dolf. "Excitation Transfer on Communication-Mediated Aggressive Behavior." Journal of Experimental Social Psychology, Vol. 7, No. 4, 1971, pp. 419-434.

An experimental test of the amount of influence of emotional arousal apart from violent content. Angered male subjects were exposed to neutral (non-arousing), aggressive (moderately arousing), or erotic (highly arousing but non-aggressive) films. Erotic material produced the most aggressive response (measured by the apparent administration of electrical shock to the provoker). The effect of the aggressive film was midway between that of the erotic and the neutral film.

670. Zillmann, Dolf. "Television Viewing and Arousal." In David Pearl, Lorraine Bouthilet, and Joyce Lazar (eds.), Television and Social Behavior, Vol. 2, Technical Reports. Rockville, MD: National Institute of Mental Health, 1982, pp. 53-67.

A review of research in the field of psychology extending the examination of observational learning of aggression from media portrayal to account for an existing physiological state of arousal. Certain TV fare can increase, perpetuate, or reduce level of arousal of viewers. Some behavioral effects are due to this excitatory effect regardless of content. Research on emotional habituation to violence is discussed, along with what appears to be a contradiction between media cultivation effect research (which supports a positive relationship between viewing and attitudes such as fear of crime/victimization) and behavior modification theory (which supports a negative relationship between media exposure and certain phobias).

671. Zillmann, Dolf, James L. Hoyt, and Kenneth D. Day. "Strength and Duration of the Effect of Aggressive, Violent, and Erotic Communications on Subsequent Aggressive Behavior." Communication Research, Vol. 1, No. 3, 1974, pp. 286-306.

An investigation of the effect of exposure to a neutral, an aggressive, a violent or an erotic communication on provoked individuals. The effect of erotic communication significantly exceeded those of all other types, yielding more intense aggressiveness. Measures of excitatory changes correlated highly with those of measured aggressiveness; the excitation-transfer paradigm was employed to account for this phenomenon.

672. Zillmann, Dolf, Richard T. Hezel, and Norman J. Medoff. "The Effect of Affective States on Selected Exposure to Televised Entertainment Fare." Journal of Applied Social Psychology, Vol. 10, No. 4, 1980, pp. 323-339.

Subjects were experimentally placed in a negative, positive, or neutral emotional state and were then either exposed to particular types of television programs or not exposed. Subjects in a negative state avoided hostile comedy over a ten-minute test period, while those in a positive emotional state were more likely to prefer action drama. Findings supported the hypothesis that viewers select media content that promises the most immediate relief from a negative affective state.

673. Zillmann, Dolf, Rolland C. Johnson, and John Hanrahan. "Pacifying Effect of Happy Ending of Communications Involving Aggression." Psychological Reports, Vol. 32, 1973, pp. 967-970.

An aggression-involving communication was manipulated such that, with the total duration and amount of aggression displayed held constant, one version depicted a typical happy ending and the other version did not. In a pretest, the happy ending significantly reduced excitation and thus induced relaxation. Subjects were aggravated by a confederate, exposed to one of the two versions of the communication, and then given an opportunity to retaliate against their earlier tormentor. Aggressive behavior, as measured in the intensity of ostensibly delivered electric shock, was significantly lower after exposure to the communication with the happy ending.

Pornography and the Media

674. Abramson, Paul R. and Haruo Hayashi. "Pornography in Japan: Cross-Cultural and Theoretical Considerations." In Neil M. Malamuth and Edward Donnerstein (eds.), <u>Pornography and Sexual Aggression</u>. Orlando, FL: Academic Press, 1984, pp. 173-183.

   A review of Japanese pornography and a discussion of differences in comparison to American pornography. Important differences are the degree to which pornographic material is available and the level of consistency in media presentations of sexuality. The relatively low frequency of rape in Japan is striking, given the existence of abundant rape stimuli within the society. The cross-cultural variations are accounted for by a difference in emphasis on internal and external restraints on individual behavior. A number of policy directions for the United States are proposed.

675. Beattie, Earle. "Magazines and Violence." <u>Report of the Royal Commission on Violence in the Communications Industry</u>, Vol. 4, <u>Violence in Print and Music</u>. Toronto, Canada: The Royal Commission, 1977.

   Violence was a significant element in a cross-section of magazines, including family magazines. Police file magazines were a particularly violent medium, featuring beatings and torture. Men's and women's magazines blend violence, sex, and stereotyping in ways that dehumanize and set the stage for violent conflict.

676. Commission on Obscenity and Pornography. <u>The Report of the Commission on Obscenity and Pornography</u>, New York: Bantam Books, 1970.

   Congressional commission conclusions which indicate no support for contentions that pornography has antisocial effects. Almost excluded from the study were stimuli that involved rape or other forms of coercive sexuality. When the commission conducted its research studies in 1967, aggressive-pornographic materials were relatively infrequent.

189

677. Court, John H. "Correlational and Cross-Cultural Studies on Pornography and Aggression." In Neil M. Malamuth and Edward Donnerstein (eds.), Pornography and Sexual Aggression. Orlando, FL: Academic Press, 1984, pp. 143-172.

The possibility of a negative correlation between the availability of pornography and the incidence of sexual offenses was widely accepted in the 1970s; this position now lacks experimental support. Porno-violence is identified as a subcategory of pornography which is especially powerful in its potential to generate antisocial sexual behavior and attitudes. Experimental work suggests that porno-violence directly affects specific types of response and attitude change. In other respects, a ripple effect (propagation of a hostile, exploitive view of women) is believed to occur. The containment of porno-violence, especially in view of the increasing exposure of young people to pornography, is advocated.

678. Donnerstein, Edward and Daniel Linz. "Mass Media, Sexual Violence and Male Viewers." American Behavioral Scientist, Vol. 29, No. 5, 1986, pp. 601-618.

The authors examine the research on aggressive pornography and the research that examines nonpornographic media images of violence against women, the major focus of recent research and the material that provokes negative reactions. The final section examines the research on nonviolent pornography. There is no evidence for any harm related effects from sexually explicit materials, but the research does support potential harm effects from aggressive materials.

679. Donnerstein, Edward and Leonard Berkowitz. "Victim Reactions in Aggressive Erotic Films as a Factor in Violence Against Women." Journal of Personality and Social Psychology, Vol. 41, No. 4, 1981, pp. 710-724.

An investigation of how the behavioral characteristics of the people in erotic films and the nature of the targets available for later aggression can affect subsequent aggression. Eighty male subjects were angered by a male or female confederate. They were then shown a neutral film or one of three erotic films. The erotic films differed in terms of their aggressive content and the reactions of the female victim. Subjects were then allowed to aggress against the confederate via electric shock. Results indicated that the films had no effect on male targets whereas both types of aggressive erotic films increased aggression toward the female.

680. Donnerstein, Edward and Neil Malamuth. "Pornography: Its Consequences On The Observer." In L. Schlesinger and E. Revitch (eds.), Sexual Dynamics of Anti-Social Behavior. Springfield, IL: C. C. Thomas, 1983.

A review of research dealing with the relationship between aggressive erotica and violence against women. The authors find highly consistent data which indicate that exposure to aggressive forms of pornography can change attitudes concerning violence against women and increase the probability that male subjects will overtly aggress against females.

681. Donnerstein, Edward. "Aggressive Erotica and Violence Against Women." Journal of Personality and Social Psychology, Vol. 39, No. 2, 1980, pp. 269-277.

In an examination of the effects of aggressive-erotic stimuli on male aggression toward females, 120 male subjects were angered or treated in a neutral manner by a male or female confederate. Subjects were then shown either a neutral, erotic, or aggressive-erotic film and given an opportunity to aggress against the confederate via the delivery of electric shock. Results indicated that the aggressive-erotic film was effective in increasing aggression overall, and it produced the highest increase in aggression against the female. Even non-angered subjects showed an increase in aggression toward the female after viewing the aggressive-erotic film.

682. Donnerstein, Edward. "Pornography and Violence Against Women: Experimental Studies." Annals of the New York Academy of Sciences, Vol. 347, 1980, pp. 277-288.

A review of experimental research on pornography and violence against women. While research has been directed at the effects of erotic media presentations on behavior, the issue of whether such presentations can in some manner be related to increased aggressive attacks against women has been only recently of concern. It is generally believed by a large proportion of the population that many sexual materials can precipitate violent sexual crimes.

683. Donnerstein, Edward. "Aggressive Pornography: Can It Influence Aggression toward Women?" In C. Albee, S. Gordon, and H. Leitenberg (eds.), Promoting Sexual Responsibility and Preventing Sexual Problems. Hanover, NH:, 1983.

This paper examines recent research on the effects of aggressive pornography and subsequent aggression toward women. The author suggests that nonaggressive erotic or pornographic images have really no measurable effect on aggression toward women; it is only the aggressive forms that seem to produce negative effects.

684. Donnerstein, Edward. "Erotica and Human Aggression." In Russell G. Geen and Edward Donnerstein (eds.), Aggression: Theoretical and Empirical Reviews, Vol. 2. New York: Academic Press, 1983.

A review of research on the subject of the effects of erotica on human aggression. It is acknowledged that research strongly supports the position that exposure to certain types of erotica can actually reduce aggressive responses in people who are predisposed to aggress. The differing aspects of erotic material -- arousing versus nonarousing, pleasing versus disturbing -- all seem to affect the way in which individuals respond to the material.

685. Donnerstein, Edward. "Pornography: Its Effect on Violence Against Women." In Neil M. Malamuth and Edward Donnerstein (eds.), Pornography and Sexual Aggression. Orlando, FL: Academic Press, 1984, pp. 53-81.

Overview of research reveals that it is difficult to make a straightforward definitive conclusion about the relationship between pornography and aggression toward women. Certain types of pornography can influence aggression and other asocial attitudes and behaviors toward women; others, especially nonaggressive pornography, do not. The aggressive content of pornography is the main contributor to violence against women.

686. Dziki, Sylwester, Janina Maczuga, and Walery Pisarek (eds.). World Directory of Mass Communication Researchers. Cracow, 1984.

An international listing of mass communication researchers.

687. Eysenck, Hans J. and D. K. B. Nias. Sex, Violence and the Media. New York: Harper and Row, 1978.

A comprehensive review of research relating to the effects of media violence in both the United States and the United Kingdom. Examines the possible influence viewing and reading overtly pornographic and violent material may have on behavior. It examines the methodology used in this area of research and the results of field and experimental field studies, and laboratory experiments. Evidence indicates that media violence increases viewer aggression, and perhaps viewer sexual libido; that effects of pornography, while variable, cannot be disputed; and that the portrayal of violence in media can incite some viewers to violence.

688. George, W. H. and G. A. Marlatt. "The Effects of Alcohol and Anger on Interest in Violence, Erotica and Deviance." Journal of Abnormal Psychology, Vol. 95, No. 2, 1986, pp. 150-158.

The influence of situational antecedents on viewer interest in video entertainment were investigated in this study. Alcohol expectancy, alcohol content and anger provocation were factorially crossed to investigate their influence on male interest in viewing four types of slides: neutral, erotic, violent and violent-erotic. Alcohol expectancy emerged as most potent of these manipulated variables, facilitating viewing times for the nonneutral slides and overriding the impact of alcohol content.

This expectancy effect was more pronounced with the violent erotic slides than with slides that were violent only.

689. Howitt, Dennis. The Mass Media and Social Problems.
Oxford: Pergamon Press, 1982.

Posits that mass media research has been social problem oriented (role of the mass media in causing crime, violence, civil disturbances, etc.) rather than academic and theoretical. Looking at research in Great Britain and the United States, the author emphasizes the "no effects" point of view. Likewise the review of research on sex, eroticism, and pornography suggests that evidence is not really available to support a link between pornography and sexual deviance or sexual crime. Finally, the review of research on crime and the mass media revealed no simple relationship between amount of exposure to crime in the media and criminal behavior and no simple link between coverage of crime in the news media and the audience's perception of the amount of crime in society.

690. Linz, Daniel Gerard. "Sexual Violence in the Media: Effects on Male Viewers and Implications for Society." Dissertation Abstracts International, Vol. 46, No. 4,1985, p. 1382B.

Four studies were conducted to investigate effects of exposure to filmed sexual violence. Study 1: Men viewing 5 movies depicting violence against women have fewer negative reactions to films, perceive them as less violent, and consider them significantly less degrading to women than a control group who saw no films. The exposed group judged the victim of violent assault and rape as less injured, and evaluated her as less worthy than control group. Study 2: Examined exposure to R-rated slasher films, R-rated teenage sex films, and X-rated sexually explicit non-violent films, across two exposure periods (2 or 5 films). Found no difference in desensitization between exposure groups. Study 3: Examines relationship between individual differences in psychoticism and hostility, and exposure to movies with sexual violence and rape. Those subjects high in psychoticism and exposed to rape films were more likely to endorse force in sexual relations, and have lower esteem for victims. Study 4: Measured effectiveness of debriefings in Studies 2 & 3. Results indicate that even after 7 months, debriefed subjects' attitudes about sexual violence showed significant positive change.

691. Linz, Daniel, Edward Donnerstein, and Steven Penrod. "The Effects of Multiple Exposures to Filmed Violence Against Women." Journal of Communication, Vol. 34, No. 3, 1984, pp. 130-147.

A continuation of research on pornography and attitudes toward women. Five commercially-released, feature-length R-rated movies depicting violence against women were shown to 52 men. The impact of this exposure on judgments about the victim of a violent sexual assault was measured. As predicted, subjects' perceptions of the violence portrayed in the films changed over the five days of the study. The films were perceived to be significantly less violent by the last day of viewing; ratings of how degrading the films were to women and of offensiveness also were significantly lower by the last day.

692. Linz, Daniel, Charles W. Turner, Bradford W. Hesse, and Steven Penrod. "Bases of Liability for Injuries Produced by Media Portrayals of Violent Pornography." In Neil M. Malamuth and Edward Donnerstein (eds.), Pornography and Sexual Aggression. Orlando, FL: Academic Press, 1984, pp. 277-304.

This article explores the possibility for a plaintiff to claim injury through a third party as a result of exposure to violent pornography. An overview of tort law is provided highlighting cases dealing with the effect of television violence and subsequent injury. The means by which current psychological research on violent pornography might be incorporated within a civil trial is explored. Greater reliance by the courts upon researchers working on the relationship between exposure to violent pornographic material and behaviors is predicted. A successful civil suit of this nature might have important ramifications in limiting the proliferation of violent pornographic matter at a broad social level.

693. Malamuth, Neil M., and Edward Donnerstein. "The Effects of Aggressive-Pornographic Mass Media Stimuli." In Leonard Berkowitz (ed.), Advances in Experimental Social Psychology, Vol. 15. New York: Academic Press, 1982, pp. 103-136.

A review of the literature on "aggressive" pornography (depictions in which physical force is used or threatened to coerce a woman to engage in physical acts).

694. Malamuth, Neil M., and Edward Donnerstein. Pornography and Sexual Aggression. Orlando, FL: Academic Press, 1984.

A collection of articles focusing upon pornography and sexual aggression. Includes experimental, correlational, and cross-cultural studies. Implications for men and women and the role of the mass media are also explored.

695. Malamuth, Neil M., and James V. P. Check. "The Effects of Mass Media Exposure on Acceptance of Violence Against Women: A Field Experiment." Journal of Research in Personality, Vol. 15, No. 4, 1981, pp. 436-446.

An experiment on the effects of exposure to films portraying sexual violence as having positive consequences employed 271 students as subjects. The subjects were randomly assigned to view, on two different evenings, either violent-sexual or control feature-length films. Results indicated that exposure to films portraying violent sexuality increases male subjects' acceptance of interpersonal violence against women. For females, there were nonsignificant tendencies in the opposite direction--women exposed to the violent-sexual films tended to be less accepting of interpersonal violence and of rape myths than control subjects.

696. Malamuth, Neil M. and Victoria Billings. "The Functions & Effects of Pornography: Sexual Communication versus the Feminist Models in Light of Research Findings." In Jennings Bryant and Dolf Zillman (eds.), Perspectives on Media Effects, Hillsdale, NJ: Lawrence Erlbaum Associates, 1986.

Discusses problems of defining pornography, and presents two theoretical models proposed to describe functions and effects of pornography, followed by consideration of empirical research findings relevant to the theoretical models.

697. McCormack, Thelma. "Deregulating the Economy and Regulating Morality: The Political Economy of Censorship." Studies in Political Economy, Vol. 18, Fall, 1985, pp. 173-185.

The current agitation in Canada for stronger censorship laws reflects a return to a more conservative political environment, with emphasis on deregulating the economy and regulating morality. The preoccupation with "violence" by antipornography activists is seen here as an attack. It is also suggested that the problem from a feminist perspective is not the eroticization of violence, but that of power, which may take many benign forms. The Fraser report on pornography and prostitution in Canada rejects the claim that exposure to pornography leads to acts of sexual aggression such as rape; instead it directs attention to the obstruction of women's aspirations for equality. The question is raised as to whether equality and freedom of expression are tradeoffs or are necessary for each other.

698. National Coalition on Television Violence. NCTV News. Champaign, IL: NCTV, 1980 to date.

This newsletter reports on many aspects of violence in society: research on media content and effects, ratings and reviews of programs, scholarly and popular commentary, citizen and governmental action relating to media, industry viewpoints, and crime statistics vis-a-vis TV portrayal. Monitoring results of violent content--classified by network, program, and sponsor--are a regular feature, along with reviews of current theatre films. NCTV also expresses concern about other aspects of violence and aggression in society, including violence-related toys and games, sports, pornography, and interpersonal aggression.

699. Nelson, Edward C. "Pornography and Sexual Aggression." In Maurice Yaffe and Edward C. Nelson (eds), The Influence of Pornography on Behavior. London: Academic Press, 1982, pp. 171-248.

Discussion of research regarding effects of exposure to sexually
explicit material upon sexually aggressive attitudes and behavior.
Discusses definitional problems, different research approaches,
measures of sexual arousal, exposure, sexual fantasies, sex and
aggression, aggression toward women, sex offenses and offenders,
deviant sexual arousal. The research clearly shows that observing
violent sexuality can facilitate aggression in the observer.

700. Nias, David K. B. "The Effects of Televised Sex and Pornography."
In Michael J. A. Howe (ed.), Learning From Television: Psychological
and Educational Research, London: Academic Press, 1983.

Based on the theory that the portrayal of violence is almost
always potentially harmful, but that the portrayal of sex is not
necessarily so, the author suggests that a case for sex on
television can be made on the grounds of entertainment and
education, pointing out that most commercially available
pornographic films at present are antilove and antiwomen.
Discusses widely differing research results on effects of erotica
and pornography regarding imitation, disinhibition,
desensitisation, treatment procedures, sex-aggression link, ethics
and censorship.

701. Otto, Herbert A. "Sex and Violence on the American Newsstand."
Journalism Quarterly, Vol. 40, 1963, pp. 19-26. Also in Otto N. Larsen
(ed.), Violence and the Mass Media. New York: Harper and Row, 1968,
pp. 82-90.

Analysis of print material available at a city newsstand in 1961
to determine the extent of coverage of sex and violence. A
significant increase was found for the preceding ten years in the
number of magazines specializing in sexual and violent themes.
Police-detective and men's magazines contained the largest amount
of violent incidents--including torture and rape--followed by
romance magazines, which frequently linked sex and violence.
Examination of paperback book covers revealed that these books,
including those in the police-detective category, were more likely
than similar type magazines to portray sexual themes; while
violence was a less significant element. On the sample day, the
ten major daily newspapers allotted about 5 percent of column
inches to violent topics--including war (the most common
category). One newspaper contained a significantly greater amount
of violence-related material (33 percent).

702. Penrod, Steven and Daniel Linz. "Using Psychological Research on
Violent Pornography to Inform Legal Change." In Neil M. Malamuth and
Edward Donnerstein (eds.), Pornography and Sexual Aggression. Orlando,
FL: Academic Press, 1984, pp. 247-275.

An historical overview of current American law on the regulation
of pornography and obscenity. Differences between Great Britain
and the United States are discussed. Utilization of social
science research in legal proceedings within both countries has
met with little success. Newer research on pornography and the

possibility of its incorporation into current constitutional law are examined.

703. Reisman, Judith A. "Mass Media and Civil Rights." In Ann Wolbert Burgess (ed.), Rape and Sexual Assault, NY:Garland Publishing, Inc., 1985, pp. 365-373.

Suggests evidence is surfacing which links certain sex/violent media with possible murder and mutilation of women and children, as well as citing use of sexually explicit media in entrapment of children in sex and pornography rings. Advocates serious investigation into components of mass media which may be facilitating an increase in rape and sexual assault of women and children, citing evidence which supports the relationship between some mass media and seduction/abduction/murder of women and children.

704. Sapolsky, Barry S. "Arousal, Affect, and the Aggression-Moderating Effect of Erotica." In Neil M. Malamuth and Edward Donnerstein (eds.), Pornography and Sexual Aggression. Orlando, FL: Academic Press, 1984, pp. 85-113.

A review of research on the consequences of exposure to both nonaggressive and aggressive sexual stimuli. A two-component model, incorporating both arousal capacity and affect-eliciting qualities of an erotic stimulus, is proposed as a means of examining the impact of nonaggressive sexual stimuli on aggression. The affective component of responses to erotica emerges as the primary determinant of a stimulus's aggression-moderating effects. The major influences upon the affective responsiveness of the individual to such stimuli are also explored.

705. Slade, Joseph W. "Violence in the Hard-Core Pornographic Film: A Historical Survey." Journal of Communication, Vol. 34, No. 3, 1984, pp. 148-163.

Analysis of erotic films in the Kinsey Institute archive (dating from 1920 to 1970) and of loops sampled in Times Square arcades during the early 1980s indicate that about 10 percent of these films combine violence and sex. The degree of violence in these films increased somewhat after the mid-1970s, generally avoiding brutal force. The author posits that eroticism has unique dramatic requirements and that while graphic aggression is a standard element of "legitimate" feature films, it has been accepted only on the fringes of the pornography market. However, a new genre -- pornographic feature films -- may blend sex and violence in increasing amount and degree.

706. Wheeler, Hollis. "Pornography and Rape: A Feminist Perspective." In Ann Wolbert Burgess (ed.), Rape and Sexual Assault, NY: Garland Publishing, Inc., 1985, pp. 374-391.

Elaboration upon the theme that the fundamental aspect of pornography from the feminist perspective is that it is one element in a system of violence against women, which system is, in itself, but an element in the larger social system of male dominance and female subordination.

707. Wober, J. Mallory,. "See As You Would Be Seen By: 'Video Nasty' Antagonists In A Personality Mirror." Psychology News & In Mind, 1984, pp. 7-8.

A discussion of the controversy surrounding TV "video nasties," video cassettes featuring sadistic sexual violence. There is a division between those who are alarmed by "video nasties" and who wish to challenge them, and those who realize their unsavory nature but who believe that it is much more important to avoid legislation against freedom of cinematic expression.

708. Wober, J. Mallory,. "Viewers or Vigilantes: Options on Violent Pornography." InterMedia, Vol. 12, No. 2, 1984, pp. 20-23.

A comparison of American and European approaches to the regulation of "video nasties," pre-recorded sexually-violent video cassettes. In the United Kingdom, the government is currently supporting a radical extension of statutory licensing powers that would be more rigid than the ones now in force. The British tradition of voluntary, self-regulatory film censorship and the tenets of the First Amendment of the American Constitution are discussed as ideological hindrances to statutory regulation. These issues are debated in light of recent findings on the aggression-arousing elements of violent pornography.

709. Yaffe, Maurice and Edward C. Nelson (eds.). The Influence of Pornography on Behavior. New York: Academic Press, 1982.

A collection of papers that presents a broad perspective on obscenity and pornography, including chapters focusing upon aggression and pornography.

710. Zillmann, Dolf and Jennings Bryant. "Effects of Massive Exposure to Pornography." In Neil M. Malamuth and Edward Donnerstein (eds.), Pornography and Sexual Aggression. Orlando, FL: Academic Press, 1984, pp. 115-138.

Almost all experimentation to date concerning the consequences of massive exposure to pornography has concentrated on the effects on aggression directly subsequent to erotic stimulation. A two-component model of erotica effects on motivated aggressive behavior is proposed, modified to incorporate behavioral response changes which occur as a result of repeated exposure. The methodology employed in prolonged-exposure work is summarized and the research findings reported. Numerous non-transitory effects of massive exposure on the perception of sexuality and on sex-related dispositions are reported. Further understanding of the nature and consequences of these effects is predicated upon conducting longitudinal investigations.

Terrorism and the Media

711. Adams, William C. "The Beirut Hostages: ABC and CBS Seize An Opportunity." Public Opinion, Aug-Sept, 1985, pp. 45-48

    Examination of the coverage these Networks gave to the 1985 Beirut Hostage crisis, which examines the volume and the view events and issues were given.

712. Alexander, Yonah. International Terrorism: National, Regional, and Global Perspectives. New York: Praeger, 1976.

    The collaborative efforts of U.S. and Canadian scholars to present a general overview of the problem of international terrorism. This collection of essays presents views on national, regional and international perspectives of terrorism. The main questions addressed are what acts constitute terrorism, the underlying causes for this phenomenon, and how society can and should deal with it.

713. Alexander, Yonah. "Terrorism, the Media and the Police." Journal of International Affairs, Vol. 32, No. 1, 1978, pp. 101-113.

    Asserts that modern media provides terrorist groups with a critical communication instrument which willingly or unwillingly serves their general or specific propaganda and psychological warfare needs. This paper elaborates on the specifics of how and why this occurs. Research results are presented regarding the role the media should take in combating terrorism.

714. Altheide, David L. "Iran vs. U.S. TV News: The Hostage Story Out of Context." In William C. Adams (ed.), Television Coverage of the Middle East. Norwood, NJ: Ablex, 1981, pp. 128-158.

The objective of this analysis was to determine the degree to which network news reports reflected "reality" and various production values by examining format, mode of emphasis, themes, topics, and visual images of reports about the holding of American hostages in Iran. Clusters of 375 reports included in network early evening newscasts from November, 1979 to June, 1980 were analyzed. Overall, the content and style of these reports--including emphasis on release of the hostages rather than on socio-political conditions in Iran and emphasis on conflict--served to support official U. S. policy during the crisis, documenting an important role of the media in diplomacy.

715. Altheide, David L. "Three-in-One News: Network Coverage of Iran." Journalism Quarterly, Vol. 59, No. 3, 1982, pp. 482-486.

Analysis of a saturation sample of 368 evening newscast reports concerning the holding of United States hostages in Iran. The sample, from the Vanderbilt University Television News Archive, dates from November, 1979 to June 1980. There was overall similarity among networks in the number of reports devoted to the hostage situation and similar patterns of fluctuation in this measure of coverage over the period examined. However, amount of time devoted to coverage varied considerably during sampled clusters of broadcasts for all three networks and, overall, for one network. There was general consistency in emphasis of various topics, with reports about the hostages themselves the most prominent. Activities of Iranian students in the United States received more attention than did internal socio-political events in Iran. The effect of this homogeneity in coverage amounts to a "national news service," which presents a very limited view of events and issues.

716. Altheide, David L. "Impact of Format and Ideology on TV News Coverage of Iran." Journalism Quarterly, Vol. 62, No. 2, 1985, pp. 346-351.

A content analysis of 925 reports about Iran from two waves of selected newscasts broadcast from August 4, 1979 to June 7, 1980 and from July 3, 1980 to January 24, 1981. The Iranian hostage crisis of 444 days received extensive coverage by the major American networks. The reporting of selected events was consistent with production considerations such as accessibility, visual quality, drama and action, and thematic unity. This corresponded with selection of themes resonant with cultural stereotypes and images already familiar to the journalists. In this way, political and ideological value judgments became part of news coverage.

717. Atwater, Tony. "Network Evening News Coverage of the TWA Hostage Crisis." Terrorism and the News Media Research Project, Paper No. 6, Louisiana State University (undated).

Study to investigate the nature of the network evening news coverage devoted to the TWA hostage crisis by ABC, CBS and NBC. Questions included amount and percentage of newstime devoted to the crisis, specific topics emphasized, types of stories and locations of report origination. A comprehensive visual analysis of story content indicated 17 days of intensive coverage; 491 stories comprising 12 hours of newstime. Topics characterizing coverage were hostage status and official U.S. reaction.

718. Avallone, Franco. "Analisi Psicologico-Sociale del Comportamento Comunicativo del Rotocalco Televisivo Sul Terrorismo." [Social-Psychological Analysis of Communicative Function of Television Programs on Terrorism]. In RAI Radiotelevisione Italiana, Terrorismo e TV Vol. 1, 1982.

A psychological perspective on portrayal of terrorism on television supporting Ronci's analysis, explaining the reductionist image of terrorism as a distortion inherent in the medium. The author also discusses the public service function in the representation of terrorism.

719. Barcus, F. Earle. "Newspaper Coverage of Violence in Boston Public Schools, August 1981 - April 1983." Boston, MA: Report for the Safe Schools Commission, 1983.

Coverage of violence in Boston schools by two daily newspapers was the focus of this content analysis. Of approximately 1,000 newspaper items pertaining to Boston schools, 13 percent dealt with school-related violence. These stories were not given more prominence than other education items.

720. Bassiouni, M. Cherif. "Terrorism, Law Enforcement, and the Mass Media: Perspectives, Problems, Proposals." Journal of Criminal Law and Criminology, Vol. 72, No. 1, 1981.

Comparison of the scope of impact of acts of terrorism with that of a widespread condition, such as common crime, suggests that the psychological effect of terrorism is more significant than the specific violent action. This effect may be more a creation of the media than an intrinsic element of such violence.

721. Bassiouni, M. Cherif. "Media Coverage of Terrorism: The Law and the Public." Journal of Communication, Vol. 33, No. 2, 1982, pp. 128-143.

An examination of the issues involved in the media's coverage of terrorism -- when the public's right to know interferes with their protection; when the First Amendment privileges of the media conflict with law enforcement; and how the media should regulate themselves when it comes to portraying terrorism.

722. Bell, J. Bowyer. "Terrorist Scripts and Live-Action
Spectaculars." Columbia Journalism Review, No. 17, 1978, pp. 47-50.

The author expands the conventional description of the
media-terrorism relationship as one of mutual gain in presenting
the view that the amount of coverage of their actions is more
important to terrorists than consideration of any underlying
issues. Whether the action itself succeeds or fails is less
important than causing sensation among the public, which is
implemented by the communications media.

723. Bormann, Ernest G. "A Fantasy Theme Analysis of the Television
Coverage of the Hostage Release and the Reagan Inaugural." Quarterly
Journal of Speech, Vol. 68, No. 2, 1982, pp. 133-145.

A rhetorical critical analysis of the TV coverage of the hostage
release and the Reagan inaugural address, using the method of
fantasy theme analysis to examine how the dramatization of
unfolding events on TV creates a social reality for those caught
up in the portrayal. Compares the subliminal impact of the public
affairs inaugural coverage and coverage of the hostage release, in
working together to reinforce and amplify the core fantasy of
Reagan's speech.

724. Brown, William J. "Mediated Communication Flows During a
Terrorist Event: The TWA Flight 847 Hijacking." Paper presented at the
International Communication Association, Montreal, May, 1987.

Potential international effects of a single terrorist event can be
augmented by news media mediation and control during such an
event. A theoretical approach proposed here describes how the
mediation process can alter discourse as it moves through channels
of communication that are regulated by the mass media. A case
study of the TWA Flight 847 Hijacking of 1985 is used for this
analysis. By combining semiotic concepts with an understanding of
mass communication flows, this paper analyzes the terrorist
discourse disseminated by the news media during this event. The
nature of the mass media's role as mediator, and the critical need
for communication scholars and government leaders to understand
this role is considered.

725. Burnet, Mary. The Mass Media in a Violent World (1970 Symposium
Proceedings). Paris: UNESCO, 1971.

Specialists in mass media, sociology, psychology, criminology,
social work and education, from 18 countries met to examine the
definition of violence, the relationship between real-life and
media violence, and the means of expanding the use of reason in
the conduct of human relations. Topics included content and
impact of civil disturbance and personal violence in news; the
dramatic context of violence in media entertainment; and the
particular status of media and related problems in developing
countries. Participants called for examination of industry
processes which determine content, and of the political, economic

and social influences on these processes. They also sought media
promotion of increased understanding of social and international
conflict.

726. Catton, William R. "Militants and the Media." Indiana Law
Journal, Vol. 53, 1978, pp. 705-713.

New threats posed by the media's availability to terrorists. The
author addresses the possiblility of preventing terrorists from
taking illicit advantage of the existence and nature of the mass
media. He suggests that denial of access to the media to these
groups challenges the nature of the first amendment of the United
States Constitution. The trends in terrorism and the media's role
in terrorism in light of these issues are examined.

727. Clutterbuck, Richard. The Media and Political Violence.
London: The MacMillan Press, 1981.

An examination of the power and role of the media in the context
of political violence. The author discusses the influence of
television on scenes of violent demonstrations, and asks if one of
the aims of such violence is to provoke or discredit the police,
and whether the media unwittingly further this aim. He also
debates whether the BBC should broadcast interviews with
terrorists, and examines the effect of the media on violence in
Northern Ireland. Finally, the author discusses the issue of
whether the journalistic profession should enforce its own
standards, or whether there should be Parliamentary legislation
regulating the conduct of the media.

728. Covert, Lorrie Schmid. "A Fantasy-Theme Analysis of the Rhetoric
of the Symbionese Liberation Army: Implications for Bargaining With
Terrorists." Dissertation, University of Denver, 1984.

Analysis of the "vision" of the Symbionese Liberation Army
illustrated in its rhetoric, identifying and explaining the
motives that compelled its members to action.

729. Czerniejewski, Halina J. "Terrorism and News: In Search of
Definable Boundaries." The Quill, April,1977, p. 12.

How news media should handle hostage/terrorist stories, and who
should be making news decisions. Though problematic, guidelines
are suggested which do not encroach upon news judgment, that deal
with complexities of coverage helping or hindering terrorists or
victims, and that clarify the situation for newspersons to deal
responsibly with fast-breaking life-and-death situations.

730. Dader, Jose Luis. "Periodismo Y Pseudocomunicacion Politica: Contribuciones del Periodismo A Las Democracias Simbolicas." [Journalism and Political Pseudo-Communication: Contributions of Journalism to Symbolic Democracies]. Pamplona, Spain: Ediciones Universidad de Navarra, 1983.

   Various theses on the use of the communications media by terrorists are discussed.

731. Dominick, Joseph R. "Crime and Law Enforcement in Prime-Time Television." Public Opinion Quarterly, Vol. 37, No. 2, 1973, pp. 241-250.

   A content analysis of one week of dramatic and comedy television programs. Two-thirds of prime-time programming portrayed at least one crime and violent crimes were most prevalent. Murder, assault, and armed robbery accounted for 60 percent of TV crimes. Compared to real life, crimes against property and violent crimes against family members were underrepresented on television.

732. Dowling, Ralph E. "Terrorism and the Media: A Rhetorical Genre." Journal of Communication, Vol. 36, No. 1, 1986, pp. 12-24.

   Only certain terrorist activities fall within the domain of rhetorical acts. Therefore, crusaders, who practice terrorism for political ends, are the essay's subject. The author identifies the situational demands influencing political terrorists, the recurrent forms of a terrorist genre, the rhetorical purposes of terrorists, and the probable results of proposed responses to terrorism. The violent acts required to obtain media access constrain terrorist rhetoric while at the same time achieving rhetorical purposes that ordinary forms of discourse could never achieve. The violent deeds and distinct messages to the two main audiences of terrorism: the dedicated followers of the movement (insiders) and the mass audience (outsiders). Having succeeded in gaining the attention of the mass audience, crusader terrorists then seek to make themselves credible. Although this credibility is intended to create "an emotional state of extreme fear in target groups," terrorism has not succeeded in creating a climate of repression in Western nations, because terrorists have failed to create sufficient fear.

733. Dziki, Sylwester, Janina Maczuga and Walery Pisarek (eds.). World Directory of Mass Communication Researchers. Cracow, 1984.

   An international listing of mass communication researchers.

734. Elliot, Philip, Graham Murdock, and Philip Schlesinger. "Lo Stato e il Terrorismo alla Televisione Britannica." In RAI Radiotelevisione Italiana, Terrorismo e TV, Vol. 2. Rome: RAI, Verifica del Programmi Trasmessi, 1982.

British research for this international study of television and
terrorism presents three points of view on terrorism as mediated
by television. The first view, that of officials and authorities,
regards terrorism as illegitimate and repression as the only
political solution. The second view is that terrorism, while
illegitimate in "liberal democracies," may be legitimate in other
political systems. Social and political action based on an
understanding of the causes of political violence is proposed as
the most effective approach. The third view, that of opponents of
the state, justifies violent action by general condemnation of the
existing system or by a claim of self-determination or national
liberation.

735. Elliott, Deni. "Family Ties: A Case Study of Coverage of Families
and Friends During the Hijacking of TWA Flight 847." Terrorism and the
News Media Research Project, Paper No. 7, Louisiana State University,
(undated), .

   Family and friends were an important part of the coverage of this
   event. This paper focuses upon how some of these people dealt
   with the event and the media and how the media focused upon them.

736. Francis, Richard. "La Politique de la BBC en Matiere de
Presentation de La Violence." [BBC Policy Regarding the Presentation
of Television Violence]. Revue Internationale de Criminologie et de
Police Technique, Vol. 36, No. 4, 1983, pp. 91-99.

   Describes guidelines developed by the British Broadcasting
   Corporation (BBC) concerning the representation of violence on TV.
   The inclusion of violent scenes in news broadcasts depends on
   factors such as its importance to the broadcast and public
   sensibilities. The treatment of stories on terrorism, bomb
   alerts, and accidents and catastrophies is considered, as well as
   requests for the suppression of specific information.

737. Friedlander, Robert A. "Iran: The Hostage Seizure, the Media, and
International Law." In Abraham H. Miller (ed.), Terrorism: The Media
and the Law. New York: Transnational Publishers, 1982, pp. 51-66.

   Examination of events during the 14.5 month (Nov. 1979 to Jan.
   1981) period in which 52 Americans were held as hostages in
   Tehran, with particular reference to the impact of these events on
   the U.S. political administration. The media's role in this event
   is described as one of exploitation.

738. Gallup Organization, The. "The People and the Press: Part 2." An
Ongoing Times Mirror Investigation of Public Attitudes Towards the News
Media, Los Angeles: Times Mirror, 1986.

An investigation of public attitudes toward the press in a variety
of areas, to measure changes which focus on public opinion of
press coverage of specific issues and events. Regarding
terrorism, results measure rating of press coverage of various
terrorist events, appropriate coverage amount, perceived effects
of coverage, and reasons for failures of good coverage.

739. Graber, Doris A. "Evaluating Crime-Fighting Policies: Media
Images and Public Perspective." In Ralph Baker and Fred A. Meyer,
Jr. (eds.), Evaluating Alternative Law-Enforcement Policies, Lexington,
MA: Heath Lexington Books, 1979, pp. 179-199.

Comparison of amount of coverage of types of crime in several
Midwestern U.S. newspapers and TV newscasts with public
perceptions concerning the frequency of these crimes during
1976-1977. Reports of political terrorism accounted for 5 percent
of press reports and 8 percent of television news reports and
ranked fourth out of eight news topics. Respondents' daily
viewing diaries, in which summaries of news items were recorded,
revealed a similar pattern.

740. Heath, Linda, Margaret T. Gordon, and Robert LeBailly. "What
Newspapers Tell Us (And Don't Tell Us) About Rape." Newspaper Research
Journal, Vol. 2, No. 4, 1981, pp. 48-55.

A content analysis of 8,015 crime stories in newspapers published
in Philadelphia, Chicago, and San Francisco revealed that
newspapers give a fairly accurate picture of rape when they
present the details. Newspapers must rely upon police blotters
for information thus many rapes or attempted rapes are not
reported. A serious concern is that rape stories often lack
details and thus hinder the public's understanding of rape.
Readers must then fill in the details which can lead to a very
frightening and erroneous view of rape. Newspapers need to run
stories that will more adequately inform the public about rape.

741. Herman, Edward S. The Real Terror Network. Boston: Southend
Press, 1982.

Examination of the ways in which western media emphasize a network
of terrorist action which challenges important western interests
rather than that of supported authoritarian states.

742. Hoge, James W. "The Media and Terrorism." In Abraham H. Miller
(ed.), Terrorism: The Media and the Law. New York: Transnational
Publishers, 1982, pp. 89-105.

An examination of the media's responsibilities in covering
terrorism using specific examples in several countries to back a
claim for expanded rather than restricted coverage of such events.
While calling for professional restraint and outlining those
guidelines that exist among the various news organizations, the

author points to the similarity in effect of voluntary guidelines and enforced censorship.

743. Holz, Josephine, Eric Cardinal, and Dennis Kerr. "The Achille Lauro: A Study in Terror." Paper prepared for the 42nd annual conference of the American Association for Public Opinion Research, Hershey, PA, May 14-17, 1987.

Study based on the June 17, 1986 NBC News Special examining the events surrounding the hijacking of the Achille Lauro cruise ship in October, 1985. This broadcast was unique in terrorist media coverage in affording considerable coverage of the hijackers' political goals and beliefs. A national sample of adults was recruited for a panel study. Prior to the broadcast, two hundred and eleven respondents were interviewed about their beliefs and opinions regarding terrorism and the news media, and then reinterviewed subsequent to the broadcast. Findings show no support for the argument that terrorists are humanized by news coverage, or that legitimacy is lent to their cause. Regarding the claim that news coverage of terrorism may increase the viewers' sense of personal risk and fear, findings were mixed and inconclusive. Some support was found for the hypothesis that coverage results in viewer identification with the victims rather than with the terrorists.

744. Jaehnig, Walter B. "Journalists and Terrorism: Captives of the Libertarian Tradition." Indiana Law Journal, Vol. 53, No. 4, 1978, pp. 717-744.

A discussion of the ethical dilemmas confronting the news media surrounding terrorism, hostage-taking, and other violent incidents. Those who use violence or threats of violence to attain their objectives, have recognized that the best guarantee of coverage lies in appealing to traditional news values, making full use of the news industry's attraction to dramatic, conflict-laden, and tragic events. News judgments regarding the coverage of terrorism are made quickly, often with less than full cooperation of police authorities, and usually under the pressure of commercial competition.

745. Jaehnig, Walter B. "Terrorism in Britain: The Limits of Free Expression." In Abraham H. Miller (ed.), Terrorism: The Media and the Law. New York: Transnational Publishers, 1982, pp. 106-129.

An examination of media-law enforcement-government relationships in regard to the coverage of terrorism. Violent acts related to the political dispute between England and Northern Ireland is covered specifically. Media self-regulation by the British Broadcasting Corporation is examined against the background of the 1974 Prevention of Terrorism Act and a 1979 agreement with London's Metropolitan Police concerning "sensitive" programming.

746. Joyce, Edward M. "Reporting Hostage Crises: Who's in Charge of Television?" SAIS Review, Vol. 6, No. 1, 1986, pp. 169-176.

Reviews the debate which deals with the role of television in hostage- taking acts of terrorism. Examples are cited of arguments regarding media coverage as helping or hindering the cause of terrorism, and commenting upon the public's right to information.

746. Knight, Graham and Tony Dean. "Myth and the Structure of News." Journal of Communication, Vol. 32, No. 2, 1982, pp. 144-161.

An analysis of Canadian press coverage of the British recapturing of the Iranian embassy in London. The work reveals that myths work through news accounts by developing abstract notions of expertise and legitimacy. The authors compare the accounts of the embassy takeover in two of Toronto's dailies -- the Globe and Mail and the Sun.

748. Larson, James F. "Television and U. S. Foreign Policy: The Case of the Iran Hostage Crisis." Journal of Communication, Vol, 36, No. 4, 1986, pp. 108-130.

A number of general propositions about television and foreign policy provide backdrop for interpretation of U.S. TV news coverage of Iran, and especially the hostage crisis between 1972 and 1981. Nine propositions regarding the role of television news in foreign policy result from selective review of existing literature on media and foreign policy. These are organized along key concepts of the role of the press in the foreign policy process as observer, participant and catalyst. To examine these propositions, content data are analyzed in five major time phases of network news coverage of Iran from 1972 10 1981. This data comes principally from the Television News Index and Abstracts. The role of TV news is noted to have implications for 1)scholarly conceptualization of the news media to foreign policy; 2)policies and practices of TV news organizations and; 3)the conduct of foreign policy and international diplomacy.

749. Lule, Jack. "The Myth of My Widow: A Dramatistic Analysis of News Portrayals of a Terrorist Victim." Terrorism and the News Media Research Project, Paper No. 8, Louisiana State University, (undated), .

This paper explores news portrayals of terrorist victims and discusses the implications of such portrayals for public policies. The Dramatistic analysis suggests a relationship between the news stories and myth, if myth is defined not as a false or incredible tale, but as a symbolic narrative that attempts to explain and give meaning to practices and beliefs. A compelling mythic image -- the heroic victim -- is given dramatic portrayal by news accounts of the victim's widow. Mythic images in the news may help create a powerful climate for prevention and reprisal against terrorism.

750. Martin, L. John. "The Media's Role in International Terrorism."
Paper presented to the Association for Education in Journalism and Mass
Communication, Corvallis, Oregon, 1983.

This study revealed that the mass media may quote someone using
"terror" or "terrorism" in reference to an act performed by a
group toward which the medium is either neutral or opposed. The
press, however, will never use these terms in a headline unless it
not only disapproves of the act but has no sympathy for its
perpetrators. Five newspapers were studied, four foreign and one
American, on five alternate days in late June and early July,
1983.

751. Mickolus, Edward F. Transnational Terrorism: A Chronology of
Events, 1968-1979. Westport, Conn: Greenwood Press, 1980.

A massive and authoritative compilation, including lists of
locations of incidents, and organizations believed to be involved.

752. Midgley, Sarah and Virginia Rice (eds.). Terrorism and the Media
in the 1980s (Conference Proceedings). Washington, DC: The Media
Institute and Institute for Studies in International Terror, 1984.

A discussion of the relationship between news coverage and
terrorist events. Many experts in this field propose guidelines,
such as those used at CBS, that leave the media responsible for
policing its own actions and using its judgment as to what extent
coverage will be given to each terrorist act. However, others
feel that the media, by virtue of their nature, will not be firm
enough and suggest that formal legislation is necessary to keep
the media in hand. There is strong support for the position that
the public's right to know is secondary to the safety of the
people involved.

753. Miller, Abraham H. "Terrorism, the Media, and the Law: A
Discussion of the Issues." In Abraham H. Miller (ed.), Terrorism: The
Media and the Law. New York: Transnational Publishers, 1982,
pp. 13-50.

A brief discussion of several of the issues relating to media
coverage of terrorism. Media access to sources, relationships
with government and law enforcement are examined, including ways
in which these relationships are moderated by the law. Specific
terrorist incidents are used to elucidate areas of conflict
between institutions. The author also provides an overview of
questions concerning the depiction of terrorists in the media.

754. Miller, Abraham H. (ed.). Terrorism: The Media and the Law. New
York: Transnational Publishers, 1982.

Journalists, legal scholars, and police officers address the issues of media access and portrayal in relation to terrorist groups, with particular reference to the holding of American hostages in Iran (1979-1981) and coverage of the IRA in England. A number of guidelines enacted by particular stations, newspapers, and organizations are included, along with results of three surveys of U.S. police and media representatives evaluating coverage of terrorism.

755. Morcellini, Mario and Franco Avallone. Il ruolo dell' informazione in una situazione di emergenza - 16 marzo 1978: il rapimento di Aldo Moro. [The role of information in an emergency situation - March 16, 1978: The Kidnapping of Aldo Moro]. Rome: RAI Radiotelevisione Italiana, Verifica Programmi Trasmessi, 1978.

A content analysis of news reporting in public and private broadcasting and in both the Italian and foreign press on March 16-17, 1978. On this day, Aldo Moro, president of the Christian Democratic Party, was kidnapped and his escorts killed by the Red Brigades.

756. Moreland, Richard L., and Michael L. Berbaum. "Terrorism and the Mass Media: A Researcher's Bibliography." In Abraham H. Miller (ed.), Terrorism: The Media and the Law. New York: Transnational Publishers, 1982, pp. 191-215.

The fields of communications, journalism, law, psychology, and sociology are represented in this bibliography of approximately 500 works relating to media violence and the coverage of terrorism.

757. Ozyegin, Nejat. "Construction of the 'Facts' of Political Violence: A Content Analysis of Press Coverage." Unpublished Master's Thesis, The Annenberg School of Communications, University of Pennsylvania, 1986.

A study of the role played by the Turkish press in the creation of public images of political violence during five years of rising political turbulence prior to the 1980 military coup.

758. Paddock, Alfred H. "Psychological Operations, Special Operations, and U.S. Strategy." In Frank R. Barnett, B. Hugh Tovar, and Richard H. Schultz (ed.), Special Operations in U.S. Strategy. New York: National Strategy Information Center, 1984, pp. 231-251.

A comparison of the Soviet media and American media. The former adheres strictly to the Bolshevik concept of socialist realism -- reporting not what is, but what should be. The latter is passive, leaving itself vulnerable to terrorist exploitation.

212

759. Paletz, David L., John Z. Ayanian and Peter A. Fozzard.
"Terrorism on TV News: The IRA, the FALN, and the Red Brigades." In
W. C. Adams (ed.), <u>Television Coverage of International Affairs</u>,
Norwood, NJ: Aben, 1981, pp. 143-165.

   Histories, ideologies, goals and tactics of these three terrorist
   groups are presented, and a content analysis done on every story
   ABC, CBS and NBC evening news carried in their regard, from July
   1, 1977, to June 30, 1979. Dimensions of news content were coded,
   explanations for depictions offered and explanations of media
   effects suggested.

760. Paletz, David L., Peter A. Fozzard, and John Z. Ayanian. "The
I.R.A., the Red Brigades and the F.A.L.N. in <u>The New York Times</u>."
<u>Journal of Communication</u>, Vol. 32, No. 2, 1982, pp. 162-171.

   This study analyzes the <u>New York Times'</u> coverage of the I.R.A.,
   the Red Brigades, and the F.A.L.N., during the period from July 1,
   1977 to June 30, 1979. The authors found that despite charges
   from several quarters, there is no evidence to suggest that media
   coverage (as exemplified by that of the <u>Times</u>) legitimizes the
   cause of terrorist organizations. Although violent organizations
   can influence frequency of news coverage by the nature of their
   actions, authorities hold greater influence over how violence is
   portrayed because of the frequency with which they are sources and
   the interpretations they offer.

761. Palmerton, Patricia R.   "Terrorism and the Media: A Call for
Rhetorical Criticism." Paper presented to the Speech Communication
Association, Mass Communication Division, 1983.

   The author discusses the media-terrorism interaction, arguing that
   terrorism is a rhetorical endeavor and that the rhetoric of
   terrorism is in part created by the response of the news media.

762. Palmerton, Patricia R.   "Terrorism and Institutional Targets as
Portrayed by News Providers." Paper submitted to the Speech
Communication Association, Mass Communication Division, 1985.

   Terrorism, to be an effective strategy depends upon coverage by
   the news media for part of its impact. This study examined the
   news media's portrayal of terrorist action upon governmental
   representatives and institutions. Includes an analysis of CBS
   evening news coverage of the taking of American hostages in Iran
   from 1979-1981. Results indicated that CBS news' image of the
   situation showed that while actions taken by the United States
   were responsible for whatever happened to the hostages, control
   over the outcomes of actions remained external to the United
   States.

763. Picard, Robert G. "The Conundrum of News Coverage of Terrorism." Terrorism and the News Media Research Project, Paper No. 1, Louisiana State University, (undated), .

General discussion of the dynamics of terrorism from a political perspective. Concludes that the media support the existing social, political, and economic orders.

764. Purnell, Susanna W. and Eleanor S. Wainstein. "The Problems of U.S. Businesses Operating Abroad in Terrorist Environments." Rand Report R-2842-DOC, November, 1981.

Terrorist assaults on United States business firms abroad have become an escalating threat. As U.S. investments have grown, so has terrorists' dissatisfaction with local regimes and U.S. business interests, which are seen as allies of the Government they are trying to overthrow. Among the demands that terrorists impose upon kidnap victims is payment for newspaper or press conference statements, in which a corporate representative admits guilt for exploiting workers, supporting an oppressive regime, and promoting the terrorists' cause.

765. Quarantelli, E. L. "Realities and Mythologies in Disaster Films." Communications: The European Journal of Communication, Vol. 11, No. 1, 1985, pp. 31-44.

This paper examines 36 films with substantial footage on disaster phenomenon, excluding war/terrorism films, science fiction films and comedies. Considerably more time was devoted to preimpact period than to trans or postimpact periods. Disaster agents portrayed were usually highly unlikely, with frequently occuring natural disasters seldom depicted. Disaster agents rarely appeared unexpectedly.

766. Rabe, Robert L. "The Journalist and the Hostage: How Their Rights Can Be Balanced." In Abraham H. Miller (ed.), Terrorism: The Media and the Law. New York: Transnational Publishers, 1982, pp. 69-75.

An argument for the primacy of law enforcement agencies in responding to terrorist actions, citing court decisions which limit the constitutionally-granted freedom of the press. These decisions involve restricting access to information. This perspective, in which the safety of hostages is central, calls for limiting the media's role to factual reporting of information made available by police public information offices.

767. RAI Radiotelevisione Italiana. Metodi di Ricerca e Risultati Sul Rapporto Tra Violenza in Televisione e Criminalita'. [Research Methods and Results Concerning the Relationship Between Violence in Television and Criminality]. Torino, Italy: ERI, 1975.

The record of proceedings of a meeting in Florence in September,
1974, organized by the Prix Italia Secretariat. Various studies
conducted in several countries were discussed at this meeting.

768. RAI Radiotelevisione Italiana, Verifica dei Programmi Trasmessi.
Terrorismo e TV: Italia, Gran Bretagna, Germania Occidentale [Terror
and TV: Italy, Great Britain, West Germany], 2 Vols. Rome: RAI, 1982.

Research proposed at a 1980 seminar on the way terrorism is
presented on television. Descriptive, comparative studies provide
information on the delicate and important role television plays in
socially- and politically-complex phenomena. The first volume
incorporates studies relating to portrayal of terror in Italy.
Terrorism in Great Britain and West Germany is the focus of
research reported in the second volume.

769. Rath, Claus, and Dagmar Jacobsen. "Produzione di immagini sul
terrorismo alla televisione tedesca occidentale." [Production of
Images on Terrorism in the TV of West Germany]. In RAI
Radiotelevisione Italiana, Terrorismo e TV, Vol. 2. Rome: RAI,
Verifica dei Programmi Trasmessi, 1982.

Research on television portrayal of terrorism in West Germany
examined programs broadcast from May to October in 1981.
Examination of the creation of these mass media events proceeds
from reflection on the concept and history of Germany's political
system and the concept of political violence to dominant forms of
violence on German television and the nature of terrorism as it
functions in a specific society. These perspectives are
incorporated into a matrix which provides a cohesive framework for
the image of terrorism presented on television.

770. Ronci, Donatella. "Terrorismo e Sistema Politico nel Rotocalco
Televisivo." In RAI Radiotelevisione Italiana, Terrorismo e TV,
Vol. 1, Italia. Immagini del Terrorismo nel Rotocalco Televisivo.
Rome: RAI, Verifica del Programmi Trasmessi, 1982.

This analysis of TV portrayal of terrorism examines the
relationship between terrorism, information, and power. The way
in which information mediates the representation of the
institutional political sphere when this sphere is challenged by
another, negative, political power is clarified.

771. Savarese, Rossella and Antonio Perna. "Strategic Arms and
Guerrilla Weapons: A Content Analysis of Articles from Italian
Newspapers of the 70s." Paper presented to the International Peace
Research Institute Association, Orillia, Canada, 1981.

A critical discussion of the Italian press' coverage of armament
issues and the uses of conventional or nuclear weapons for acts of
terrorism. The authors hold the view that the Italian daily press
lacks an appropriate communication strategy concerning these
issues, and that its main objective is to "make news" and attract

readers. An analysis of about 2,700 headlines of the <u>Corriere della Sera</u>, the independent mass circulation newspaper and one of the most important newspapers of Italy, is included.

772. Scanlon, Joseph. "Domestic Terrorism and the Media: Live Coverage of Crime." <u>Canadian Police College Journal</u>, Vol. 8, No. 2, 1984, pp. 154-178.

Presents 2 case studies of the role of media at hostage-takings in Calgary and Edmonton, Canada. The incidents suggest that the police must pay attention to the role of the media here, and that the media create certain problems. Police contingency must include plans for dealing with the media, and trained personnel must include hostage commanders, a task force, and public relations officers along with negotiators.

773. Schlesinger, Philip. "'Terrorism', the Media, and the Liberal-Democratic State: A Critique of the Orthodoxy." <u>Social Research</u>, Vol. 48, No. 1, 1981, pp. 74-99.

The role of the state (the United Kingdom) in advancing anti-terror images is explored in this complex interpretation of the relationship between terrorists and the media. The author also examines the similarities in effects of industry self-regulation and legislative control.

774. Schlesinger, Philip, Graham Murdock and Philip Elliot. <u>Televising Terrorism: Political Violence in Popular Culture</u>. London: Comedia Publishing, 1983.

A detailed examination of television examining how different perspectives on terrorism are presented. The authors take issue with the prevailing orthodoxies of both the Right and the Left. They reject the rightist claim that television gives extensive publicity to terrorist views and mobilizes sympathy for their causes as well as rejecting the radical characterization of broadcasting as a largely uncritical conduit for official views. Rather, they draw attention to the diverse ways in which television handles terrorism and the problems this question poses for liberal democracies.

775. Schmid, Alex P. and Janny de Graaf. <u>Violence as Communication: Insurgent Terrorism and the Western News Media</u>. Beverly Hills: Sage Publications, 1982.

An extended study treating the relationship between insurgent terrorism and the Western news media. The authors have tried to identify those elements in the Western information order which invite the use of violence, and have suggested ways to transform this information order.

776. Shaheen, Jack G. The TV Arab, Bowling Green, Ohio: Bowling Green
State University Popular Press, 1984.

A review and examination of the portrayal of Arabs during eight
seasons of TV shows reveals that TV perpetrates four myths about
Arabs: they are all very wealthy, barbaric and uncultured, sex
maniacs, and revel in acts of terrorism.

777. Silj, Alessandro. Brigate Rosse-Stato: Lo scontro spettacolo
nella regia della stampa quotidiana. [Red
Brigades-State: Confrontation Spectacle Directed by the Daily Press].
Firenze: Vallecchi, 1978.

Analysis of coverage of the kidnapping of Aldo Moro, president of
the Christian Democratic Party, in five Italian newspapers
indicated that the press was used by various political forces for
ideological ends. Results indicated that political ideology was
the basis for immediate beatification of Moro in the press and
denial of the authenticity of letters from the "People's prison."

778. Silj, Alessandro. Stampa, Radio e TV di Fronte Al Processo Moro,
Ai Casi La Torre, Delcogliano, Cirillo e Ad Altre Storie Di Terrorismo.
[Press, Radio and Television Before the Moro Trial, the Cases of
LaTorre, Delcogliano, Cirillo, and Other Stories of Terrorism].
Rome: RAI Radiotelevisione Italiana, Verifica dei Programmi Trasmessi,
1982.

A study comparing the RAI information on the problems of Italian
terrorism with information published in nationally-distributed
newspapers. The study shows that the information on terrorism
broadcast or published by eight media groups during a four-week
period in 1982 seems to be neither a response to a concern for an
exhaustive review of terrorism and related events nor, in the
majority of the cases, a response to orientations and choices that
are continual and coherent. It is suggested that this type of
information has not yet found its own code of behaviors and that
the performance of broadcast groups and newspapers is often the
result of conflict.

779. Stephens, Lowndes F. "Press and Public Reaction to 'Special
Bulletin'." Paper presented to the Association for Education in
Journalism, International Communication Division, 1983.

An evaluation of "Special Bulletin", a made-for-television movie
about a group of anti-terrorists who take hostages. Episodes in
the movie were analyzed as a television news scenario. The script
was also analyzed to determine if the fictitious news scenario had
a structure similar to "real world" accounts of similar
activities.

780. Terrorism and the Media. (Report of Conference Proceedings) Terrorism, Vol. 2, No. 3, 1979, pp. 59-60.

A general overview of modern terrorism is followed by a case presentation and analysis of the TWA hijacking by Croatian nationalists, the Itanaf raid in Washington, D.C., and the South Moluccan cases. The subsequent debates address the role of the media in handling these situations. The final section deals specifically with the role of the media, what it has learned from experience and its responsibility for the future.

781. Terrorism and the Media. (International Seminar held in Florence, Italy, 1978) Rome: International Press Institute with Affari Esteri, 1980.

This collection of papers raises fundamental questions about the conflict between the responsibility of the media to cover terrorism, the public's right to information, and the necessity of low-profile police investigations. While the media play a role in advancing terrorist aims by publicizing their terms, editors also recognize a duty to inform the public.

782. Wardlaw, Grant. Political Terrorism. London: Cambridge University Press, 1982.

The author examines the relationship between terrorists and the media, which is described as a symbiotic one. In this perspective, terrorists gain attention to their cause, and media reap the commercial benefits of sensational coverage.

783. Weimann, Gabriel. "The Theater of Terror: Effects of Press Coverage." Journal of Communication, Vol. 33, No. 1,1983, pp. 38-45.

An examination of the effects of press coverage of terrorist events on readers' attitudes regarding the terrorists. Semantic differential scales were used to measure evaluative attitudes before and after 80 students read press clippings describing 2 separate terrorist events. Comparison of the scores before and after exposure shows exposure did tend to enhance the evaluations of the terrorists. Shifts in evaluation were found on several image dimensions, mostly toward a more positive evaluation than before exposure. Thus, the important function of media coverage as the theater of terror is highlighted. Staging a terrorist event that will attract the mass media will, in turn, guarantee worldwide awareness and recognition.

784. Wurth-Hough, Sandra. "Network News Coverage of Terrorism: The Early Years." Terrorism, Vol. 6, No. 3, 1983, pp. 403-521.

Using the Vanderbilt News Archive, this study examines the image of terrorist activities in reports by ABC, CBS, and NBC. Includes a comparison of story emphasis and depiction, frequency, length of coverage, and location of newscasts. Results indicate that the electronic media influence public opinion by defining which national and international issues become significant.

Author Index

Includes authors and joint authors.

Entries refer to individual entry numbers.

Abel, J.D., 1
Abeles, R.,P., 256
Abramson, P.R., 674
Adams, W.C., 2, 710
Adoni, H., 3, 328, 329
Alabert, J.A., 4
Albert, R.S., 269
Alexander, Y., 5, 712
Alioto, J.T., 299
Altheide, D.L., 6, 7, 9
Andison, F.S.,
Aner, K., 9
Applefield, J.M., 614
Arnetz, B.B., 272
Askins, C.D., 224
Atkin, C.K., 119, 273, 274
520, 541
Atwater, T., 10
Avallone, F., 184, 717
Ayanian, J.Z.

Baarda, B., 656
Bachman, J.G., 577
Bailey, G.A., 12
Bailyn, L., 276
Baker, R.K., 13, 14
Ball, S.J., 13
Baldwin, T.F., 15
Bandura, A., 279-286
Barcus, F.E., 16-18, 718
Barlow, G., 287
Barnes, G.E., 288
Baron, J.N.,289
Baron, L., 290, 291
Baron, R.A., 372, 500
Barrett, G., 359
Bart, L., 674

Bassionni, M.C., 292, 721
Baxter, R.L., 19
Bear, A., 293
Belson, W.A., 294
Beninson, M.E., 1
Beattie, E., 20
Becker, J., 21, 22
Bell, J.B., 721
Belvedere, E., 385
Berbaum, M.L., 186
Berkoiwitz, L.,295-303,
367, 396, 496, 550
Berndt, T.J., 330
Billings, V., 515
Bjorkqvist, K., 304
Blanchard, D.C., 305
Blanchard, R.J., 305
Blankenburg, W.B., 45
Boemer, M.L., 23
Bogart, L., 306, 307
Bollen, K.A., 308, 309
Bonfadelli, H., 310, 588
Bormann, E.G., 24
Bouman, H., 25
Bouthilet, L., 198
Boyd, D.A., 206
Bravo-Corrada, M., 37
Brice, P., 377, 465
Brody, S.R., 27
Brown, R.L., 438
Brown, W.J., 28
Brubaker, T., 385
Bryant, J., 29, 313, 314
620, 668
Burnet, M., 30

Liebert, R.M., 372, 498, 499, 500, 587
Lindholm, B.W., 175
Linne, O., 501, 502
Linton, J.M., 170
Linz, D., 352, 503, 504, 505, 690, 702, 749
Lippincott, E.C., 628
Lometti, G., 264, 265
Lovaas, O.I., 506
Lovibond, S.H., 507
Loye, D., 508
Lule, J., 171
Lyle, J., 590
Lyness, P.I., 172

Maccoby, E.E., 173, 509
MacDonald, G.E., 361, 362
MacDonald, P.T., 78, 79
Maczuga, J., 72
Malamuth, N.M., 288, 354, 511, 512, 513, 514, 515
Malan, J.C., 54
Maloney, S., 578
Malstrom, E.J., 372
Mancini, P., 129
Mane, S., 3
Manning, S.A., 516
Manzolati, J., 131
Markham, J.W., 569
Marlatt, G.A., 88
Martin, L.J., 174
Mattern, K.K., 175
McCann, T.E., 176
McCarthy, E.D., 518
McCombs, M., 53
McConahy, J.B., 155
McCunnachie, G.A., 235
McCormack, T., 177, 178
McCutcheon, J., 644
McDermott, S., 275
McIntyre, J.J., 442, 519
McLean, M.S., Jr., 569
McLeod, J.M., 520
Medler, J.F., 211
Medoff, N.J., 672
Menard, B.S., 521
Mermelstein, R., 377
Messner, S.F., 522
Meyer, T.P., 523, 524, 525
Meyerson, L.J., 526
Mickolus, E.F., 751
Midgley, S., 179
Milavsky, J.R., 527
Milgram, S., 528
Miller, A.H., 280, 754

Miller, J.B., 181
Miller, N.L., 182
Mirams, G., 183
Mitchell, T.H., 152
Morcellini, M., 184, 185
Moreland, R.L., 186
Morgan, M., 101, 102, 103, 104, 105, 231, 405, 531
Motto, J., 532
Mueller, C.W., 533
Murdock, G., 132, 734, 774
Murray, J.P., 52, 187, 274, 534, 535, 536, 537, 538, 539, 541
Musonis, V., 578
Mussen, P., 542

Naon, R.L., 65
National Coalition on Television Violence, 188
Nayman, O.B., 274, 541
Neale, J.M., 497
Nel, E.M., 344
Nelson, E.C., 666, 699
Nelson, J.L., 73
Newell, D.S., 223, 593
Nias, D.K.B., 378, 544
Noble, G., 545

Osborn, D.K., 546
Oppenheim, A.N., 141
Orzeck, L., 518
Oho, H.A., 189
Otto, U., 272

Paczkowski, A., 191
Paddock, A.H., 192
Paletz, D.L., 193, 194, 195
Palmer, E.L., 196, 548
Palmerton, P.R., 197, 761
Parke, R.D., 303, 496, 550
Parker, E.B., 590
Parnes, P., 228
Pearl, D., 198, 551
Penrod, S., 504, 505, 702, 749
Perna, A., 216
Pfuhl, E.H., Jr., 553
Phillips, D.P., 308, 309, 554, 555, 556, 557, 558, 559, 560, 561, 562
Picard, R.G., 763
Piepe, A.J., 563
Pierce, C.M., 564
Pietila, V., 565

225

Subject Index

Entries refer to individual entry numbers.

accidents, 245, 264, 556
accuracy, 110, 259
Achille Lauro, 743
adolescents, 42, 47, 77, 172
  173, 205, 206, 268, 294, 321,
  324, 350, 389, 412, 426, 442,
  519, 520, 577, 606, 626, 629
  630, 645, 651
advertisements, 21, 220, 239
African Americans, 625
alcohol, 88
anger, 88, 295-303, 523, 524
  623, 645, 646
antisocial, 119, 685
Arabs, 221
army, 507
arousal, 168, 199, 288,
  649, 669-672, 704, 710
attitudes, 36, 52, 211, 213
  254
attitudes toward press, 738
Australia, 11, 76, 128, 137
  370, 371, 444, 445, 487, 507
  566, 629

behavioral effects, 272, 412
  424, 679
Beirut, 342, 711
Belgium, 496
bibliographies, 32, 33, 52
  72, 157, 186, 249, 535, 541,
  635, 756
Brazil, 243
business terrorism, 764

cable TV, 38,
Canada, 20, 32-36, 39, 77, 85,
  109, 112, 113, 143, 152, 170,
  246, 253, 476, 590, 657, 697,
  747,
capital punishment, 557, 558
cartoons, 73, 96, 138, 151,
  223, 248, 267, 373, 392, 440,
  447, 467, 542, 596, 611, 637
catharsis, 15, 337, 382-384,
  414, 462, 477, 516, 649
censors, 15
censorship, 27, 60, 65, 166,
  178, 255, 697, 700, 708, 742
Chicago-7, 592
child abuse, 491
children, 1, 11, 15, 18, 31,
  34, 43, 58, 68, 77, 80, 100,
  102, 121, 138, 141, 159, 168,
  172, 175, 182, 187, 196, 199,
  215, 220, 248, 267, 269, 279,
  286, 316, 317, 330, 339, 342,
  343, 344, 347, 351, 363, 365,
  366, 368, 371, 373, 374, 377,
  384, 386, 387, 390, 392, 414,
  425, 427, 440, 447, 456, 457,
  463, 465, 467, 468, 483, 487,
  496, 500, 501, 506, 509, 525,
  526, 545, 548, 566, 568, 569,
  575, 578, 594, 595, 600, 603,
  604, 611, 612, 614, 627, 628,
  641, 642, 643, 655, 656
chronology, 751
civil disturbance, 134, 315
  486

229

About the Compilers

NANCY SIGNORIELLI is an Associate Professor in the Department of Communication at the University of Delaware. She is the author of *Role Portrayal and Stereotyping on Television* (Greenwood Press 1985), *Images of Men and Women in the Mass Media: A Comparative Analysis, Drinking, Sex, and Violence on Television: The Cultural Indicators Perspective*, and has contributed extensively to the *Journal of Communication*, *Gazette*, and *Society*.

GEORGE GERBNER is Professor of Communication and Dean of the Annenberg School of Communication, University of Pennsylvania. He is the editor of the *Journal of Communication*, co-editor of Oxford University Press Communications Books, and the recipient of numerous awards and prizes for his work in communications.